The Real McKay

The Real McKay

The Remarkable Life of
Alexander McKay, Geologist

Graham Bishop

Otago University Press

Published by Otago University Press
PO Box 56/Level 1, 398 Cumberland Street, Dunedin, New Zealand
Fax: 64 3 479 8385. Email: university.press@otago.ac.nz

First published 2008
Copyright © Graham Bishop 2008

ISBN 978 1 877372 22 3

Cover image: Alexander McKay.
Te Papa Tongarewa/Museum of New Zealand E4664/14378

Maps by Allan K. Kynaston

The publisher thanks Ross Armstrong, John S. Dennison,
Wendy Harrex, Ralph Lawrence, Emily Rainsford, Richard Reeve
and Taryn Tait for their work on this book.

Thanks to these organisations for financial support:
Genesis Energy
Geological Society of New Zealand
Royal Society of New Zealand

This book is printed with vegetable-based inks on
ECF-bleached paper from sustainably managed forests.
Printed in Aotearoa by Astra Print Ltd
Wellington

Contents

Acknowledgements *7*
Introduction *9*
Prelude: Long Lens *13*

1   Scotland – An Austere Beginning *15*
Carsphairn, Woodhead, McKay's Early Years, Braidenoch

2   A Child of the Southern Uplands *29*
School Days, Paying His Way

3   Prying & Trying *41*
Words and Stones, Love & Poems

4   Emigration *51*
A Near Miss

5   New Horizons *61*
Looking for Work, Looking for His Brother, Looking for Gold

6   Australia – The Grass is Greener *77*
Outback Queensland, Malaria, Tropical Storms

7   Lake Ohau – The Turning Point *87*
An Incredible Journey, … and a Job …, … and a Wife …

8   The Door Opens *99*
The Three 'Hs', The Fossil Collector, The Body in the Cave Affair

9   A Career is Born *115*
Working for Hector, The Catlins, West Coast, Poverty Bay

10   Into His Stride *129*
Field Geologist, The Routeburn & Hollyford, Waitaki to the Matukituki

11   THE PEAK OF HIS POWERS *143*
       Marlborough, Glenn Wye Earthquake, Coal at Rowley's Farm, Photography

12   GOVERNMENT GEOLOGIST, FGS *161*
       Fiordland, Family, Coromandel, Cheviot Earthquake, Ill Health

13   WINDING DOWN *177*
       Retirement & Remarriage, The End of the Road, Last Will & Testament

14   THE LEGEND AND THE REAL MCKAY *187*
       His Achievements, The Legend, The Real McKay

       APPENDICES

          1 In Memoriam 196
          2 McKay Hammer Award 197
          3 Epic Poems by Alexander McKay 199

       BIBLIOGRAPHY *213*

       NOTES *225*

       INDEX *243*

Acknowledgements

This work would not have been possible without an Award in History from the New Zealand History Research Trust Fund of the Ministry for Culture and Heritage, and grants from the Charles Alexander Fleming Trust and the Brian Mason Scientific and Technical Trust. These grants allowed me to familiarise myself with McKay's origins in Scotland and many (but by no means all) of the localities of special importance in New Zealand. They also enabled me to spend time researching the archival material at the Alexander Turnbull Library, National Archives, Te Papa Tongarewa, and the Institute of Geological and Nuclear Sciences in Wellington. It is a pleasure to acknowledge the assistance and professionalism of the staff at these institutions.

In Scotland, I am indebted to Anna Campbell and Anne Rutherford of the Carsphairn Heritage Centre and Carsphairn School respectively and also Charlotte Brown (Glasgow), the present owner of the McKay cottage in Carsphairn. The help and hospitality of these three women was of enormous value.

The contributions of my former colleagues with their specialised knowledge of important localities was also of great importance, especially the commentaries on McKay's work by Dr David Skinner (Coromandel) and Dr Michael Isaac (Bay of Islands) and the broad-ranging help and interest from Nick Perrin.

Other important sources of mainly unpublished information were Dr Rodney Grapes (faulting in Marlborough) and John Patterson and Bill Main (photography).

Alan Mason unselfishly provided me with copies of the results of his very considerable archival investigations and also reviewed the manuscript.

Other reviewers included Drs I.M. (Mo) Turnbull and M.J. Isaac, and Peter Wood (with special thanks for his hospitality and encouragement) and Jean Strachan, of the McNab (New Zealand) Room of the Dunedin Public Library. All have contributed in no mean fashion to the final calibre of the manuscript.

My good friend Mary Miller is especially thanked for her companionship, tolerance, and involvement, in places both here and there. Natasha Szeto helped to restore order out of imminent chaos. Roger Smith, Mary Browne, and Bob Entwistle helped with illustrations. Support for the publication from the Royal Society, Geological Society of NZ, and NZ Geological Survey (now GNS) is also gratefully acknowledged.

A detail here, a detail there, help to find a waterfall, permission to go on land: all were contributions for which I express my gratitude. Those involved are not forgotten, even if not named.

Friendly, helpful people and institutions, from Scotland to the Bluff have added a special dimension to the satisfaction of undertaking this work.

And finally to Bek, especially when the going got really tough and I was ready to throw the whole thing in the bin.

GRAHAM BISHOP
Dunedin 2008
dgbishop@paradise.net.nz

Introduction

It is almost impossible to start geological work anywhere in New Zealand without discovering Alexander McKay has been there first. I used to fantasise about meeting this shadowy character behind whom I always trailed. I have long known that his life was a prime target for a historical biography, but the years rolled on before I was ready and it was with relief and some surprise that I found, when I did start, that it was still an unclaimed area. Once I had begun, however, there was no putting it down as the enigma of the man unfolded, and the enormous written resource he had left became apparent. For almost every year of his life there is some output, and I had to get to the end before I could truly start at the beginning. On the way, I came across some extraordinary coincidences. Both of us started our careers in South Otago, and had them terminated prematurely by heart problems. Both of us were fully sighted in only one eye. Both of us married at twenty-seven and had two sons. Both of us remarried at the age of sixty-five. Both of us spent a short unsuccessful period in Australia. Both of us were occasional poets, and we each wrote a long narrative poem involving the last moa!

Like McKay I was also a geologist, and I am familiar with many of the places he worked, and the conditions he experienced. This familiarity has provided me with a considerable advantage in understanding the forces driving him. However, although McKay and I share a number of coincidental similarities, I do not imagine we were much alike, with major physical and intellectual differences. I do not possess the same dogged determination, nor his exceptional ability to find fossils, nor do I share his legendary affinity for whisky.

Although this is a book about a geologist, by a geologist, it is not a geological book. It is written to appeal to all those interested in the history of exploration, science, and the colonisation of New Zealand. It is about a man, his trials, tribulations, achievements and personality. A secondary focus is the dramatic changes that occurred during his lifetime, and also those that have occurred since.

The resource he left has two distinctly different aspects. One is the 291 pages of typed transcript of unfinished autobiography that he wrote when he was in his seventies. This covers his early life in Scotland, from infant to young man, then his emigration to New Zealand, and his early days, both here and in Australia. It ends just before his meeting and subsequent marriage to Susannah, when he was twenty-seven. There are fragmentary records for the next few years, until at the age of thirty-two he began his professional career with New Zealand Geological Survey, and commenced his prolific series of technical reports, 202 in all. McKay's technical writing, especially in the early part of his career, is not easy reading, even for geologists. Compounding the difficulty of marrying his autobiography with his professional reporting was his habit of seldom mentioning his companions, means of travel, accommodation, or other items of general interest in the latter reports. Nevertheless, buried in these thousands of pages of technical data there are occasional personal glimpses of the man and aspects of his life.

His autobiography is drawn on heavily in the first half of the book. It was an extraordinary experience going back to Scotland and seeing the places he had written about fifty, sixty, even seventy years since he last saw them. McKay was justly proud of his memory, and it was a delight to find the features of his youth so accurately described.

Distilling his professional work down to a form that was both manageable and able to be appreciated by readers with no specialised geological knowledge was a major challenge. Much basic information of where and when in the reports is given as maps and tables that all but the enthusiast will probably pass over lightly. However, all his reports are identified, and are available in major libraries for those who want to delve deeper.

Although the work has been a labour of love, it has not been without its frustrations. Susannah, his first wife, remains a shadowy figure, recorded only in a smattering of official documents. Neither domestic correspondence nor photographic records of her have survived, and the period of their meeting and marriage is the most poorly documented segment of McKay's life.

The concentration of archival records in Wellington poses considerable difficulties for an impecunious researcher based in Dunedin. The open-ended cost of employing a 'search agent' to track down a land title that might not exist was a gamble I was not prepared to risk after a significant initial outlay was fruitless. It was made doubly galling when Land Information New Zealand staff admitted they could do the search but were not permitted to do so.

Undoubtedly there is more incidental material, perhaps in the papers of his contemporaries, in local or regional newspapers, or other records, but eventually enough must be enough. Alexander McKay had a remarkable life, and left a remarkable record. I hope you find it as interesting as I did.

I have used the following conventions. Quotes in text from McKay's autobiography 'Fragments in the Life History of Alexander McKay' are enclosed "…" or, in the case of longer quotes, the source is given. Quotes from other sources are enclosed '…'. Where I have inserted an explanatory word or phrase within a quote it is enclosed […]. I have made approximate conversions of pounds into dollars (year 2000 values) by multiplying by 150; hence McKay's salary of £280 after twelve years' service converts to $42,000.

Prelude: Long lens

For a moment in 1886, a beam of light passed through an array of homemade lenses, lenses painstakingly ground from the bottoms of whisky bottles. At that instant, an astonishing image was locked on to a photographic plate and preserved for posterity.

The image was of a Russian warship, the *Vjestnik*, anchored in Wellington harbour. Clearly visible were its open gun-ports, the Russian flag, lifeboats, and other details such as individual rigging lines. This unexpected visitor was of some concern to the citizens of Wellington. The booming explosions accompanying the eruption of Mount Tarawera a few days later were attributed to the *Vjestnik* shelling coastal settlements as it sailed north up the east coast of the North Island. Completely overlooked was the fact that the first successful telephoto picture ever – one of outstanding quality – had just been taken in Wellington from a distance of about two and a half kilometres from the ship.

The man behind the camera had emigrated to New Zealand from Scotland twenty-three years before, after a formal education that finished when he was eleven years old. He arrived in New Zealand when he was twenty-two, and educated himself through his own observations and prodigious reading. After a decade of chasing dreams of gold, he established himself in science and society. His experiments with photography and his invention of the world's first successful telephoto lens were a second-phase activity: a hobby that further occupied his ever-active mind. Alexander McKay's contribution to geology will long be remembered. His contribution to photography, however, is almost unknown.

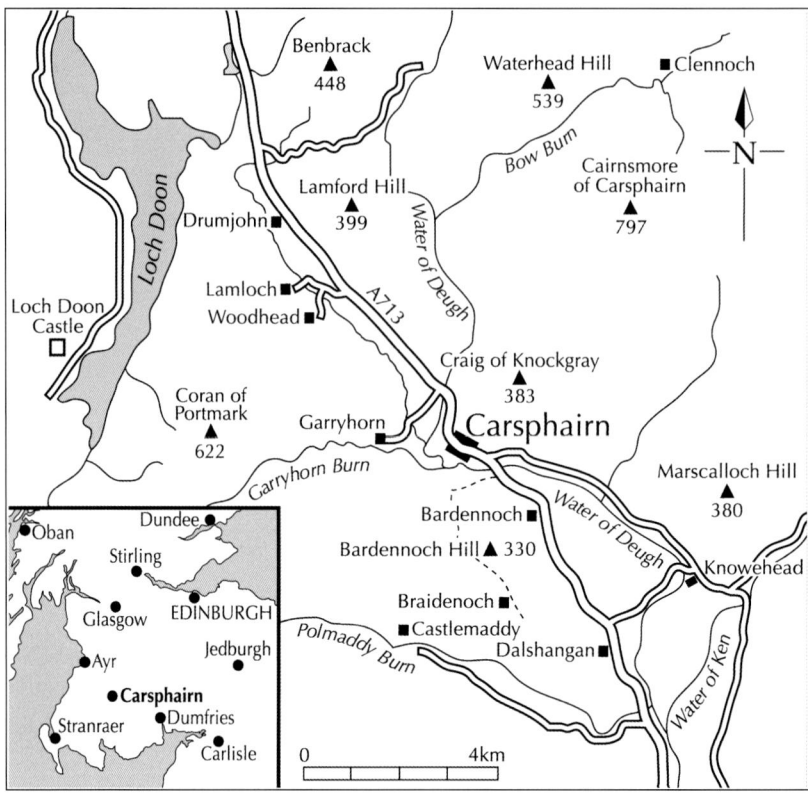

Map of Galloway. The village of Carsphairn is close to the crest of the Southern Uplands, between Ayr and Dumfries, about 100 km southwest of Edinburgh.

The tiny village of Carsphairn, consisting of a straggle of cottages astride the A713. The McKay cottage, school and church are obscured by the trees at the north (right) end. In the left foreground, immediately beyond the stone dyke, is Cairn Avel, a large Neolithic burial mound, one of a number of Neolithic features in the area.

1. Scotland – An Austere Beginning

Carsphairn

The isolated village of Carsphairn is near the crest of the southern Scottish uplands, in Galloway. When Alexander McKay was born there in 1841, it had a population of 161 and consisted of a straggle of stone cottages extending along both sides of what is now the A713 for about 100 metres. Many of these were semi-detached, in rows of up to five, but a few stood alone. The largest building was the Salutation Inn.

At the southern end of the village are the kirk and school. Across the road, in the first cottage on the right as you enter the village, Alexander McKay was born. His father, William Sloan McKay, built this cottage about 1836, when he married Agnes McClellan. Apparently he had not wanted to take his bride to the bleak moorland home of his parents at Braidenoch (a full hour's walk from the village), nor had he wanted for himself the hard and lonely life of a shepherd.

William had leased the plot for the house and garden from the Craigengillan Estate. It had a street frontage of 35 feet 10 inches (11 metres) and extended up the hill for 167 feet 10 inches (51 metres). It contained the remains of an old house, which he converted to a workshop, and he may also have used it as a cow byre. Friends and family would have rallied around, bringing in rocks from near and far – from collapsed dykes (stone walls) on moving hillsides and the ruins of old huts and houses – and sledging them to the site. As was customary, the front of the new cottage was built right to the edge of the footpath and across the full width of the section. However, it was detached from the house of their neighbour, Rab Hastings, and a short lane between them allowed Wiliam access to his workshop. The communal water pump was about seventy metres away, towards the centre of the village.

The slate-roofed cottage – which would eventually house three adults and ten children – has two floors. It has four large rooms, two downstairs, and two upstairs. All have fireplaces. The downstairs room on the right (south) as you enter has a wooden floor, and was probably the family living room. The other room has a flagstone floor. A passage runs from the front to the back door, with a narrow flight of stairs leading up from near the back door. Downstairs at the back are two smaller rooms, perhaps originally a pantry and/or a dairy. There is another small room at the head of the stairs between the two upstairs rooms.

At first glance, Carsphairn today does not seem to have changed much in a century and a half. The turnpike road from Dumfries to Dalmellington, which passes through the village, is now sealed and a scattering of cars is parked along it. The McKay cottage has dormer windows, which were not there originally, but were installed before 1905, and there are larger panes of glass in the windows. A store and Post Office agency are located near the water pump. The Salutation Inn has been enlarged and converted into flats for welfare beneficiaries. Television aerials sprout from most buildings. The current hostelry, the Greystone Inn, occupies what was Rab Hastings' house.

In the churchyard across the road from the McKay cottage, nine people lie buried in the McKay plot, including Alexander McKay's parents, William and Agnes, his paternal grandparents, John and Janet, and his sister Agnes, who died as an infant. The death in 1937 of his sister Margaret (who would have been only seven when Alex emigrated) brought the McKay lineage in Carsphairn to an end. The headstone of the plot, a slab of Old Red Sandstone, is inscribed:

IN MEMORY OF

John McKay who died 20th March 1848 aged 87 years and his wife Janet Welsh who died 8 June 1852 aged 71 years Elizabeth their daughter died 4th August, 1828 aged 4 years Also Agnes daughter of William McKay who died 17th of June 1850 aged ten months The above William McKay died 6th of April 1883 aged 74

Also Agnes Mclellan wife of said William McKay, who died at Carsphairn 9th of July 1892 aged 79 years Annie daughter of above John McKay who died at Carsphairn 11th Jan 1900 aged 82 years. Barbara (?) daughter of the above John McKay who died at Carsphairn 16th Jan 1905 aged 51 years Margaret McKay daughter of above William McKay died 14th April 1937 aged 81 years

Carsphairn had its heyday in the early part of the twentieth century, before the McKays had quite died out and when the Salutation Inn was 'replete with every modern convenience.'[1] There was a nine-hole golf course, and the area was popular with walkers and fishermen. The Carsphairn Heritage Centre, a few hundred metres north of the village, offers some tantalising glimpses of these and earlier days. Today, there is an absence of activity in the village with few, if any, people on the street. It was no surprise to learn that the population has shrunk to about sixty.

There is something enigmatic about Carsphairn. To me, it seemed a community that was disconnected from its environment. It was not until

1. SCOTLAND – AN AUSTERE BEGINNING   17

Carsphairn Village in about 1900. The McKay cottage is the first on the right side of the road. The school (partly obscured by trees) is opposite. The largest building is the Salutation Inn. Garryhorn Farm is above the tall chimney of the inn, and in the distance beyond are the deserted buildings of the Woodhead mining settlement. Photo from The Upper Glenkens *by Jack Hunter*

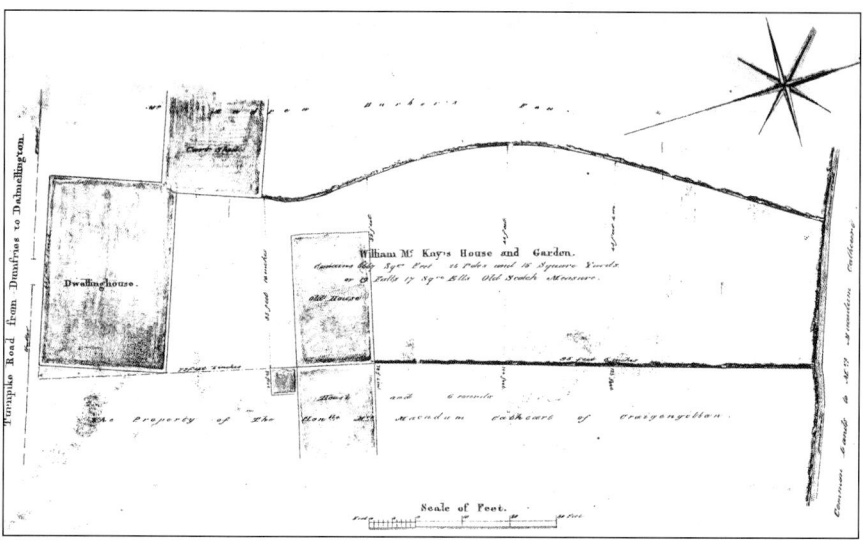

Plan of the McKay house and garden, 1846. Courtesy of Carsphairn School

Little had changed in Carsphairn by 1905, more than forty years after McKay had left the village. The cottage of his birth is on the right with the two-storeyed Salutation Inn beyond. The kirk and school are hidden behind the walls on the left.

The fireplace in the McKay cottage. An open fire of smouldering peat was the only source of heat and means of cooking for a family of three adults and ten children.

Tinklers Loup was named because a thieving tinker evaded capture by leaping the five-metre chasm containing the Water of Deugh. The gorge and the bridge are now submerged beneath the waters of the Galloway hydroelectric scheme. Photo from The Upper Glenkens by Jack Hunter

after I left that I realised the full implications of its story, one so familiar in New Zealand. Gone are the natural flow and fall of rivers, rapids, gorges, and rushing water, gone too are the quiet places and dark pools, all submerged beneath a neutralising sheet of water, which has rendered the landscape impotent. This story is repeated around the world, a story justified by the convenience of electricity, but for which the consequences have yet to be determined. The spread of pine plantations and the cross-country march of power pylons strengthen the likeness to New Zealand's landscape.

These developments had nothing to do with Alexander McKay. He was long gone, and indeed long dead in a distant land, before they came to pass. It took time, however, to understand that the setting of his early years that I had come to see for myself was vastly changed. The present was no longer a guide to the past: the whole basis of the physical environment had been displaced by hydroelectric development. So I had to take a fresh look at the waters of the Deugh and Loch Ken and imagine the hydro dams emptied of water and the pylons and plantations stripped from the hills.

In New Zealand, McKay was early attracted to the Mackenzie country in the headwaters of the Waitaki catchment. This great basin, surrounded by tussock-covered, treeless hills, upstream of the now-submerged gorges of the Waitaki, may well have kindled memories of the Carsphairn bowl in the upper part of the Water of Deugh.

Woodhead

There has been another important change in Carsphairn since McKay's time. The Woodhead lead mine has closed and the mining community, which at one stage numbered three hundred, considerably more than the population of the village at the time, has drifted away.

In 1838, three years before McKay was born, the tenant of Woodhead Farm made a discovery which was to have a significant social effect on the village and its inhabitants. He discovered a large amount of lead ore near the surface and reported this to his landlord, Colonel McAdam Cathcart. Within months, shafts had been sunk, houses built for thirty workmen, and sixty men employed.

By 1841, there were twenty-two houses at Woodhead and a population of two hundred, which increased to fifty houses and three hundred and one people in the next ten years.[2] A smelting complex and powder magazine had been constructed, tracks laid for the bogies to move ore to the smelter, and a water wheel thirty feet (eight metres) in diameter and a complicated system of water races ('lades') to bring water to the wheel had been built. 'Shops' for the wheelwright and blacksmith were also built. A surveyor in 1848 reported that the 'houses [were] all one story in height, slated, and in good repair and wholly inhabited by miners.'[3] Initially, very few local men were miners but, because of crowded conditions at Woodhead, a number of mine workers had lodgings in Carsphairn – some in the McKay house – and elsewhere around the district.

Unfortunately mine production began to slump from 1852 as the ore ran out, and the population declined swiftly. The school closed in 1853, and by 1861 the population had shrunk to eighty-eight. Although it increased again to 109 in 1871, by 1891 only three houses at Woodhead were occupied; the mining community had all but disappeared.[4]

Woodhead historian Anna Campbell relates how the owner 'Colonel Cathcart's care for the community he created was reflected in the school built in 1843, described as "more ample and commodious than any in the district".'[5] A liberal salary was paid to both the schoolmaster and the female teacher.

> Colonel McAdam Cathcart was a capitalist who fostered good industrial relations by his interest and benevolence. Not only had he built a model village and school, but he also encouraged the miners to have a library, as in many other mining communities. The Library Society started in 1840 and by 1849 the catalogue listed over 800 volumes … Colonel McAdam Cathcart had presented the miners with … a splendidly bound copy of the Encyclopaedia Britannica and gave the library occasional grants.[6]

Not only the miners benefited from the library, as everyone within a ten-mile (fifteen-kilometre) radius of the mines was allowed to borrow from it.

Although Colonel Cathcart was deeply concerned about his workers' housing and education, he did not share their religious views. After a meeting of the miners to see how much interest there would be in setting up a Free Church, he refused to allow them to meet again at the mines, or on any land he owned. They met instead in the kitchen of a neighbouring landowner.[7]

For a brief period, the lead mines had brought increased population, prosperity and industry to the region. Through the school and the library they also offered more – the opportunity for enhanced education and knowledge throughout the community. Colonel McAdam Cathcart was a farsighted man.

McKay's Early Years

Such was the environment into which Alexander McKay was born on Monday 12 April 1841, the third of the ten children that William and Agnes produced:

1 John b 15 March 1837, d 1917
2 Catherine [Kate] b 1 December 1838, d c. 1916
3 Alexander b 12 April 1841, d 8 July 1917
4 George b 1843
5 James b 1845
6 Duncan b 1847
7 Agnes b 1849, d June 1850
8 Agnes b 1851
9 Janet b 1853
10 Margaret b 1856, d 1937

Alexander was a spring baby, and when he was born the snow patches that lay around the houses would be melting fast as the chill faded from the winter air. As he relates in his autobiography, his mother found him "a troublesome, fretful child, clearly addicted to the belly-ache and decidedly inclined to let other people be aware of the fact".[8] He was late walking and teething, and was wet-nursed through his second year.

McKay described his mother as "a good mother, a good housewife and good looking; the Venus [de] Milo of the village, wonderfully quiet, much respected, and fond of mashed potatoes and buttermilk: she had no other vices."[9] Given that Agnes had ten children, she was probably 'eating for two' for most of her adult life and such indulgences were of necessity.

William McKay was the son of a shepherd, but became a joiner and wheelwright in Carsphairn. "According to his lights my Father was a good man, but he lived spiritually in a state of continual alarm (especially on Sundays) because of his unalterable belief in the doctrine of predestination, then generally accepted by Calvinists of the Auld Kirk in rural districts such as ours … He was industrious, honest, and conscientious in all his dealings, and succeeded in bringing up a large family on comparatively small means."[10] His exemplary conduct was duly recognised and he was offered a vacancy in the eldership of the Kirk when one occurred. And so "his ambition was gratified and he lived and died worthily."[11]

Jenny Welsh, McKay's grandmother on his father's side, was to have a significant influence on his childhood, perhaps more than his mother in the circumstances. She was "wee, but wiery, vigorous and determined. She was also a storehouse of information".[12] Alexander was to spend much of his childhood with his Granny. There was an occasional clash of strong wills, but McKay remembered her with deep affection. He was less entranced with his other grandmother: "she died in her 99th year. That was almost the only notable fact of her life history, except that she went to bed to die 29 years before she actually did".[13]

When Alexander was two years old, an outbreak of typhoid fever in the village was to have major repercussions on his upbringing. He writes in his autobiography, "Hygeia was a lady quite unknown in the village of Carsphairn … and anything like systematic sanitation was undreamed of",[14] although the village was fortunately elevated, with plenty of fresh air. Given the general lack of sanitation and running water in rural villages, it is likely that some 'typhoid' outbreaks involving gastric disorders were the result of food poisoning or pollution of the water supply. No typhoid-related deaths were recorded in Carsphairn at this time.[15]

Nevertheless, it was decided that the young Alexander, being prone to bellyaches, was best removed from the scene and sent to "a place of safety in the country".[16] His paternal grandfather John, the immediate patriarch of the McKay dynasty, was a shepherd at Braidenoch, an isolated upland farm an hour's uphill walk to the west of the village and it was quickly arranged that little Alex would go to his grandparents: "my Grannie came to the village and took me away with her. I was tucked up in a shepherd's plaid – a la Maori".[17]

There were two possible routes to Braidenoch, the shorter being the steeper: a climb of 150 metres from Carnavel Farm almost over the top of Braidenoch Hill. The longer, easier alternative followed the line of the pack road to Polmaddy. Given that Alexander's Granny was sixty-two at the time, her choice of the less demanding route was not entirely surprising but, as McKay relates, they came across a mob of a hundred highland cattle:

> My Grannie undid the hasp and boldly entered amongst the cattle. At first they gave way, astonished at the somewhat unusual sight which my Grannie and her burden presented, but growing bolder they closely surrounded the good

lady and became so demonstrative, threatening violence, that perforce my Grannie was compelled to stop and act on the defensive, and the needs of the case were such that I had to be set at liberty to act as an independent unit. My Granny was knocked down and in part her clothes were torn, but she sustained no other damage – the bullocks appear to have been more frolicsome than dangerous. By-and-by she succeeded in driving them off, but in the meantime I had mixed with the mob and the business was to get hold of me without afresh exciting the bullocks to further overtures. It appears that I had made my peace with the bovines and was unnoticed of them whether straying between them or passing under their bellies. I was recovered, and the bullocks desisting from further attack, the journey to Braidenough House was completed without other incident worthy of note.[18]

Braidenoch

Alex spent at least three or four years at Braidenoch. It is a bleak, windswept spot, a broad moorland saddle between Bardennoch Hill and Gairy Crag. For the first few months, his redoubtable Granny had to carry him every time she went away from the house. On one such excursion he believes the cornerstone of his geological career was laid:

One day my Granny had occasion to scour a piece of wool, and the final process was a thorough washing in clear water. To do this it was handiest to take the fleece to a pool in the burn not distant from the house, and as usual, perhaps of necessity, I accompanied and superintended. My Granny did the work and I sat where placed in the midst of a bush of heather which grew on the right bank of the stream and overlooking the pool. From this vantage I watched the process my Granny was engaged in completing, and made other observations likewise. Much of my after life has been devoted to geology and here my geological studies began. From where I sat I observed certain peculiarities of the bed of the stream and its rocky banks, and the description which I will now give, though employing the language of after years, will speak only of the facts relating to the place and time. This indeed must be, since I have no recollection of again visiting the exact spot, and certainly never did so with the purpose of being able to describe the nature of the rocks present. I am well aware how easy it is to deceive oneself but there are cases, as in this instance, in which self-deception is impossible, unless indeed the description which follows is wholly a fabrication, and with me there is no reason why I should invent that which can easily be disproved. The pool was formed by the water tumbling as a rapid and the lower part a cascade over several strata of rock, the total height of which might be five or six feet; the lower part forming the cascade was 3 feet 6 inches to four feet in height, the pool might be five feet in width, and scarcely more in length. Down stream a bank of shingle barred the water for three-fourths the width of the pool, the water escaping on the north-western (right-hand) side of the pool under the high bank on which I sat. The strike of the strata at the cascade and rapid is nearly at right angles to the course of the stream, and for some distance farther up the stream the banks are near enough each other to enable them to be stepped across.[19]

The isolated upland farmhouse of Braidenoch, where McKay spent his first few years. The hills in the background are the Rhinn of Kells. The house is at an altitude of 750 metres and is about an hour's walk from the village of Carsphairn.

From McKay's description, it was not hard for me to find the pool. It was about 100 metres from the house. The stream was, as he said, in most places narrow enough to be stepped across. The higher true right bank where he had sat ensconced in a chair of heather is now littered with forest prunings. Only one detail is at variance with the remarkable observations of a two-and-a-half-year-old: the rocks in the stream are morainic boulders, not strata *in situ*. Given his lack of formal training at the time (or at any time), such an error is easy to overlook.

Braidenoch must have been a lonely place for a small boy with no companions of his own age. His Granny, however, soon began to teach him to read and write: "I was taught the alphabet from an old tattered Bible that had served and suffered at many a conventical ... First I had to master the plain letter, but was always impatient to get at the ornamental initial letter commencing the Chapter."[20] Today, McKay's beautiful copperplate manuscripts are a testament to her foresight and patience.

McKay's account of his life with his grandparents is rich in detail. He records his integration into the little circle around the fireside and the preparation of a simple meal of rummeled or rauchled (mashed) potatoes:

> On a peat fire was a three-legged pot in which potatoes were being boiled. When the potatoes were cooked the water was drained off and the pot was again put on the fire to dry the potatoes. This done the pot was taken off the fire and the potatoes broken by a large four-pronged fork called a 'rauchle'. Butter, cheese dreed [rind?], and one or two onions cut up small were added, and the whole was

McKay believed he made his first geological observation at this pool at the tender age of two and a half, while he was 'supervising' his Granny scouring wool. His description of the pool, made seventy years later, is amazingly accurate. The Braidenoch farmhouse is at upper right.

again put over the fire long enough to melt the butter, soften the cheese and cook the onion as far as taste required. Then the potatoes were once more rauchled till they had assumed a fine and even-grained condition. Then milk was added and the whole stirred by a long, two-handled potstick until a perfect paste was formed and of the desired consistency. The rauchling and the rummeling were done by the men and considerable dexterity was displayed, especially in the rummeling part of the business, the forming of the figure 8 being a favourite and effective mode of mixing. This being the final stage of preparation, three live peats were placed on the floor, the pot set over these, and the meal began. Each one was provided with a bowl of milk and a ram-horn spoon, and for the most part had a three-legged stool to sit upon. … I was provided with the smallest spoon in the kit and a porringer and stool to be my own.[21]

Another culinary delicacy McKay recalls was a slice of bannock or thick scone, thumb-spread with butter, and covered with sugar. This was a placatory offering, to still his tears after he had been cuffed for tormenting the cat, but had over-balanced and cut his ear.

Village Life

The Braidenoch era came to an end when his grandfather became too old and frail for the position he held and moved back to the village "to end his days",[22] which he did in 1848, when Alex was seven.

But then Alex became unwell: "I was ill and of the very complaint I was taken to Braidenoch to avoid. I gather that I must have been dangerously ill and for a considerable time."[23] He remembered being the only recipient of chicken broth, and having no hair on his head. When eventually he recovered, he renewed acquaintance with his Granny who was by now installed in an upstairs room of the McKay house, where she made a little money by spinning. Alex became more and more dependent on her company, for "I never had had other children of my own age to associate with, and such as I could find my own age were a great deal more advanced in boyishness than I, and consequently I herded not with them, but more and more kept the company of my Granny."[24]

When he was about ten, Alex was offered a kitten. He had to collect it from Braidenoch, but once he got it back to Carsphairn, it thrived on a diet of porridge and milk and "grew to be a cat of respectable dimensions and lived much with my Granny and I. When it grew to man's estate it displayed, for a cat, considerable intelligence … the cat saw how the door was opened and soon learned to open it for himself."[25]

> This cat did a little poaching which, at the time I write about, was not considered a very heinous crime. I have even known my father being out of a night 'leistering' … And where was the sin? If our cat did bring home a ger-cock or a moor hen. What was my Granny to do with them? She could not sell them having no confederate, so she burned the feathers and the bones also,

The village pump. It is possible the ground water it tapped was sometimes contaminated by uncontrolled effluent, which contributed to the outbreaks of gastric disorders experienced by the villagers in the 1840s.

and fairly admitted it was wrong of the cat to bring them home. Sometimes, and not so infrequently either, the cat would bring home a hare, but it was mair than he could manage to drag a big one upstairs, but he could always make my Granny understand there was something about, and usually there was little difficulty in finding it. Tom was very proud of these doings, and was always rewarded with a share of the spoil.[26]

So, while Alexander's Granny taught him to read and write, gave him a passionate view of his Scottish heritage, and instilled values and and a sense of traditional ethics, there were shades of grey in the teaching. She also taught him that love was more important than anger:

> On one occasion my mother asked me to bring some water [from the village pump], but I disregarded the request. ... My Granny ... determined that I should get that water, and she came towards me with an air I did not like. I ran away, and went up the village as fast as I could run, and when just clearing the last of the houses on the east side of the road I looked round ... sure enough, there was my Granny hot on my trail, and coming slowly, though quick as she could after me. ... I clambered over the dyke, and coming through the garden reached the stables of the 'Salutation Inn', and getting into a manger covered myself over with the straw ... I was unearthed, and with a firm grip on my jacket, I was led forth as a prisoner ... In at the front door, through the house, and right to the back door I was led. Here the stairs ascended to my Granny's room, and here I concluded my last stand for liberty must be made. ... I held on to the bannister, I clutched the post, and made desperate efforts to be free. It was a real battle royal and long continued. ... But while we struggled my

> Granny exclaimed: 'Oh I could hold you were you were as strong as a bull calf.' This lost me the battle … The mental force of my Granny, not her physical strength, was triumphant.[27]

Alexander was then led upstairs and into her room, whereupon she pocketed the key. He waited in trepidation. "[She] opened the big oak kist [chest], the contents of which I thought I knew. Out came the bannock, and I had a thumb-spread one, well sugared. I could not help it – not for the life of me I could not help it. If she had thrashed me I would have been content, but a thumb-spread ane, well sugared – that fairly broke me down. I wept."[28]

McKay became a remarkable man, but he had a remarkable Granny. She died later that year, at the age of seventy-one, on 8 June 1852, when McKay was eleven.

2. A Child of the Southern Uplands

School Days

At school McKay was "an indifferent scholar".[1] His arithmetic was poor (although eventually he mastered enough maths to cope with the optical physics of camera lenses) and his grammar worse. "Even now I write only the grammar of common sense, and I fear the scholar who will read these pages with wonder and disgust."[2] However, "I soon developed a great liking for reading, and having a more than ordinary memory and equal facility for recollecting, I had little trouble in getting such lessons as depended upon these qualities, and thus I had often spare time which I used for promiscuous reading in the Bible or reader in use at the school."[3] Once, when reading the Book of Genesis, he was so overwhelmed at the plight of poor Joseph, thrown into a pit without his coat, that he began to cry. As he was unable or unwilling to explain why, "by a smart application of the cane the Master said he would give me something to cry for. That was auld Sloan, a hard man, though at times he could be jocular when he had in him just the required amount of whiskey."[4]

Sloan frequently thrashed the children. On one morning,

> When the school door was opened I was the only scholar – all the rest, boys and girls alike, were at the curling pond sliding on the ice which was new and smooth, I think the first of the season. I was sent to tell them to come to school, and they came. The Master armed with a stick that would not easily break placed himself behind the outer door, and as each scholar passed him, boy or girl it mattered not, he or she got at least one blow from this stick. The boys wisely rushed the door and some escaped and were not afterwards punished. I was among the last to enter and hoped for my services to escape punishment, but I got my share of the stick as the rest had done.[5]

The spring examinations were an important part of school life, when the children were questioned by ministers of the parish and adjacent parishes of the Auld Kirk of Scotland. "For a time there was great doubt whether I could be present at this examination mainly on account of the want of clothes … I was not anxious to be present but rather pleased at the prospect of a day off. But alas the tailor was got, and out of an auld pair of breeks that my Father had done with ... contrived to manufacture a jacket".[6] At the end of the day, the children's knowledge of "Scripture History" was individually tested in front of interested villagers.

> I made my way to the Master's desk and halted at a safe distance in front of a great big burly presence ... This man had hair gie grizzly and plenty of it standing straight on end, and otherwise he was fearsome to look at. When he spoke I did not feel any better, for I had my courage dashed when I passed Miss ... who said to her neighbour 'that one will not do much', and I heard it.[7]

McKay excelled. He was examined on aspects of the Gospel according to St Luke and after several recalls and re-examinations, was eventually pronounced the winner. Aggie Stewart's aunt, however, was less than happy, and eventually the examiners agreed to present her with a second prize of greater value than the first, and "her auld Auntie was satisfied. Singular to say my old Granny was not much elated at my success, but merely remarked 'there might be something in the McKays after all.'"[8]

School had other high moments, of which Candlemas (2 February, commemorating the presentation of the baby Christ to the Temple) stood out in McKay's memory:

> That was a great day at school. Then it was that the children one and all, rich and poor, gentle and simple, brought their coin or coins to the schoolmaster, who received them on a table in front of his desk and made it plain to all the scholars who had contributed the most, and the name of the boy or girl heading the list was duly announced. Then, according to the number of scholars and the amount of the contributions, were two or three bottles of whisky produced and converted into weak toddy, well sweetened with white sugar. ... Then two girls of his household, filling jugs with the liquor, went round the benches and gave each of the scholars a wine glass full of toddy and some bread and butter; the dose was repeated, and if that did not exhaust the toddy, then as a half measure it was sent round as far as it would go. This done we were all turned loose for the day.[9]

At home McKay had quite a different education: "I had passages of scottish history given me, or my Granny's version of such, and in every case the scot was a hero and the Englishman deserved all he got."[10] He helped her with her work, carding as she spun, but "in the evening she rested and told me stories and so we might have been engaged till bedtime, but for my impertinent curiosity in asking for explanations which the good old lady could not give. This was a habit of mine and always irritated her".[11]

One of the local legends concerned the building of the first Kirk at Carsphairn. The "Deil" (Devil) was most upset and did everything in his power to stop it. Once it was built, he set about demolishing it:

According to my Granny he stationed himself at the top of Cairnsmuir, the highest mountain in the parrish, the top of which is formed of loose granite blocks. These were of all sizes up to 20 feet in diameter. From the top of Cairnsmuir the Deil commenced throwing stones at the Kirk and must inevitably have destroyed it had not the Craig Hill directly in a line with Cairnsmuir and the village, risen, or by some power been raised, several hundred feet or sufficiently higher to prevent the Deil from seeing what he was throwing at.

On an occasion more than ordinary a numerous congregation had assembled and the Deil a' morning had been particularly busy throwing stones clearly with the intention of interrupting the meeting and service then going on, and some of the stones straight in the line intended came parlously near the Kirk. Every time that the Deil launched forth a big stone he flew up in the air to see where it would light, hoping of couse, that it would hit the Kirk. But an unseen hand guided the stones as before, and they fell near and far to the one side or the other ... The last one that the Deil threw was well calculated as to direction, but his judgment was out as regards the weight of the stone and it fell short by something more than 100 yards. It lighted in Rab Hastings' garden as a mass of granite rock some 20 feet in length and breadth and there it remains to the present day.

The Deil, finding that he could not hit the Kirk ... came straight for the Kirk, running as it were for his very life. ... He came down the side of the Craig Hill with such speed and momentum that it seemed the Kirk must gang and a' that was in it, but fortunately for Cairsphairn and Carsphairn Kirk the big stone in Rab Hastings' garden was in the way and he had to swerve a little to one side to avoid that. ... before he could get himself put right in line for the Kirk he was past it, and gaed plump into the water-o'-Deuch, at the time in flood, and his Deilship being hot from Hell and hot with running, so disturbed the water and caused it to boil, that Carnevel Pool was the result.[12]

Many people saw the man they thought was the Devil enter and struggle in the swollen river. They ran for ropes to help him, until out strode the minister, John Semple, who saw at once who the man was and called, "'Leave him alone. He may burn, but he winna drown.' And so it was. He gaed sailing down the water, and while John Semple lived he no more bothered the people of Carsphairn."[13] (In another version of this story, the man was an innocent stranger trying to cross the river in 1677. His fate was sealed by the preacher's rhetoric!)[14]

McKay's education about the supernatural was extensive:

Carsphairn, according to my Granny, was a deuce of a place for witches, and their works were various and not always bad. They were of use often in connection with the dicovery of lost or stolen articles. Of course one had to be careful not to offend them, or one felt the pins in the wax figure and pined away as it melted slowly before the fire. Witches were not quite extinct in my time, and … Mary G … was the professional witch of the parish. She was rather proud than otherwise of her compact with the Deil, and took it not ill to be called a witch. This is explained by the fact that drowning and burning for witchcraft had been abolished, and it may be that this also accounted for the less malevolent character of the witches.[15]

McKay's boyhood in Carsphairn was not restricted to attending school and helping his Granny. There was some time for adventure:

Winter had come and gone, and the ice on the curling pond was rapidly breaking up, in fact had broken into fragments which were drifting about on the open waters. William Young and I ventured on some of these. We had independent commands and both of us set sail on a voyage of discovery. Commander Young's vessel got stranded on some unknown land before it had got half round the circuit of the pond. Mine made a deep sea voyage, and according to my own account I discovered America but had a great difficulty in landing on that distant shore on account of intervening sheets of ice which it was very dangerous to traverse, but I got safely to terra firma.[16]

The next time the boys went to the pond the ice was melted and they decided to use William Young's mother's washing tub as their vessel. Needless to say, it was not a success. McKay could not swim and had to be rescued. "I had to let my Granny know what had happened, and she assisted me to get my clothes dry. I have never been much inclined to follow the life of a sailor since the adventure of the tub."[17]

On another occasion, McKay's father was away working on a farm and Alex took the opportunity to use his carpentry workshop. While making a pot lid, he broke the bow saw he was using. When his father returned, "preparations for my punishment were in a forward state when my Granny appeared, very opportunely for me, and told my father how many times she had saved him from chastisement, and that in this case I was to be forgiven. Nothing worse happened than that I was sent suddenly to bed, and I was very glad it ended so."[18]

Eventually McKay discovered the library at the mines and "gained some knowledge of what was going on in the outside world."[19] The available texts covered chemistry, geology, arts, medicine, astronomy, religion, travel, fiction, and included atlases, dictionaries, the *Encyclopaedia Britannica*, and periodicals.[20] It was certainly sufficient to stimulate the interest of a young lad who found "Reading books was indeed the only thing that I could be said to be fond of."[21] Some of the villagers shared a subscription to the *Ayr Advertiser*. As his father was last on the reading list, McKay was able to read it too. "From perusal of this I learned that great quantities of gold were obtained in California, and I entertained my Granny with bulletin announcements to that effect ... I was often told that there were things of greater worth than gold."[22]

Paying his Way

One of Alex's first jobs outside the family was burning heather at Furmiston, a local farm. On Whitsunday 1852, however, at the age of eleven, he started work in earnest as a cowherd for the summer at Waterhead, a farm about six kilometres north of the village. The term was six months, for which he would be paid seventeen shillings and sixpence (in today's terms, about $5 per week) "and as much yarn as I could weave into stockings [long ones, extending to the groin] during the period of service."[23]

This farm was occupied by the brothers James and Alexander Shaw, "who were men of the old school, making no distinctions between themselves and their servants – eating at the same table and freely associating with them." According to McKay,

> The house in this respect was famous. In most of the farmhouses there had begun to be a separation between the farmer and his family and the servants, and when they no longer sat at the same table the breach grew wider and wider till the Parlour knew not the Kitchen further than was actually necessary for business purposes. This state of things had become general in the low grounds and agricultural districts of Galloway, but in the pastoral districts in many cases the Old Style continued to be.[24]

Alex was responsible for a dozen cows and "a great big Galloway bull".[25] They were kept in a byre at night and at dawn he drove them to the waird (an enclosure); some of this was reserved for growing hay, while the stony parts were for the animals. It was high up on the hill; even in summer frosts were frequent and McKay suffered from cold feet until he was given a pair of clogs. "At nine o'clock I had to bring the cows home to be milked, and when this was done I had to take them a certain distance farther than the cow-waird and turn them out on the hillside for the day."[26] For the rest of the day, he worked in the "kail-yard" (kitchen garden) or amongst the corn, turnip, or potato crops, unless it was haymaking time. At about six, the cows were brought in for milking again and then put in the byre or the calf-waird, a small paddock near the house, for the night.

It was fortunate that the farm was near the village as

> one Sunday morning towards the end of June word was brought that I was wanted at home. I went, and found that my Grandmother had been ill, and in fact was nigh unto death. I was brought to her bedside, and with an effort she put out her hand and bade me farewell saying that she was going away to leave

me. And I, poor me, hardly knew the meaning of what she said, but I knew that the gathering of my uncles and aunts meant something more than ordinary consequence. I had nothing to say in reply to my Granny. I looked upon the wan face in the bed and felt alarmed, yet so stood rivetted to the spot till led away. In less than half an hour the message she longed for had come and my Granny was no more. I was sorry and grieved in my own way … and it was long before a full realization of my great loss was brought home to me.[27]

McKay had to be back at Waterhead that afternoon in time for milking, and the next day was back to the usual routine. Luckily there was a distraction. At the time, people were talking about the discoveries of gold in Australia:

I like the rest, was excited. I made discoveries on my own account. My Granny had told me that gold was to be found in the neighbourhood of Wenlockhead [another lead mining area in the Southern Uplands, about forty kilometres west of Carsphairn, where gold had been found about 300 years earlier], and I thought it quite possible that it could be found nearer home. Where I herded the kye … the hill sides showed a thickness of glacial till much of which was of a granitic character, the granite material having a good deal of yellow mica. … [I] amused myself with make-believe that it was gold. I knew better, but then it was pardonable that I should try to deceive myself.

I failed entirely at the stocking-knitting business, due largely to having so many other matters on hand. My fads were trumpery affairs and half a dozen pairs of good socks would have been worth all the lot.[28]

McKay discovered a small library in a sitting room next to the kitchen at Waterhead. "Here I found Jamieson's dictionary of the Scotch language and was interested in the many scottish words I was till then unacquainted with or did not know the meaning of. Burns Poems was also there, and this I had not seen before."[29]

The farm of Durnscaw, where William Wilson was shepherd, was just across the River Deugh from Waterhead:

Mrs Wilson was cousin to my mother, and thus it was that I was often at the house. One night, the games and amusements being over, Mr. Wilson asked me which of his daughters I was going to marry – a wise-like question to ask a boy of eleven years. He had three, one much older, one younger, and one a year or so older whose name was Elizabeth. After due deliberation I said I would take Bess and was told I could have her. Bess raised no objection, and I then asked what tocher she would bring with her and was told that I must make bargain with the old woman (Mrs. Wilson), and accordingly I addressed myself to her. As a result it was promised me that Bess would bring with her plenishing to the extent of a caff [chaff] bed, three pair of hame-made blankets, a bolster, two pillows and a counterpane. Of the bed itself nothing was said and by inference that would have to be found by me. I next inquired if Bess would be provided crockery-ware pots and pans, etc., but was informed that what was promised was all that could be offered and that I must work for the rest and supply them when and how I could. Thus the business part of the arrangement ended. Then Mr. Wilson, who played on the violin, proposed that the arrangement arrived at should be followed by a dance … I said that before the dance commenced I should salute Bess the bride-to-be with a kiss and made overtures to Bess for that purpose. But Bess was bashful and would not be kissed before her parents, and perhaps imprudently I insisted on having the kiss. Bess was a big girl for her years and resisted; and in the struggle that ensued we passed from the kitchen into a sort of pantry and storeroom … there was a flood of something about our feet, and then I became aware that the large earthenware vessel called the 'cream pig' had been capsized … I did not go back to see Bess for a fortnight and then I had to submit to a good talking to from Mrs. Wilson.[30]

At Martinmas (28 November 1852), McKay finished his cow herding and returned to Carsphairn. That winter he went to school except when his father needed help with pit sawing. He did not get on with the new schoolmaster, Jock Hamilton. "My Grandmother being dead I missed her very much, and consequently I spent my lesson hours reading books obtained from the library at the Woodhead mines. Spring came, and at the school examination I gained the prize for Scripture history and this time I believe I better deserved it."[31]

He returned to Waterhead for the summer of 1853, but this time with an increased wage of thirty shillings for the six months (about $225 in today's terms). "At Waterhead the cows were the same, the bull was the same, and my duties scarcely different from what they had been the year before."[32] Alex began keeping a diary, "a cromele of daily occurrences … in rhyme too, for I had already discovered that Nature had designed me for a poet".[33] When a travelling salesman, Geordie Briery, revealed that Waterhead had been a castle and had a chamber where in olden times people had been imprisoned and murdered, it was too much for the imagination of a twelve-year-old boy:

> Geordie Briery made me eerie,
> With the story that he told;
> And I wonder if another
> From his pack he did unfold,
> What my dreams would be when sleeping
> In the garret up the stair;
> Would I waken in my terror,
> Would I grip my stiffened hair?
> Would I hide beneath the blankets?
> Or would I try to see

> If the horrid thing was still about
> And trying to catch me?
> I dinna ken, I canna tell,
> I have'na seen the thing,
> And maybe I but fright myself.
> O, when will it begin.[34]

McKay's work as a cow herd was not entirely uneventful as he describes in this account:

> From some cause haystacking was delayed longer than usual and I had still to herd the kye in the waird. After haystacking they had the run of the whole enclosure. The mornings were beginning to be frosty … I sat on the bull's back with my feet in a warm place, and the poke or bag end of my plaid over his head to keep away the flies when the sun got up. Well, one Sunday morning … feeling comfortable [I] neglected my duty and fell asleep. The cows very soon discovered what was the matter and hastened to get into mischief. They were soon among the hayricks, and in a short time capsized some half dozen of them and were having a rare time of it which might have continued till not one of that group of ricks was left standing. Fortunately auld Jamie Shaw was about, and observing what the cows were up to set his dog on them … For a time I was not to be found, but observing a heap of something that he knew was not aforetime in such place, he discovered that it was the bull with a plaid over him and something underneath the plaid … Jamie's anger was very considerable and his language was not choice. … When I brought home the cows I learnt that auld Jamie was rather pleased than otherwise with the morning's adventure, and had been telling with great glee how that after much search for me he found me fast asleep on the back of the bull.[35]

At Waterhead, McKay slept in a garret reached by a stepladder. The only window was in the roof, so that it was possible to get out onto the thatch and ridge of the roof. When his bed was found to contain some garden produce, he denied all knowledge of how it came to be there. Eventually the mystery was solved when the ploughman, who slept in the same room, found him half out the window but sound asleep, but "clearly on my way to the gooseberry patch."[36]

His sleep walking almost had more dire consequences. One night after a nocturnal wander McKay thought he was lying back down in bed when in truth he was at the top of the ladder. Falling to the bottom, he was stunned and could not make out who or where he was. "Had I come head first I had had no more adventures nor this to tell."[37]

From Waterhead one Sunday, Alex and Jock McCrae were sent to deliver a letter to a shepherd's cottage at Clennoch, a very isolated spot in the high hills north of Carsphairn. They saw several children at the cottage as they approached, but there was no answer to their knock. They went inside to leave the letter on the mantelpiece. On turning around, they saw three small heads peeking out from under the bed but as soon as they tried to explain their mission the children were out the door and took to the hills like wild goats. "These children were thoroughly wild and had evidently seldom seen other than their father and mother. I have seen children both in Australia and New Zealand that were as much isolated from intercourse with other than their parents, but were not wild and shy as these were."[38]

Martinmas came again and McKay returned home to Carsphairn for the winter of 1853–54. Again he felt the absence of his Grandmother. "My mother did not attract me in the same way, good and kind mother though she was. There were too many of us for her to give special attention to one, besides altogether she was a different type of woman to my Granmother".[39] He continued to read anything and everything, from the Bible to the *Ayr Advertiser* and the *West County and Galloway Journal*, in addition to books from the miners' library. But his father now kept him at knitting stockings in the evenings, and expected to see some progress made each night.

Sunday afternoons were free and he managed to find a little time each day to write up his diary. As he had no money to buy paper, he used paper scraps and the margins of old newspapers sewed together to form 'books'. Some of these books he destroyed and some were lost. The ones surviving at the time he emigrated, he gave to Auld Duncan McMurtie, with whom he had become friendly and who in a measure took the place of his Granny. Duncan could recite old songs and the poems of Burns and Byron and for more than three years the boy and the old man formed an association that brought them both comfort and company.[40]

That winter Alex went to school once more but helped his father in the sawpit when needed. He was 'broken in' on ash and oak and Scottish fir, but kept away from the more precise task of converting Canadian logs to one-inch and half-inch deal. He was glad of the work and glad to stay away from school, as his relationship with the schoolmaster was no better than it had been the year before.

The next summer (1854) he was hired as a cowherd at Garryhorn Farm, only one or two kilometres west of the village. Once again he had about a dozen cows and a bull to supervise. It was easier ground and looked as if it would to be an easy six months, so he kept with him a supply of reading and writing material in the crown of his Kilmarnock bonnet. His master, William Somerville, was not excited about his reading on the job and took him off to the cultivation paddock to pull weeds from the potato and turnip crop. McKay was displeased as he felt this was not part of his contract.

Garryhorn Farm, scene of one of McKay's less successful ventures into the workforce: '... that devil of a boy McKay put the bull on me.'

He also objected to Somerville's habit of leading him by the ear. The next day Alex hid but was tracked down and led off to the paddock once more. Each time the cows wandered, and each night he had to find them. This continued for some time until one day he hid himself so well that the master could not find him. "The cows were all round me and I could see what was going on. Presently [Somerville of] Garryhorn was in the close vicinity of the bull, who resented him being there at all, and with a loud bellow rushed towards him tail up and with no friendly intention."[41] The master fled with the bull in pursuit. Alex emerged from hiding as quickly as possible to watch. Somerville raced through a ford without slowing down, "the water splashing as high as himself", and after some minutes reached Holm House [Holm of Daltallochan] in a state of terror. Restored with a tot of whisky, he exclaimed "Oh, that devil of a boy McKay put the bull on me."[42] The next day the bull was removed and put in a strongly fenced paddock, as a 'dangerous animal'. "After that I had no more visits of Garryhorn."[43]

McKay was at the age where he needed action and the cultivation paddock was not to his taste. Acquiring some gunpowder from the village shop, he entertained himself with small explosions. Tiring of this, he planned a larger explosion, with the master's son in tow. "I got a peat from the kitchen fire and handed it through the back window to Jock who was outside. I had just done so when his mother called me and in such a tone that it was clear I must go and without delay. I therefore asked Jock not to set the powder off till I came."[44] Unfortunately the boy did not obey and when Alex returned he found the powder had gone and Jock's face was blackened. "I took him to the burn, a cold mountain stream, and put his face in the water as long as he could hold his breath, and when he stood up he said the pain was better, so I led him towards the house. We had gone but a few yards when Jock's face was as painful as before and I had to take him back and put his face in the water once more." Eventually he took Jock back to the house, where he was confronted first by Mrs Somerville and then by the master, who gave him a cuff on the side of his head, "knocking off my Kilmarnock. The blow was of such force that the contents, – pamphlets and broadsheets, songbook and so on were spread across the kitchen floor. … The news spread rapidly and during the afternoon my Mother went to Garryhorn and the matter was settled in some fashion."[45] But McKay had acquired the reputation of being a bad boy and after another incident, in which he killed a laying hen, he could not be pardoned and Alex left Garryhorn a month before his time was up.

Nothing was said by his parents about the fracas at Garryhorn. He went back to helping in the sawpit and once the potato harvest was over he went, at the age of fourteen, to school for the last time.

3. Prying & Trying

Words and Stones

As McKay grew into adolescence, so too grew his interest in poetry and young women, to the extent that he fantasised about becoming a successor to Robert Burns.[1] His dreams extended to the discovery of vast mineral riches, as another way of avoiding the conventional occupations available to him locally: a carpenter in the footsteps of his father, or a farm labourer. Although in his 'Fragments' he does not present himself as an able and willing worker, in a few years he saved enough to go to New Zealand.

For literature, he was able to spend more time with Auld Duncan McMurtrie, provided his father approved the current rate of stocking production. Auld Duncan was a great admirer of Burns, Scott and Byron. Alex delighted in his company, and they spent much time in reciting ballads and poems. Once, in the fields of Carsphairn, while he was digging potatoes with his mother and an older brother, he felt the approach of the Poetic Muse, and asked his mother (who believed in his poetic genius) to run to the house for paper, pen and ink. When she had done so, he sat on a potato drill and wrote:

> It wun'd, it rained, it hail'd, it snaw'd,
> It thundered away like anything,[2]

McKay's brother was not impressed, and with a burst of scornful language frightened "away the coy lady [the Muse] and she never returned to finish the stanza."[3] However, McKay was determined to distinguish himself "if not among the great, at least among the local poets."[4] He was distracted from this when Robert Hastings found a mass of lead ore on the back of Holm Hill, where it slopes down to the Deugh and Knockengorroch:

> I had already read some articles and notices of geology in books from the Mines libary [sic], and been attracted by the Spar minerals [crystalline minerals] in the waste materials excavated from the mines, and I was determined to know something more of local geology and mineralogy. I knew that gold had been got from upper Clydesdale and Wanlockhead districts, and now I must needs discover a lead mine or a gold mine. Others, including skilled miners, made a search, and failing to find anything more than what had been found by Robert Hastings, the exceitement [sic] soon died away. My search resulted in the finding of a seam of soft claystone (calmstone) exposed in the banks of Bank Burn [Benloch Burn] at the back of Knockgray Craig. This was a discovery

neither valuable nor important, but it provided the excuse for myself and other boys making trips to the locality to get some of the material for the making of slate pencils.[5]

The following year, 1854, the potato crop was east of the road between the village and Lagwyne (now across the road from the Heritage Centre). McKay was again one of the gatherers. Finding some unusual stones in the gravelly soil, he took a couple home and, using his father's grindstone and oil stone, produced a flat, polished surface. He could see that the stones consisted of bundles of small rods, with a different material between the rods. He called the stones 'rush roots',[6] but in reality they were fossil corals of Silurian age (400–440 million years ago). As a geologist, McKay was to add tens of thousands of fossils to museum collections in New Zealand, so the time and place of these first finds assumes special significance. He was then thirteen years old.

During the next year, 1855, McKay worked on various jobs: stone-gathering, peat-casting (cutting and stacking), turnip-thinning, sheep-shearing, haymaking and harvesting. As a growing adolescent, he also associated with more persons of his own age, though with mixed effect:

> I was not always a favourite with the others and sometimes had to put up with thrashings from those who were bigger or more expert than myself. That, off the boys, I did not much mind because I thus learned how to fight. At one place where a number of boys and girls were employed at turnip thinning a girl there was who belaboured me most unmercifully, not once or twice, but once or twice daily. I put up with this for a time and until the thing became unbearable, till finally I had to complain to the man in charge of the field, and he advised me to retaliate, giving me instructions as to how I might successfully wrestle with her. I practised on some of my smaller brothers, and by Monday morning I was prepared for Jean Ferguson, and before dinnertime had an opportunity of displaying my skill, and was not further molested.[7]

He was still reading the local newspapers and interested in events in the outside world. The Crimean War was being fought and he followed its battles (Alma and Inkerman). He would listen eagerly as the newspaper was read out in the smithy, sometimes turning events into doggerel verse, once Auld Duncan had explained their significance to him:

> On Alma's height the Russian sat
>   And thought himself secure,
> And some said he was right in that
>   And some were not so sure.
> But right or wrong our soldiers' speed
>   Across the rushing stream
> And up the hill whence yet ahead
>   Did bullets whiz and scream.
> Yet up and up our heroes sprang

> Though some behind remained,
> The Russian fled, and thus my man,
> The Alma heights were gained.
> Shout then for victory and declare
> How well the field was won,
> Ah, but how many still lie there,
> Where the brave deed was done.[8]

Love & Poems

As a teenage successor to Robbie Burns, he naturally expanded into love poems, but not about Bess Wilson (with whom he still had some arrangement but apparently little contact):

> O Miss Mary Ballantine
> I love thee more than blood-red wine;
> Although a tippler I may be,
> Yet more than whisky I love thee.
> I love each bonnie glowing cheek,
> And kisses which thou dost bestow.
> Thou art the only thing I seek
> Of all the blessings here below.
> Your crusty father disna wish
> That I your lover ere should be
> He says that I'm a drunken fish –
> You know that is not true of me.
> Oh, were I married to my love
> I'd gain the height of happiness
> And more: I then would ever prove
> A husband which the wife could bless.
> So I will love and love thee still
> Till time shall give thyself to me,
> Till bent will be the stubborn will
> That will not let my love go free.[9]

McKay showed the love poem to Leezy Curry, the girl next door, with whom he was "rather thick",[10] and who was also writing poetry. Leezy may have been expecting something addressed to herself, for she "took it waur than anything I had ever seen ... she tore it up and threw it on the fire ... I had no comings and goings with Leezy for nearly a week after that ..."[11]

A later literary venture was to write love letters on contract. It transpired that a lassie wanted a repeat of the previous night's encounter with her young man. Once the time and place of a tryst had been sandwiched between romantic encouragements, the letter was duly signed, sealed and delivered. Alex then hid at the appropriate spot, to witness the outcome. It was apparently successful, although neither Alex nor the lassie could agree on the number of times she had been kissed![12]

Then it was summer and he was fifteen. He was to work again on Furmiston farm, where he had begun his career as a heather-burner. John Harper was a considerate master and McKay did well under his care. Once again his duties were various. Some days he was a shepherd, or a cultivator, or whatever was most pressing. After haymaking and the corn harvest, he was occupied with stone-clearing, draining, and fencing the more fertile land. Some of the stones to be moved were so large that blasting was necessary, and for this Auld Guffie had to be brought in from the village. Auld Guffie was a carter, but was experienced in quarrying or raising stones for building walls or fences.

Guffie also happened to be Preceptor (teacher or instructor) in the local Kirk on Sundays. A light-hearted prank taught the young McKay something of the tribulations of love. During a lively conversation at midday dinner one day, Alex's arrangement with Beth Wilson was mentioned. Auld Guffie took great interest, and dictated a form that Alex signed – with little thought for the consequences. It authorised Guffie to proclaim in church a proposal of marriage between Elizabeth Wilson of Durnscaw and Alex McKay of Carsphairn. Auld Guffie went home that evening and the news spread like wildfire. A shepherd, John Cowan, even went post-haste to Knockgray farm where Bess was working, in order to tell her before she went to bed.

Despite Bess's declaration that "lines or no lines … she would not have [him]",[13] the senseless joke, fuelled by the Guffie family, went on and on. On Sunday her tormentors explained to Bess that, thrice cried, she was bound to him, whether she liked it or not. Her mistress found her in tears and urged her to get down to the Kirk and object. Meanwhile, Alex's parents pointed out that as he was under age the banns would not be cried.[14]

The Guffie girls, however, shielded Bess from both this information and from the fact that other banns were to be cried that day. When Auld Guffie rose to announce the advertised intentions of marriage, Bess sprang to her feet and shouted, "I won't hae him":[15]

> Instantly all eyes were turned to Bess and there was such movement and rustling all over the Kirk that the dogs, thinking the Service was over, rushed into the passages and with much snarling and growling a real genuine dog-fight concluded this part of the proceedings, and it was some time before order could be restored.[16]

Though she could not know it then, this rejection was to end their relationship.

Bess left the area for several years and Alex continued in much the same fashion as before. Winter came and went but spring brought a heavy snowfall, just as lambing was due. On Furmiston, not a single sheep could be seen and Mr Harper was very apprehensive:

> Clearly it was a case for dogs and digging. All worked with a will … There were but four of us and the auld man. The dogs soon let us know where to dig and about two thirds of the sheep were set free without much trouble. They had drifted before the storm into a sheltered gully, the lower part of which was swept by the wind, and here the deposit over the sheep was but a few feet thick. Farther east the sheep had a very great thickness of snow over them, the gully being quite levelled. After one or two sheep were taken out the others came out of themselves. At another place the dogs located sheep and here the rest of the flock was liberated with almost as much ease as in the first case, and thus every sheep on the place was accounted for. In other parts of the mountain district between Ayrshire and Galloway there were serious losses, the heaviest being on the Star farm in the valley above Loch Doon. Here three hundred sheep were driven before the storm and drowned in Star Lane.[17]

The following summer Alex was at Carminnows, a farm about three miles down the river, on the opposite side from Carsphairn. He was now sixteen. There were two girls at Carminnows, N.G. and her older sister B., who had been jilted when her young man ran off to Australia without her. Poor B. in despair ran away from home. After a week she was found and brought home, where she shut herself in her room for nine days with neither food nor drink. By the time haymaking came round, she was about and doing a little, although lacking her former vitality. Despite her own ordeal, B. with delicacy and tact arranged for Alex and N.G. to be frequently left alone. As a result of this practical encouragement – and a natural attraction – he became very close to N.G. Looking back, McKay regarded her "as my first love".[18]

By 1857, when he was sixteen, McKay had shown little indication of how he might ultimately earn a living. His parents, "at their wits end", decided that he should become a carpenter like his father.[19] As reading books was the only thing he was fond of, this seemed as good as anything else to Alex. Much of the work that winter was outdoors, on the Holm of Daltollochan, where Mr Jamieson needed rough farm timber sawn up.

Helping his father with casual work on farms around the district gave Alex the opportunity to increase the number of young women he knew in the parish. In 'Fragments', he reported that he "made love" to one of them, a serving girl at Knockgray farm.[20] His attentiveness to the young women he encountered was by no means unique. Knockgray was only two miles from the village and often troubled with night prowlers seeking to make the acquaintance of the female servants in the house. Jock Wallace, the son of the tenant farmer, hit on an effective plan. He loaded a gun, but instead of shot, wad, or ball he used bullock blood. From the shelter of some trees he surprised the prowlers at such close quarters that one of them received the contents of the gun on a pair of white moleskins. Once clear of the scene, the one who was hit ran his hand down his thigh, discovered it was covered with blood, and cried out to his companions who were fast fleeing the scene, "I may rin a wee bit, but I winna rin far." However, he made it to his lodgings and did not die.[21]

In 1860, when McKay was nineteen, the schoolmaster who had succeeded Jock Hamilton brought his bride back to the village. At about midnight someone began to toll the bell of the Kirk next door as if for a funeral. As McKay commented in his autobiography, "I was innocent as the new born babe but I could not exactly state that I was in my bed at the time this outrage was committed, and thus till I left home at least, I was accused and credited with the disgrace."[22] From a distant time and place he could reveal his alibi:

> I gaed at night to see a lass,
>   I'll no say where nor when,
> Ance by itsel haith this time was
>   An' werdy o' a song.
>
> I gaed for to fulfil a tryst,
>   And kiss my lassie dear,
> I was resolved and had devised
>   That night of her to speir.[23]

Another year passed at the sawpit, with Alex sawing the stubborn Scotch fir on Holm Farm in the winter, and renovating shepherds' cottages during the summer. On one occasion, while he was repairing a cottage at Castlemaddy, near Braidenoch, he climbed Carlin's Cairn (807 metres) because he wanted to see the granite country that lay beyond the Rhinn of Kells. It was a day of fierce wind, so strong that it brought him to a standstill on his way down and he let it blow him back up the hill just for the fun of it.

Later that year he reported a great thunderstorm with torrential rain swept across the hills northwest of Carsphairn. As many of the hillsides were drained with open ditches which channelled and concentrated the runoff, there were flash floods in the larger burns. McKay notes one where a wall of water five to seven feet high (about two metres) came roaring down a stream. The rain was particularly heavy around the road between Carsphairn and Dalmellington, and the Glenmuck and Mossdale bridges were swept away. In some areas crops were destroyed, although one shepherd remarked that "he lost a patch of potatoes valuable to him but he had the consolation of having had a field of fish instead, but it cost him all his salt to preserve part of the latter crop."[24]

The Green Well of Scotland, a deep pothole formed by the river (visible lower right). The well was rumoured to hold a treasure trove. Alex McKay and his friend attempted to drain it by tunnelling in from the far side, but their attempt in the middle of the night to blast apart a rock barring their way so terrorised the local inhabitants that the two deemed it prudent to desist. Photo: Anne Rutherford

Where the road crosses the Deugh at the Holm Bridge, about a mile north of the village, there is evidence that the river once ran at a higher level. On the north bank are several churns (potholes), which are formed when stones get caught in a hole and are spun round and round by the water. The stones act as millstones, grinding the hole deeper. On the south bank, at a higher level, there is an even larger churn eighteen to twenty feet (six to seven metres) across.

McKay reported in his 'Fragments' that this hole was filled with putrid water with green scum and that it went by the name of the 'Deil's Well'. (It is now officially known as the Green Well of Scotland.)

> Of the Deil's Well all sorts of stories were told: how that at times past it had at various times received valuables that otherwise were likely to fall into the hands of the enemy, and therefore other than its being unfathomably deep and containing much rubbish, it would yield these treasures again were it pumped dry and cleaned out. Its great depth however was a deterrent as it had swallowed up several chains of a stone dyke ... and yet apparently could swallow up as much more. Also it was said that slaughter and murder had been committed here, and the bones of the dead might not with impunity be disturbed.[25]

Alex and his friend Samuel Gracie visited the Well frequently and discussed the probability of its containing vessels of silver and gold, and gold and diamond rings. Some of the ground around the well sounded hollow; they decided it was more likely that the valuables reportedly thrown in the well had been hidden in a secret chamber. They were faced with difficulties, as the farmer would never let them dig it up and they dared not let on to anyone else what they were doing. The two boys decided to see Mary Gordon, reputed witch of the parish, who had recently been credited with saving Auld Guffie, his horse and cart from a horrible death in a bog hole, about the matter. She advised them to go back the next night and think about their plans and act on their conclusion, "'for that will be the right thing ta dae, and mind ye never come to see me again for if ye doe sae that will spoil a'.'"[26] Alex and Samuel met and discussed their plans, but the greatest stumbling block was Samuel's concern about parting with the pair of diamond earrings they had agreed to give to Mary Gordon's daughter, a hurdle which was solved only by Alex offering to supply them from his share of the booty.

The next night, armed with a pickaxe and spade, Alex and Sam commenced digging into the bank where it sounded hollow. On the third night they came to a smooth face of rock. They concluded that this stone had been placed there deliberately to guard the treasure, and the only way past was to blast it. Alex took a hand drill from his father's workshop and Samuel got some blasting powder from the mines. After several nights' hard work they were ready. They set the charge carefully in the hole they had drilled, lit the taper and cleared out. They made for the terraces opposite the houses at the Brig end and lay down to wait the result. Samuel's father came out in his nightdress just as there was a roar as if the heavens were rent, and he leaped three or four feet in the air. The silence of the following moment was awful. Other residents emerged, with Betty Barber crying, "'Flee unto the mountains for this is the Crack of Doom.'"[27]

When Alex and Samuel were able to get back to the stone they found it "as sound as ever". The shot hole had not been deep enough and the charge had blown out. As other people had also heard the extraordinary noise, the pair deemed it not politic to be seen around the Deil's Well for a while.

As it turned out the treasure was to remain undisturbed, for Alex was to get work out of the village, first with James Wight at Dalmellington, a small town about sixteen kilometres north of Carsphairn, and finally in Dumfrieshire, to the southeast. His final employment in Scotland came to an unfortunate end, when one evening some green fruit was brought to the house:

> I partook of some with an unfortunate result. On the following morning I had to travel some eight miles to do some special work. I set out on the journey, but was fit neither for the journey nor the work when I got there. On the way I passed a country inn and there, as my condition warranted, I had a glass of

whisky, and without delay proceeded on my journey. When I got to where I was bound for I was no better, perhaps worse, and though I got through my work it had to be with the assistance of others … Shortly after I was sent for by my employer; the poor man was sick and in bed, so I had to see him in the bedroom. Apparently he had little to say to me, for on my being brought to his presence he handed me my wages and added that I was a young man who, disregarding the example of worthy forebears had elected the downward path and in due time my reward would be, not according to grace, but what I merited. I understood the purport of this sufficiently to endeavour to explain what had been the cause of my apparent backsliding, but was interrupted by his exclaiming: 'Not a word; as you have chosen so be it; my hands are "clean."' I didna think so, for he had a bonny daughter that through him was responsible for my being in that part of the country at all. And for my ain and her sake I was determined to make another effort, so I repeated what I had before said and asked him to hear me in defence. But sitting up in bed with his hand he waved away, and said: "Not one word, sir; leave my presence," and it was clear that I must do or create a scene.[28]

The "bonny daughter" sided with her father so he found no comfort there.

McKay left his lodgings the next morning and returned to Carsphairn, there to think out some plans for the future. Reviewing his life and future in Carsphairn, he began to realise that "so far I had not been a success",[29] and when he examined his outlook he made the decision to emigrate. He was twenty-two years old. His brother had emigrated to New Zealand a year before, as had several other young men from the region. All things considered, there were several points in favour of emigration: "I then had the wherewithal, and I might never have it again" and although "it might be a case of out of the frying pan into the fire. No matter, the frying pan was getting red-hot so the fire could not be so very much worse."[30]

At that time New Zealand (and especially Nelson and Otago) appeared to be virgin lands, where it was possible to find gold simply by raking the ground and picking up the nuggets. Alex resolved that if he made his fortune he would return to Scotland and "put some things to rights that I thought wanted mending. Clearly it was time I was out of the country."[31] He farewelled his parents: "my poor mother … That was a bit hard but it had to be."[32] He saw neither of them again.

It was less severe parting with Bess Wilson, to whom he had been 'betrothed'. She now wanted to accompany him but his response was "I'll tak' care that ye 'dinna refuse me twice'."[33] And so he and Bess parted, after what seems to have been an arranged and unsatisfactory relationship spanning at least a decade. His departure absolute from Scotland and his kin was less easy and on 3 July 1863 – "a fine sunny day while it was raining (tears)"[34] – McKay sailed from the Broomielaw in Glasgow, on board the ship *Helenslee*. His married sister Kate saw him off, and was so distressed

In the 1860s and 70s the Broomielaw on the River Clyde was a bustle of activity. In the foreground steamers queue to take day-trippers down the Clyde for a few hours respite from the grimy industrial atmosphere of Glasgow. On the far side of the river the emigrant ships created a forest of masts as they prepared to offer a more permanent change of scenery. Photo: The Herald and Evening Times, Glasgow

she would have let the ship sail without him. As the ship drew away McKay was "quite sensible that I had made the fateful move on the chess board of my life."[35] The ship drifted slowly downstream to Greenock, but the next day reached the Firth of Clyde. From there the weather was stormy; McKay and many other passengers had their first taste of seasickness:

> I did not feel quite well, but I saw lots o' folk waur than mysel'. There were six hundred of us besides the crew and the Captain. What cared I how many there were. I kenned naebody and naebody kenned me. It was a curious sensation and I canna but say I liked it. If this new venture was a success weel thanks to naebody; if it wasna weel naebody wad be any the wiser. And so with sic thoughts and half seasick I watched the rowing [angry] sea as the ship drove into the darkness.[36]

4. Emigration

This account of the 1863 voyage of the Helenslee *has been drawn from McKay's 'Fragments'[1] and from a journal by another passenger on the ship, Mrs David Bonthron.[2] However, as more details of shipboard life are available from the diary of Thomas Murray,[3] who travelled on the same ship a year later, information and quotations are drawn from all three sources. Both voyages were under the command of Captain William Brown. They carried a similar number of passengers and followed the same route (see page 52). However, the 1863 voyage departed in July and took only seventy-nine days to reach Bluff, whereas the 1864 sailing, on which Murray travelled, left Glasgow in September and took one hundred days to reach Auckland.*

The *Helenslee* was a new ship, having been built the year before by Archibald McMillan and Co. of Dumbarton, for Patrick Henderson of Glasgow. She was under charter to Shaw Savill and was apparently on her maiden voyage. According to Lloyds Register, the *Helenslee* was fifty metres long, ten metres wide, and eight metres deep. She weighed 810 tonnes. She had a crew of thirty-five and on this trip carried 315 passengers, including many children and infants. Supernumeraries included a blackbird, a hare, and a dozen rabbits, a gift to the Southland Provincial Council.

McKay wrote little about the voyage. He recorded in his 'Fragments',

> I kept nae journal of events nor of what happened from day to day. Other people did and I even now wonder what they wrote. I suppose that sort of thing goes on to the present day. I made no notes, and had I done so they would long ago have been lost. For a' that I could write a long story as to what happened, but mainly it would be a story about naething – it wasna worth putting down then and I'm sure it would not be worth paper and ink now.[4]

The accommodation on board came in several categories, matching those of present-day air travel, but relatively more expensive. A sole occupancy in the Chief Cabin was £78 /15/– (about $12,000 in today's terms). Second class was £25 ($4000). Steerage passengers had the choice of enclosed or open berths at £20 ($3000) or £16 ($2400) respectively. The berth partitions were of canvas, forming cubicles, each including several berths. Berths were arranged side by side in tiers around the perimeter of the ship, with mess tables and seats down the centre. Passengers supplied

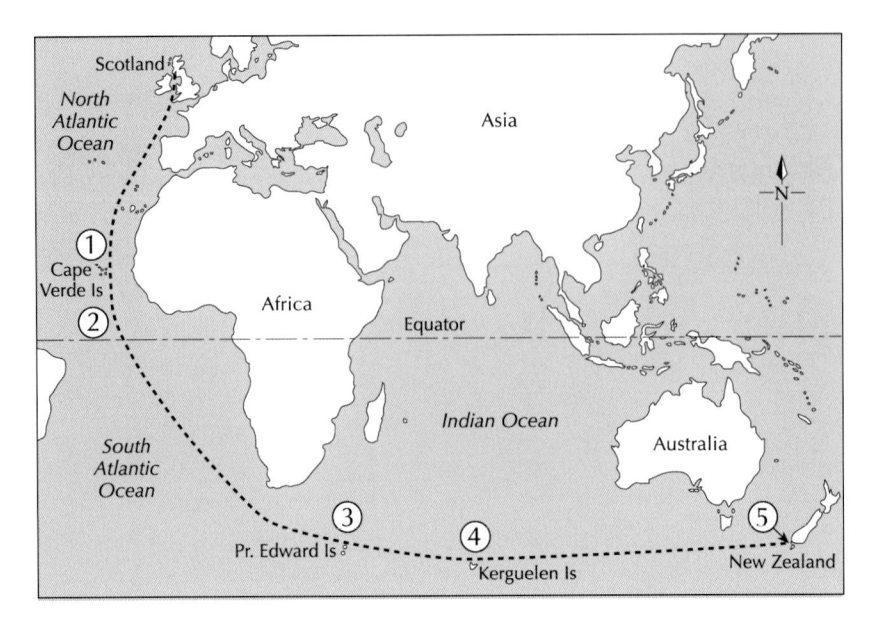

The route followed by the Helenslee *in 1863. Once out into the Atlantic Ocean, there was little to see – 'it would be a story about naething.' The first land sighted was Cape Verde (1). The Equator (2) was crossed two weeks later. The* Helenslee, *like most emigrant ships, then proceeded into the deep latitudes south of the Cape of Good Hope and Australia to capitalise on the westerly trade winds. Glimpses of the Prince Edward (3) and Desolation (Kerguelen) Island (4) were the passengers' only reminders of* terra firma, *until Solander Island (5) loomed almost too close on 25 September.*

their own mattresses to specified dimensions: fifty centimetres wide for men, forty-five centimetres for women, and for children according to their size. Single men were quartered at the bow (sharp end) of the ship, as far as away as possible from the single women at the stern, with a buffer zone of married couples and children in between. There was a water closet on each side, another in the single-women's quarters, and others in the male and female sick bays.

The segregation was not entirely successful, as Mrs Bonthron recorded:

> It seems there has been a most disagreeable affair down in the young womans division yesterday. Whispered rumors have been rife for weeks past of disgraceful doings among a few of the females and also that the Matron, a young married woman, going out to her husband instead of seeking to repress such behaviour was herself involved in it, but it now had come to such a height that some of the decent and respectable woman [sic] beside them could no longer suffer it and complained to the First Mate.[5]

Word of these 'doings' duly reached the Captain, who accepted the matron's

DINNER ON BOARD THE FIRST EMIGRANT SHIP FOR NEW ZEALAND.

In this engraving there are about forty people. On the Helenslee *about 300 would have been occupying this space, with nowhere else to go in rough conditions. Note the tiered bunks around the perimeter. Lamps or candles were not permitted when it was rough, and any loose items, including food and slop containers would have been tossed from side to side as the ship rolled. At times reverse flows of water surging up through the primitive valves of the water closets would wash across the floor.* Wood Engraving, Star Lithograph Works, Auckland. ATL, A-109-054

version so 'that this the same evil conduct will go on without check …'[6] A couple of weeks later Mrs Bonthron observed:

> [There are] Sad accounts too of the Matron using the Brandy bottle very fully in which it appears some of the ships officers partake with her, and the conduct in that quarter is a perfect scandal and grief to all who have any regard to decency and sobriety while none who are witnesses seem to have the courage to expose it at the proper quarter.[7]

No mention of these problems was made by McKay in his 'Fragments', although he did report that in the tropics the ship was briefly in the doldrums and "passengers thus early were put on a short ration of water and there was talk also of the same thing with respect to the substantials. I viewed all this with indifference; I was still half seasick and I was by no means lively."[8] There was considerable emphasis on hygiene, with an open-air bathtub on the forecastle for the men, and one of the cabin water closets converted into a bathroom for women. Bedding was aired twice a week, and the berths were scraped, scrubbed, and sprinkled with calcium chloride. Passengers were advised that four towels and two pounds of marine soap were desirable. Measles and whooping cough occurred but did not reach epidemic proportions. Bowel complaints were also common.

An astute social fabric was also set in place. Ship's constables were appointed from among the passengers to enforce the rules. "There was also a matron for the single women, who at sea had to be below by 8 p.m.; other passengers could stay on deck with their lingering thoughts until 9 p.m."[9]

The orderly distribution of meals was accomplished by creating self-governing messes, each of about ten or so persons. A concert committee was formed, and concerts and dances (to the music of the bagpipes) were held when the weather was favourable. First and second-class passengers took their entertainment separately from those in steerage.

According to Murray, passengers had 'an excellent library on board, to which everyone has access.'[10] Fishing, cards, draughts, and deck quoits all helped to pass the time. Observation of the Sabbath was another important ritual, in which both sailors and even the more unlikely elements of the passenger population sometimes participated. Smoking was commonplace amongst the men, as Mrs Bonthron noted:

> Nothing has been to me a greater source of annoyance than the almost universal practice of smoking ... I don't believe there could be ten men on board that do not smoke scores of them seem literally to do nothing but eat sleep and smoke ... It makes one almost ashamed to think that such men come from Scotland ...[11]

The quantity and range of food supplied by Shaw Savill was quite generous. Bread for each mess was baked twice a week. Thomas Murray wrote:

> We want for nothing, even the nursing children are provided for, they get sugar, oatmeal, flour, soft bread and preserved milk every week ... Some [passengers] have large cans full of tea, sugar, and butter, saved over from their rations. I have thrown [surplus] soup, beet, and potatoes overboard ...[12]

Lime juice, pickles, and vinegar were served to ward off scurvy.[13] A crate of ducks, a rooster, and a pig were carried for the menu of cabin passengers. But for those in steerage salt beef was the staple. 'Without soaking overnight it was so salty as to be barely edible, as were the preserved potatoes: they are so hard [after cooking] it would require a digester to soften them.'[14] The beef was sometimes towed astern to freshen it up. It was reported that even the sharks would veer away from it.

The calibre of the cook and his assistant had much to do with passenger satisfaction. Passengers on McKay's 1863 voyage contributed £5 ($750) as a sign of their appreciation of the meals prepared: 'it is proposed to get clothes for him when we can instead of giving it to him in money in case he melts it in grog' commented Mrs Bonthron.[15] Thomas Murray, on the other hand, reported considerable dissatisfaction the following year. 'When a passenger expressed his displeasure over the rice to the assistant cook, he replied "The rice was well enough boiled, if he was not pleased with it to chuck it overboard." Burnett, in place of throwing it overboard threw it in his face.'[16] He also reported: "The cook has mismanaged the preserved potatoes, half of them were not properly dissolved, which gave rise to a disagreeable dispute. For half an hour there was nothing but tearing and swearing, the most abominable oaths and language was made use of."[17]

The efforts of the cooks and their assistants in providing hot food and drink for 350 people on a pitching, rolling platform was quite remarkable. Their job never eased off, come fair weather or foul, whereas most of the rest of the crew had bouts of intense activity interspersed with long slack periods.

About once a week there was a significant squabble. The quality of the food, refusals to do allocated chores like standing watch or cleaning, tiffs between men whose wives felt aggrieved, the opening or closing of ventilation hatches, and transgressions into personal space and property were the main issues, beyond the underlying foundation of discomfort and boredom. The ship's surgeon was the primary arbiter in such disputes, with the captain becoming involved only in the most serious issues. Punishment frequently involved a mild form of public humiliation, such as having to respond to the ship's bell every hour through the night with a cry of 'All's Well', to the derision of one's mates. As Murray wrote, 'It is no use trying to pull against the standing orders of an emigrant ship, they will make you the laughing stock of all on board.'[18]

From the Firth of Clyde, the *Helenslee* sailed south into the Irish Sea, then out into the vast Atlantic. After three weeks they passed the Cape Verde Islands, and two weeks later, on 6 August, they crossed the Equator. While McKay's voyage rationed water in the tropics, Murray also had his difficulties a year later: as the water "from the rustiness of the tank had a colour not very pleasing to the eye; however the sailors assured us it was an excellent tonic for the stomach".[19] By the end of August, McKay's ship was in the 'Roaring Forties' and a thunderstorm relieved the water situation: "rain water filled all sorts of receptacles, some of them unnameable."[20]

Now the prevailing westerly winds were pushing them ever eastwards at a steady clip of around eleven knots. Land was sighted only twice. The Prince Edward Islands showed on the horizon on 3 September, and Desolation Island (Kerguelen) came into view six days later: "We had now snow on deck and the lasts and yards became oval-shaped from encrusting ice. It was winter and it was cauld. Some said that the Captain had gone farther South than it was allowable to take a passenger ship. Whether this was true or not I know not, but we got sight of some floating islands of ice – ice-bergs from the South Pole – and while they were visiting it was caulder than ever."[21] There were some fierce storms too. On 11 September Mrs Bonthron wrote: 'Another fearful night of rolling and pitching, water cans flying about and boxes bouncing from their fixings. No sleep to be had almost unless with the children who seem somehow to be little disturbed. Indeed it is wonderful how we all get accustomed to an extraordinary amount of tossing about by day and night but last night was rather more than tolerable.'[22]

At 50° South, they were well south of Australia and Tasmania, and running day after day before the wind, across the endless expanse of restless empty ocean. By mid-September, some seventy-five days out of Glasgow, there was talk of an imminent landfall, and Mrs Bonthron noted in her journal her annoyance at 'some of the young men next to us, separated only by a thin partition, who expressed their rejoicing at being near the end of the voyage in a very unseemly way.' Their sin apparently was to sing a boisterous version of *Old McDonald Had a Farm* in anticipation of regaining *terra firma:* 'They set up every sort of noise from the mew of a cat and crowing of a cock to the wild howling of a pack of wolves.'[23] Fortunately, the Captain, appearing 'very anxious to have sobriety and everything coming on board', had limited other forms of outrageous behaviour by raising the price and limiting the availability of grog to restrictive levels.[24]

Despite the rumours of a landfall, Captain Brown "was not quite sure of his position in longitude and offered a reward to whomsoever should first sight land".[25] Having passed 500 kilometres to the south of Tasmania, they were now on a northeast heading, making straight for Southland. Mrs Bonthron recorded on 22 September:

> Today we are in 146 degrees E longitude and 48 1/2S latitude. We are keeping now to the N.East making straight for Southland running about 8 knots per hour which is not so fast as we have been going frequently of late, but still good being 192 [nautical] miles in the 24 hours.[26]

A Near Miss

On the morning of 25 September, McKay was one of a few passengers standing at the port rail. Picture the scene – the ship was probably scudding along at its usual speed of eleven to twelve knots in the bitter greyness of the predawn. It was now the seventy-ninth day out of Glasgow, and it would seem as if they had been running with this wind forever. The following seas that accompanied the ship would surge under the ship's counter and make her pitch and yaw as uncomfortably and uncontrollably as at any previous time on the voyage. The wind wailed through the rigging, the sails slapped, and the ship's timbers creaked and groaned. From below decks came the fretful cries of sleepless children, and the sonorous rumblings of more

The volcanic rocks of the Solander Islands rear unexpectedly from the sea bed at the western entrance to Foveaux Strait and are pounded more often than not by heavy westerly swells. They are about thirty kilometres from the nearest land. The Helenslee *was within a few metres of becoming the greatest maritime disaster in New Zealand history when the islands loomed out of the dawn 'at such close quarters ... it seemed that our fate was sealed.' The Solanders were named after Daniel Solander, a Swedish botanist with Captain Cook on his voyage of exploration and discovery in 1770. Photo: Peter Johnson*

fortunate adults. Sea birds rode the wind behind, feasting on whatever was cast from the ship, adding their squabbling cries to the background sounds.

But now amongst them was a new sound, the sound of waves breaking onshore. McKay would have strained his eyes towards it. And then his stomach would have tightened, for the misty greyness beyond the ship had darkened – it now had mass and bulk and he was looking at the cliffs of Solander Island streaming with water and towering high overhead:

> In the dusk of the early morning the Solander Island at the western end of Foveaux Strait was sighted, with the ship bearing directly on to it and at such close quarters that there was every likelihood of a terrible shipwreck ... which, however, by a miracle did not come off. The ship was unruly and did not readily answer her helm, and at one time it seemed that our fate was sealed.[27]

McKay would have witnessed the shouts and frenzied activity as the crew fought the sails and aided the helmsman to control the spinning wheel. Mrs Bonthron recorded in her diary:

> Soon we were all on deck and to the left of us lay a huge rock not unlike the Bass Rock in the German Ocean to which we had come so close that escape from sudden doom seemed to onlookers almost helpless when it was seen the

The HMS Acheron *was employed on a survey of New Zealand coasts and harbours between 1848 and 1852. Beechey may well have imagined his easel set up on Solander Island when he painted this picture, which dramatically illustrates the drama of a sailing ship being too close to rocky shore for comfort. The painting, an oil by R.B. Beechey, is titled 'H.M.S.* Acheron, *Captain J. Lort Stokes, rides out a terrific gale between the South Islands [Middle and Stewart] of New Zealand, 1849'.* National Library of Australia

helm would not work on account of the violence of the storm. In an instant both Captain and first mate cast their coats on deck and were pulling at the ropes of the jib by the hoisting of which sail the vessel, got round the rock when so near that a stone might have almost been thrown at it.[28]

With sails furled and trimmed the ship slowly began to respond to the helm and the bow swung gradually south. The tension would have remained high, however, as every time a large swell rose under the ship she would have swung back a point or two closer to a collision course with the rocks that fringed the island. Then suddenly rocks and island were disappearing astern as rapidly as they had loomed ahead. 'None who saw it [the island] or when the concern of the Captain and Chief Mate could fail to realise at the moment the wonderful preservation we had experienced', gushed Mrs Bonthron.[29]

Once clear of the Solanders, the mainland was in sight, only a few kilometres to the north. Captain Brown, probably mightily relieved, may have hastened below, perhaps to fortify himself with a ration of rum after such a close shave.

McKay may well have felt some nostalgia, for the land in sight was not unlike his homeland in general elevation and steepness. The higher mountains were capped with snow but elsewhere it was thickly wooded. He was not to know that thirty-three years later he would be forcing his way through the bush to examine the geological composition of those very hills. As the day progressed and the ship got further into Foveaux Strait, the height of the land diminished although the high hills of Stewart Island appeared to the south.

By late afternoon, the wind had strengthened again and the ship was fast closing on Bluff Hill, at the base of which waves were beating furiously. At the port entrance there were some delay in obtaining a pilot; fears grew that the ship might have to stand out to sea for another night. However, to the relief of all, the pilot finally appeared and in a short time had guided the ship around the point and into the sheltered water of the port.

In the failing light there was little to be seen, but for once the motion of the ship was stilled.[30] It is tempting to think that McKay may well have slept on deck that night, thankful to be free of the crowded, fetid conditions below.

Saturday 26 September dawned fine and sunny. People on the ship could hear birdcalls across the narrow strip of water that separated them from the shore. Campbelltown (Bluff) consisted of a few wooden houses with shingled roofs. There was a larger iron-roofed warehouse, a bakery and store, a butcher's shop, hotel, and a small chapel. The population was probably less than 100, smaller than the Scottish village McKay had left behind.

The next two days would have been most frustrating as no one could go ashore until the medical inspector had given his clearance. It was not until Wednesday, the last day of September, that the nine disembarking passengers, including McKay, were able to transfer to the steamer which was to make the short trip to Invercargill.[31] The surviving animals went too. Four of the rabbits were subsequently released in the sand hills near Invercargill, their liberation being accompanied by speeches and champagne.[32] More than three hundred passengers remained on board, as the *Helenslee* was to continue on to Dunedin where, according to McKay, she "discharged the rest of her passengers, and then went to China after tea."[33]

Had McKay arrived four years later, he would have been able to take the train from the 'southernmost railway station in the world' to Invercargill. The twenty-seven kilometre track, the first in New Zealand, was completed in 1867. In other respects Campbelltown in 1875 seems not to have changed a great deal from the 'few wooden houses with shingled roofs' that greeted McKay in 1863. Courtesy Bluff Maritime Museum

5. New Horizons

When McKay arrived in 1863, New Zealand was still a frontier land for Europeans. War with Maori was ongoing in the north, but in the south, where McKay landed, men were finding gold. Roads were little more than wagon tracks, and passenger transport services, other than coastal steamer, were almost non-existent. Walking was the usual way of going places.

In the next two decades, however, there were to be major changes, fuelled by the new prosperity, the flood of immigrants, and the gold-mining industry. Soon the hurly-burly of tent-towns and the transient population of fortune-seekers would fade from the gold fields, to be replaced by a more permanent social structure. Road, rail, and telegraph links between the main centres became established, and telephone exchanges were opened in Auckland and Christchurch. Wellington became the seat of government and an Education Act provided free, compulsory, and secular education.

In Otago, towns and cities grew. Roads and railways were built. The frozen meat industry started in 1872. Land for farming was claimed from forests as they were milled, and around ports and harbours reclamation of land from the sea created space for port facilities and warehousing. In Dunedin, the building of churches, banks, schools, hotels, shops and industries following on from the gold rushes soon made it the country's most established city. A reservoir, cable car, and the University of Otago soon followed. The other main centres consolidated similarly.

In twenty years New Zealand had come of age, and the psyche of the new colonial – with the national characteristics of ingenuity and independence – was established. After a slow beginning, first on the gold fields and later as an agricultural worker, McKay eventually established roots, too. And, more significantly, although he had no scientific experience when he arrived in 1863, twenty years later he had published fifty scientific papers.

McKay had made a friend on the ship, a married man to whom he referred as 'A'. This man and his wife rented a house in the northeastern area of Invercargill, and initially McKay lived with them. They had only a very basic collection of utensils and the wooden house was unfinished inside, "but summer was coming and it would do".[1]

Invercargill, which is built on a swampy alluvial flat, was not then sufficiently drained. As it had rained incessantly for six weeks before their arrival, the partly formed streets were a quagmire. McKay noted that Tay Street, the main street, had a corduroy footpath along one side, but that the street itself "was in a state of nature."[1] Here he saw the largest team of bullocks – forty – he had ever seen, dragging a steam engine. The engine "was half-submerged and more than half of the bullocks were bogged."[2]

Looking for Work

For the new settlers, the pressure to find work soon made itself felt and was a matter of basic survival. McKay vowed his intention

> of doing anything whereby I might honestly gain a livelihood, and having one day invested half a crown [about NZ$20] in a bullock's head this was converted into brawn, and having declared my readiness to retail this among the tents that were numerous in this north-east suburb area of Invercargill, Mrs A. dished me many cups-full of this Trembling Bob, for by a liberal addition of water it was such. I made me a board, which covered with a clean white cloth, received from two to three dozen of the trembling gentlemen, and I set out to vend the goods in question. As I went along I announced that I dealt in "fine, superfine, Amalgamated Beef." That sold me my stuff as quickly as I could deliver it, for every tent I passed took some and soon I was back home empty-handed.[3]

He soon gave away this epicurean entrepreneurialism in favour of bridge building, but "scarfing [joining] o' twa sticks that were as twisted as bad as Willie Wastle's wife was scarcely a job that I was likely to make guid at."[4] He and the master soon parted.

Staying with the carpentry trades, he and 'A.' then agreed to build a house for one of their shipmates, on a section near New River on the road to Riverton, the timber for which was to be hewn from the local forest. It was too far to be convenient to travel to the site each day, so their first task was to make a shelter. Instead of pitching a tent, as was usual in such circumstances, they built a shanty for themselves with a frame of poles covered with manuka scrub and lined with sacks which they had obtained from a baker. That done, and in readiness for work in the morning, they boiled the billy and ate their evening meal, then went for a wander around the glade in which they had camped. Cabbage trees dotted the site. With the infectious and inquisitive enthusiasm of young men finally given some space, they discovered that the dry and dead foliage adorning their stems burned furiously. Then they returned to their shanty:

> It was now dark, and having prepared a featherly bed of Manuka twigs we undressed, closed our door [a split sack] against robbers and others and retired. We had not been long in bed when we became aware that we had companions of a very disagreeable sort – mosquitoes in fact, and fairly well grown ones,

too: whoppers, I might say, about from half an inch to three quarters of an inch in length. They serenaded us, they did, and they did more, they bit us, and do what what we could we could not protect ourselves from them. We had not dreamed of being pestered in this way, and finally we were compelled to light the candle and see what was the matter, as sleep was utterly out of the question.[5]

They found "the whole place full of big grey flies", with many resting three or four deep on the flour-covered filaments that hung from the sacking of the roof. However, as 'A.' examined the roof he rashly scorched a string of the insects:

on the instant the whole place was filled with one continuous flame, and fortunately for us was as suddenly in darkness again. It was more in the nature of a coal-dust explosion than anything else. Fortunately the solid sacking did not take fire, and the walls being of green Manuka they did not. But Oh, what a holocaust [sic] of our enemies! Myriads were utterly consumed and myriads lay on the floor and on our blankets. It was a great victory; we were revenged, and shortly afterwards we settled ourselves to sleep again. No; they were not all dead yet. Multitudes of them poured into the place, and in five minutes or thereabouts were as bad as ever. They got at us under the clothes, they stung and bit so that we had to get up and dress. That did not save us, and finally they got at us no matter what we did. Eventually we had to put on our boots to keep them from our feet, and I verily believe they bit us through our moleskin trousers.[6]

Morning brought problems of a different sort. They felled a tree and set about to cut scantling (small beams) and weather-boarding, but they did not know the timber, or the saw tooth to use, and it became clear they were in for a long period of experimentation. McKay suggested that 'A.' should find someone more skilled and he would resign in his favour. This was agreed and McKay took to the road.

Looking for his Brother

McKay was aiming for Christchurch, although he had little money. He had arrived in New Zealand with £7 (about $1000) which he had borrowed from a relative, but he returned this soon after arriving in Invercargill.

McKay was travelling light: "I then had not acquired the art of carrying a heavy swag … I had enjoyed the walk during the day and was delighted with the pleasant country through which I passed."[7] By about dusk on the first day he had reached a point near Gore and Langford and was looking for a place to stop when he came upon two wagons by the roadside, with the drivers sitting by a campfire. When he spoke, one of them stood, seized his hand and asked all manner of questions. The man turned out to be one of McKay's schoolfellows, one Rab McCrae. McCrae had originally gone out to Melbourne, and had then joined the rush to New Zealand. He was

McKay was impressed by the might of the Clutha, the largest river in New Zealand. 'I had but to look at it to know that I had never seen the like. Its silent but irresistible current carried its waters past with strength and steadiness that told of a vast volume of water passing seawards.'

currently a wagoner on Logan's Station in the Upper Pomahaka. As there was a possibility of work there McKay accompanied him to the station the following day. He was already aware of features in the landscape he was travelling through, noting after crossing the Mataura: "I believe [the land] to once have been a plain and the action of water to have cut it up into innumerable glens and ridges, as the ridges are all one height."[8] This comment, made in a letter to his brother in Scotland on 10 April 1864, was his first recorded geological observation in New Zealand.

The job however, turned out to be that of a boundary keeper, with thirty miles (approximately fifty kilometres) to be covered daily. "This, I thought rather more than I could undertake to do, and without a collie – to be man and dog, too – was more than I could venture upon …"[9] So McKay declined the job and once more took to the road. He slept that night in a patch of tall fern, having "arrived at nowhere and nowhere was in sight",[10] and the next under a culvert somewhere between Clinton and Balclutha. He reached Balclutha in the early afternoon. Here he was impressed by the Clutha River: "I had but to look at it to know that I had never seen the like. Its silent but irresistible current carried its waters past with such strength and steadiness that told of a vast volume of water passing seawards."[11] For a fee of one shilling he was able to cross on the punt, an ingenious affair that used the force of the current to propel it from side to side.

In the mud of the wheel ruts on the far side, McKay found a sixpence: "It was not the only one I had, but it needed this one to keep the rest warm"[12]

He came into Milton, twenty-five kilometres from Balclutha, on dusk but elected not to stop, as "it would be bad for the contents of my purse did I halt there …"[13] Some six kilometres further on, near Milburn or Clarendon, he was invited to share the tent of a German. In the time-honoured tradition of life on the road, the hospitality was greatly appreciated: "I know now that we shall never meet again in this world; all the same I shall ever hold him in kindly remembrance. I do not know his name, nor does it matter …"[14] In his autobiography, McKay gives this gentleman's nationality as Dutch, but in the letter to his brother, written from Hamilton's about six months later, he is described as German.[15] There are other minor discrepancies, but in general the two documents written nearly fifty years apart are remarkably consistent.

McKay's walking speed was about six kilometres an hour. He must have left early the next morning, for by two in the afternoon he had covered the remaining fifty kilometres to reach Dunedin. He had been given the name of a fellow townsman, David Guffie, who was now a carrier on the roads to the interior. Unfortunately he found that Guffie had left Dunedin just that morning; even worse was the news that Alex's brother from Christchurch was with him. His brother John had apparently travelled south at about the same time as Alex had started north; they missed each other by just a few hours.

As a result, McKay was on the road again as soon as possible. Dunedin is ringed by hills and his approach from the south would probably have been over Lookout Point, no mean hill to climb on foot, but from which he would have had a fine view of the harbour, crowded with ships, all bringing supplies for the thriving new city and the goldfields. Now he had to travel the other way out, by way of Halfway Bush, Three Mile Hill and Silverstream. Many people commute by car over Three Mile Hill these days, but few would be prepared to walk, especially if they had already done a fifty-kilometre warm-up trip from Milburn.

McKay made for the Taieri crossing at Outram, which he reached just as the sun went down behind the prominent hill of Maungatua. By his reckoning, he had covered forty-eight miles[16] (eighty kilometres) that day: "The doors of the Travellers' Rest stood open … yet my day's march was not done."[17] It is a long haul up the face of Maungatua, and it is small wonder that McKay's steps were slowing after another hour or two. When he eventually came to one of the crude accommodation houses that were spaced every thirty kilometres or so along the road, he elected to part with a shilling in return for a sack stretcher. But a brawl of such ferocity broke out after a couple of hours that he decided discretion was in order and slipped out onto the road again, walking through the rest of the night.

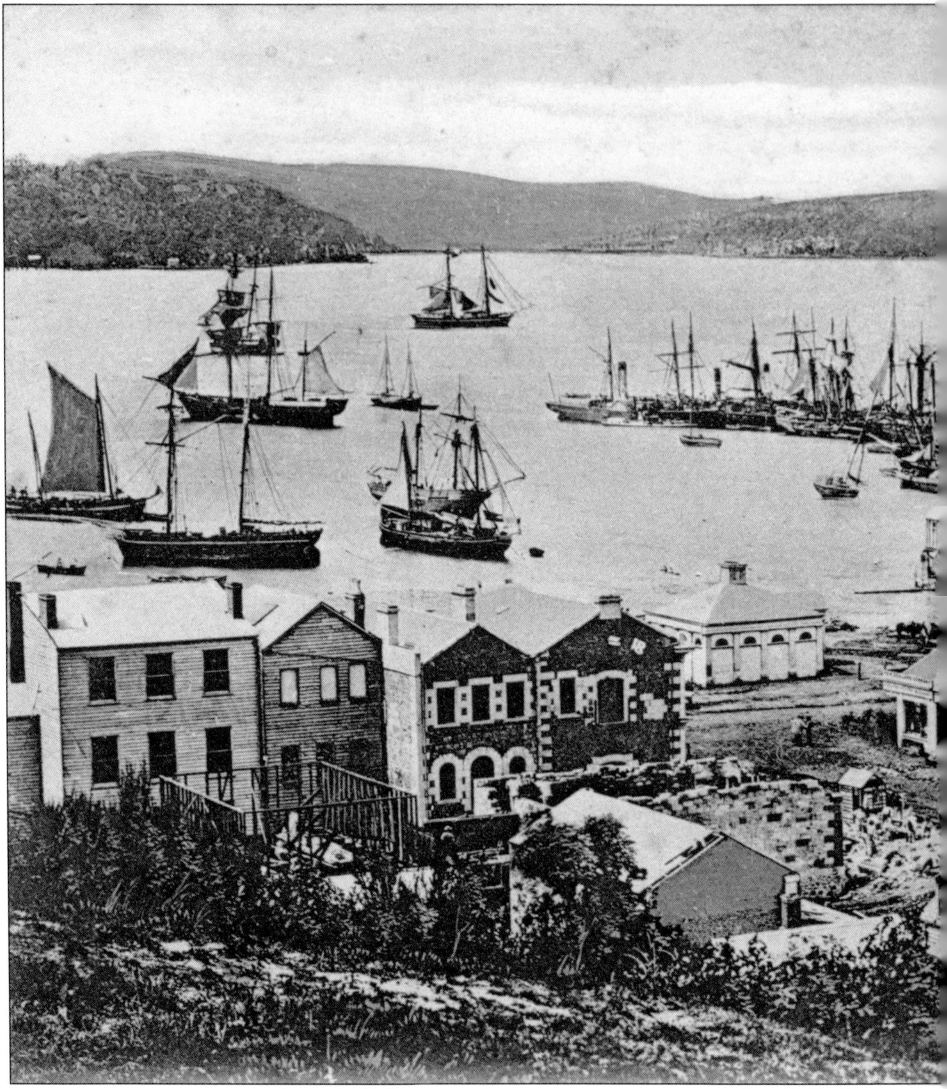

5. NEW HORIZONS 67

Even though the larger ships had to berth in deeper water at Port Chalmers, the Dunedin wharves were still busy with shipping the year following the discovery of gold in Gabriels Gully in 1861. McKay would have seen a similar view in 1863. Photograph: Gordon Burt Collection, ATL, F-36424¬1/2

The uplifted, faulted, tilted and eroded remnants of a former peneplain – a surface of low relief formed close to sea level – gives inland Otago its distinctive landscape.

When day broke he was well out on the Barewood Plateau, with wagons ahead. In excitement he hurried on to catch them before they yoked up. But his brother was not in the party and they and he soon parted company.

He was now crossing an elevated plain, with "scattered huge blocks of rock that were apparently loose upon the surface – some squat and others rising into castelated crags – and their numbers and proximity in many parts were such as to give the appearance of a forest of such rocks."[18] The Barewood Plateau is a well-preserved part of the Otago peneplain – a surface of low relief formed when the land had been eroded almost to sea level about 130 million years ago. Earth movements commenced five to ten million years ago and the surface was then broken by faults, uplifted, and tilted. The distinctive character of the landscape of Central Otago derives from the treeless remnants of this surface.

The next night was cold, and again McKay got little sleep, as he had to continue walking intermittently to keep warm. Dawn saw him near where Middlemarch now is, but it was ten in the morning before he reached the

> 'Palace Hotel', a ten-by-eight foot (3 x 2.5 metre) calico tent. Here he was able to have a meal of wild pork and bread, and a pannikin of tea, for eighteen pence (about $10).[19]

By now McKay realised that, probably during his nocturnal wanderings, he had missed the turnoff for the Dunstan Road which led inland, and was hopelessly out of his way. Eventually he was directed to a crossing of the Taieri River. There had been exceptionally heavy snowfalls during the previous winter, when scores of prospectors had perished after being trapped by snow high on the nearby Old Man Range. The river would have been running high and dirty as the snow melted.[20] Before crossing, McKay took the precaution of taking off his trousers and stockings, but unfortunately he stumbled near the middle of the river and his swag was quickly beyond his reach:

> and away down the river it went. This was a disaster indeed … I was now possessed of a somewhat meagre outfit. Fortunately I had saved my stockings and I had my boots. My trousers, blanket, and other effects were gone, even the few shillings I had left me; yet matters might have been worse, so I sat down and dressed as well as I could.[21]

His stockings would have been long, extending right up to the crutch (long johns had yet to be invented), and fortunately he had put them in the pocket of his coat, which he had strapped to his waist. His shirt would have come well down his legs, and he still had his greatcoat so he carried on. The wheel marks he was following now swung onto the top of Taieri Ridge and petered out, leaving him to follow along the flat-topped ridge "hopelessly and aimlessly" realising that now he "was completely lost in a wilderness …"[22]

Finally McKay saw a figure in the far distance. Yet the man's behaviour seemed unusual, and this may have played on his weary mind. He became concerned at the man's curious behaviour – standing – stooping – standing

Twelve years after McKay was swept off his feet crossing the Taieri River near Sutton, this fine suspension bridge was built to give access to Taieri Ridge. It features beautifully crafted pillars of hand-knapped local stone.

When the wheel marks he was following swung onto the top of Taieri Ridge and petered out, McKay was left to follow along 'the flat-topped ridge hopelessly and aimlessly, for I saw that I was completely lost in a wilderness'. He was crossing an elevated plain, with 'scattered huge blocks of rock ... apparently loose upon the surface – some squat and others rising into castelated crags ... [giving] the appearance of a forest of such rocks.'

again, and thought that he might be mad. As he came closer, it appeared that the stranger had similar fears about the trouserless figure approaching. Eventually they were within speaking distance of each other, "and yet more wonderful, discovered that neither of us was mad."[23]

McKay explained his predicament and it turned out that the stranger was cutting and stacking peat to dry. This activity had given him a sore back, so he would stoop, straighten, and then stoop the other way. In the treeless expanse of Central Otago, obtaining fuel for warmth and cooking was a major problem. Deposits of low-grade lignite were utilised in many localities, and peat in others.[24] McKay was well versed in the techniques of cutting peat, so the two got busy and had soon accomplished a fair day's work.

It was then that McKay allowed himself a moment of self-pity, which was not entirely surprising. He was a young man alone in a strange country, half a world away from home. He was tired, no doubt hungry, and he had just lost the last of his money.

> Alas for poor me! Where was my home to be? Here indeed there was prospect of a night's lodging in a station hut, but when morning came what next? A possible chance of employment, and failing that to commence my wandering again. However, I for the time being, had to consider myself fortunate. We had six miles to get over before reaching the station ... On our arrival I created something of a sensation and had to be introduced by back door methods to where I was fitted out with an old pair of moleskins, which again made me presentable in society.[25]

He enjoyed his supper, having felt that he had earned it, and being in need of some rest, he also enjoyed the first comfortable bed he had had for many days. There was even better news in the morning: it was Sunday and everyone was expected to stay put unless there was an urgent reason otherwise. McKay was not "loath to comply with the regulation."[26]

The scattered sheep stations that were the only settlements in these open empty lands had responded swiftly to the turbulent and unpredictable tide of gold seekers. In August the previous year (1862), Puketoi Station had six diggers staying one night. but the number climbed to 150 the second night, and 200 on the third. The stations set up temporary food kitchens and dormitories for the flood of miners heading inland.[27] It was in their interest to do so, as miners with a bed and food in their bellies were less likely to steal sheep. The miners were saved a dilemma too, for while acquiring an illegal sheep was easy enough in this treeless land, cooking it was a bigger challenge as dry grass was the only fuel. McKay does not mention a charge for meals and accommodation, but undoubtedly there was one. Charity was not the object of the exercise, and the least charitable became the most wealthy.

Looking for Gold

On Monday it was all bustle and go again. The dozen or so wayfarers who had straggled in the previous day resumed their journeys. The last two to leave, however, invited McKay to accompany them to the new 'rush', an invitation he was pleased to accept. They made their way back over Taieri Ridge and down towards the river. The new rush was at Fullarton's, across the river from Hyde. When they arrived there were a few tents, "a calico store, a butcher's shop of calico also, and a blacksmith's shop – all on wooden frames … there might have been some twenty men hanging about, apparently doing nothing."[28]

His party staked their claim, and then called on the store, which would have been stocked with bacon, butter, potted meat and fish, cheese, bread, tobacco and clay pipes, and Tetchford's Vesta matches.[29] The butcher too, would have been well stocked, for in 1863 135,000 sheep were slaughtered for meat, 54,000 more than in 1861.[30] The men laid in a stock of provisions, and then "dined like kings as far as the good things were concerned and like picnickers as regards place, this being the grassy slope in front of the tent."[31] McKay was impatient to start digging up the gold, but his more experienced mates laughed, and said it was better to wait and see whether the gold lead[32] was likely to pass through their ground. So he wandered about the prospect, observing a continuous stream of people arriving "as there might be at a Kirk or a theatre. Tents, simple, and calico houses on light wooden frames were going up everywhere ..."[33] It was not long before he was drawn to another like himself, standing alone, who turned out to be another school-fellow:

> This was none other than William Guffie, brother to the carrier with whom my brother had left for the Dunstan ... Our meeting was sufficiently remarkable, but more remarkable was what he told me. Owing to the new rush the destination of the wagon had been altered, and it was expected to be on the ground in an hour or so. This actually took place, and I had the satisfaction of seeing my brother by simply losing my way in my hunt after him.[34]

By evening, the population had grown from twenty or so to between 500 and 750. A township had sprung up, complete with outlets where "all the ordinary wants of man could be catered for ... all that was needed was a Commissioner's Camp and police protection."[35]

The 'protection' arrived before dark:

> in the shape of Sergeant Ryan[36] and a couple of troopers. Had they lost their way from the Hogburn (Naseby) it had been much better, but as it was they came on the ground making a great display which displeased many. Sergeant Ryan was detected [detested] by the miners, and they did everything to annoy him. He, himself, acted imprudently, and they failed not to let him understand that he himself was but mortal. There was a tent some distance apart from others wherein were sold favours not easily described. Ryan entered this, whether in his official capacity or not I cannot tell, suffice to say it was rumoured widely where the Sergeant had got to. It was now dusk and a crowd had gathered round the tent. Suddenly, at a critical moment sheath knives were produced, the fly and tent strings were cut, and all underneath them laid bare. A wrathful man was Sergeant Ryan as he rose to his feet, and he expressed his mind somewhat freely as to what he intended to do. However, he did nothing save to interest some men to put the tent in order again. This being done the Sergeant entered the tent once again, and, as before, the tent strings were cut, and again in wrath the chief of police on Fullerton's No. 1 rose to his feet vowing vengeance on those who had done this thing. Nor was this all; he drew his revolver and fired among – I should rather say over the heads of the crowd. At all events nobody was hit, but what followed was bad for the Sergeant, as the infuriated mob closed in and in to him, each one being desirous of getting the first kick at him. The crowd behind on all sides forced the foremost on top of the Sergeant and thus a buffer heap was formed which received most of the kicking, which was a fortunate thing for the policeman, otherwise he would have been kicked to death. I narrowly escaped being one of the buffer heap, but fortunately managed to squeeze my way to the outside of the crowd. Sergeant Ryan did not escape severe maltreatment. He had two teeth knocked out and a broken rib or two. Next day he was in Hospital, propped against the wheel of a waggon and attended to by his two subordinates.[37]

It was the second time within a week that McKay had taken discretionary action to avoid physical violence.

The prospect of gold at Fullarton's failed to materialise, and within a few days the inevitable exodus commenced. McKay teamed up with his brother, his uncle (Duncan McMurtie) and a fourth person, and spent a couple of weeks in an unsuccessful attempt at prospecting along the foot of the Rock and Pillar Range. Christmas was approaching and as the rest of the party was keen to spend the festive season at the Hogburn diggings at Naseby, Alex remained behind to look after the tent on the top of the Rock and Pillar Range (about 1200 metres above sea level).

Christmas Day brought what he must have thought he had left long behind – a white Christmas. Although the snow did not last long, the nights stayed cold, and his mates did not return, so after a few days he packed up and set off to follow them. When he arrived at Naseby he discovered that they had already left for the latest rush, at Hamilton's, about thirty kilometres away. Although the auriferous ground was rich at Hamilton's, there was little of it, but a lot of miners. Fights and quarrels were the order of the day.

Then it was on to Hyde, where McKay and his mates finally got onto paying ground. One wonders what they did for money in the interim. The storekeepers and carriers did a roaring trade, keeping a flow of life's necessities available at the various fields, but they would sell only to those who could pay.

At Hyde, McKay and his mates sank several prospecting holes, one near the township, to depths of twelve to twenty metres. Alex was already forming ideas on the nature and position of the gold leads, but found it difficult to convince some of his group, especially those who had had experience on the Victorian goldfields who "with the proverbial stubbornness of Scotsmen"[38] resisted his arguments to sink deeper, even when confronted with the good returns of gold that they were getting.

"But things were ever on the stir …"[39] April 1864 brought news of a great rush to the Wakamarino River in Marlborough. Two of McKay's party set off for Dunedin to catch the steamer so as to be early on the field, but McKay and his brother and about ten others decided to walk the length of the South Island, leading their horses overland. They made Palmerston on the first night. The next day they crossed the Horse Range, where McKay was impressed with the "wild and romantic scenery"[40] of Trotter's Gorge. The group stopped overnight at Oamaru and the next day were guided across the mighty Waitaki by "Jimmy the Needle".[41] That night was spent at the Waihao River in South Canterbury, where the accommodation house supplied a meal of wild pig and potatoes, which McKay noted were "of remarkably fine quality".[42] Timaru was reached the next day and in the evening McKay strolled through the town and at a bookseller bought a copy of *The Testimony of the Rocks* by Hugh Miller. He had read some of Miller's books before he left Scotland.[43]

The next day they went only as far as Temuka, fording the twin channels of the Rangitata River the following day. The township of Ashburton, where they stopped that night, then consisted only of Turton's accommodation house. They were paddled across the Rakaia River, the next major obstacle. The Selwyn River was less of a problem. McKay noted that the snowline was halfway down the mountains, so run-off was probably reduced and the rivers running low. They reached Papanui (Christchurch) in the small hours of the next morning.

From there it was to Leithfield, Amuri, Conway, Kaikoura, Clarence, Kekerengu, Blenheim, Grovetown, and finally Havelock. In seventeen days they walked a distance of 800 kilometres, about fifty each day. Considering the number of both major and minor rivers to be crossed and the lack of a defined route in places, it is unlikely that they averaged more than four kilometres an hour. To achieve such distances they must have walked for ten or twelve hours a day.

The reunion in Havelock was not joyous. Their mates had been unable to stake any claims, and the consolidated fund was now so shrunken that, McKay recalled, "my share of it was measured by a five pound note."[44] He decided to separate from his mates and head back to Otago. His brother John chose to stay in Nelson for a time and then head back to Canterbury, where he was known, if the diggings failed. So McKay joined the "great number of the disappointed and unfortunate [who] were camped on the shoreline"[45] at Picton, until a steamer going south was available.

He arrived back in Dunedin in May. There was snow on the hills and the outlook was bad so instead of heading inland to the more productive goldfields, he and his mate elected to explore some areas closer to town. For three weeks they tested Mullocky Gully in the Taieri Gorge, before working their way up the Silver Stream and eventually crossing the saddle to the South Branch of the Waikouaiti. But they had no luck there either and eventually arrived back out at the low ground next to the coastline. Here his mate decided to return to Dunedin where he had friends, but McKay had no friends and was at a loss as to what to do next.

He joined a road-making gang, breaking stone for the road a few miles north of Waikouaiti, but it did not go well. The boulders of volcanic rock collected from the ploughed fields alongside the road had a skin of soft weathered material, which made them hard to break, and after a month he found he had barely paid his keep. Near penniless, he set out for Dunedin. The road over Mt Cargill to Port Chalmers was unformed and the mud so heavy that at times he had to turn around and pull out an embedded foot before he could take another step forward. Finally he reached Dunedin, where a chance encounter led to jobbing work with James Robinson, "an indulgent and kindly man, and with him I recovered somewhat of my natural spirits and temper."[46] Work on the farms round Green Island and Saddle Hill tided him over the winter, but with the arrival of spring McKay made up his mind to leave New Zealand and see what Australia could offer.

McKay had been in New Zealand for a year. He had walked the length of the South Island with a diversion as far west as Naseby. He had earned enough money, mostly from gold, to stay alive, but he had not found the opportunity, the challenge, the opening, which would lead to a lifetime of satisfaction. With the vision of hindsight, it is clear that the missing ingredient, which may not have been clear to McKay, was intellectual engagement. It was to come, but slowly.

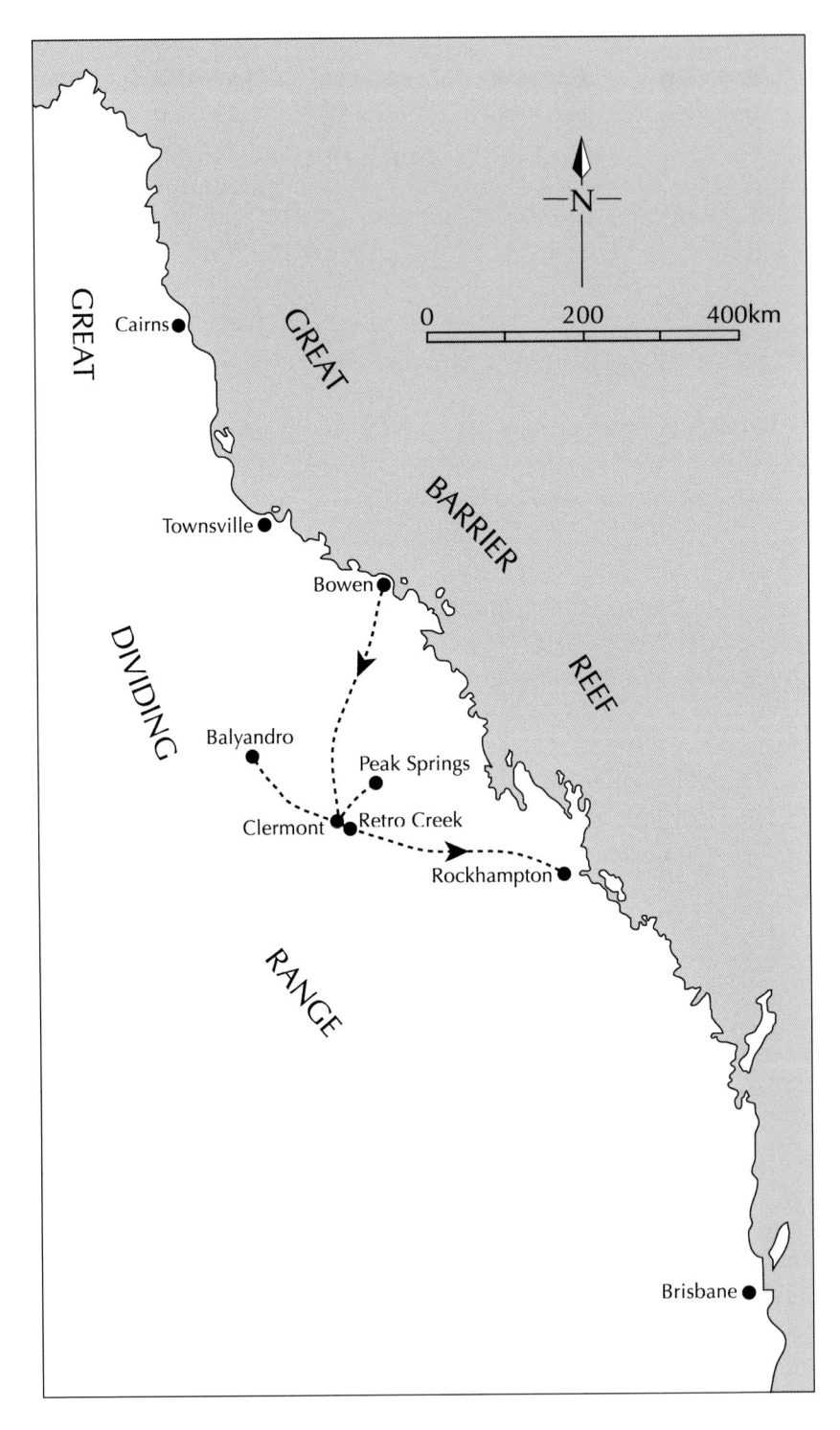

Map of southeast Queensland showing McKay's travels during 1865.

6. The Grass is Greener – Australia

As spring approached at the end of his first year in New Zealand, McKay took passage to Australia. The ship was the *Rialto*, trading in coal from Newcastle, New South Wales, and returning with ballast and passengers, most of whom – with the exception of twelve or fifteen individuals – were diggers down on their luck. McKay recorded in his 'Fragments': "they were full up of the Pig Island and glad to get out of it." Among these he became friendly with two men: a Scotsman, McLeod, and an Irishman, O'Reilly.[1]

The ship was becalmed for several days at the entrance to Otago Harbour and the three gathered cockles from the adjacent sandbanks. Next day, a light breeze allowed some progress to be made. "We enjoyed this day fairly", recorded McKay.[2] It was to be the only day they did. "The breeze freshened to what a landsman might call a gale …"[3] As the ship began to roll they retreated below to play cards in the space between the bunks rigged in their quarters on the under-deck.[4] The movement increased until a particularly strong roll sent anything movable to the port side, and a counter roll that sent everything back to starboard, with the process being repeated two or three times before the men could grab hold of something and regain their feet.

The Mate called down that if anyone wanted to be on deck, now was the time, as the hatches were to be battened down. McKay recorded: "From a blustering swearing crowd we became singularly quiet … As time went on the ship laboured more and more and was frequently on her beam-ends."[5] The next day the ship was hove to but the storm continued unabated. The men below could hear the roar of the wind in the rigging, the sound falling as the ship neared the end of each roll and then increasing again as she gradually returned to an upright position. Frequently the ballast shifted from side to side, causing even the rats to squeak. On the third day some biscuits, butter and water were hastily passed under the corner of the hatch cover, which was quickly refastened, whereupon the storm redoubled its force and they had another awful night.

On the fourth day, the weather improved a little and the passengers were allowed on deck. McKay cradled himself in the forecastle and "endeavoured to get a comprehensive and a more particular view of what was going on. ... the surface of the sea was a tangled mass of little hills with valleys between. There at hand rose higher than the main mast ..."[6] McKay had just ventured back along the deck to the waist of the ship when it was struck by another storm-blast, which again threw her on her beam-ends: the deck "was as near as may be vertical. I held onto a belaying pin and not being able to keep my feet was thus suspended hanging thereto."[7]

As the ship slowly righted, McKay and the rest of the passengers hastened below and the hatch cover was battened over them for the fourth night. Fortunately, conditions improved during the night, sail was set, and they started making good progress. At noon the next day the Australian coast came into view. But the drama was not over. They were south of the entrance to Newcastle and rapidly drifting towards the coast. To their joy, a steam tug came out to assist but the tremendous seas prevented the crew from getting a line aboard. In the nick of time, the connection was made and the *Rialto* was towed into the mouth of the Hunter River and Newcastle Harbour.[8]

Outback Queensland

After two or three days in Newcastle recovering from their ordeal, the three men took a steamer south to Sydney, where they stayed for about three weeks. Their intention was to try gold prospecting in Queensland, as soon as the dry season came to an end. Eventually they travelled north to Brisbane, and then further up the coast to Bowen, some 200 kilometres southeast of Townsville. From Bowen the men headed inland towards Clermont. They camped in the dry bed of the Don River, where they found water by digging in the sands of the river bed. After obtaining stores from a nearby station, they "baked and boiled and made ready for the morning and this done, we saw the sun go down on the first day of our acquaintance with the Australian wilderness."[9] The next day they camped by a water hole, where they shot a couple of ducks. McKay waded in with a long stick to retrieve one, but was later told that alligators in that pool had claimed the lives of most of the dogs on the station. They found swagging loads, made heavier by the need to carry water, was tiring in the heat, and sunburn was a new hazard.

The travellers acquired a less than desirable companion along the way, who claimed he was a first-class shearer and an ace bullock-driver. They off-loaded him by volunteering his services at the next station where such skills were greatly needed. The trio didn't think the squatter[10] would be very impressed with his day's tally of four! They carried on to a station in the upper Bowen, where help was needed for dipping sheep in preparation for shearing. McKay and his companions worked there for ten days. But it was still 100 kilometres to Clermont, across waterless sand. They resolved to walk in the cool of the night as far as possible.[11]

"At this time the eastern seaboard of Australia and parts of the hinterland were infested by a number of bush rangers": Johnnie Dunn and his party, Captain Thunderbolt, Morgan, and Gardener among them.[12] While McKay and his mates were filtering water from an uninviting pond, a stranger rode up, mounted on a thoroughbred. He had three or four revolvers in his belt, but no swag other than a valise to which was strapped a light rifle in a brown canvas case. He accepted their invitation to join them for tea and a bite to eat. After he had finished his meal and puffed on his magnificent scrimshaw pipe, they braced themselves to be robbed of what little they had. Instead he simply thanked them, unhitched his horse, and rode off into the night.[13]

Eventually the group reached the township of Clermont. It consisted of a single street about 100 metres long, with several bars. "The houses were built of logs, in some cases of bush sawn timber and roofed with bark or … galvanised iron. … Water must have been available but whether from a creek bed or rain waterhole I do not now remember."[14]

McKay and his party then examined the prospects for gold at Peak Springs, where there were a number of claims, with the owners all anxiously awaiting the coming rain, so that they could wash the ore for gold.[15] McKay and company were not impressed and returned to Clermont to ponder their next move.

They learned that gold was being obtained even in the dry weather in the upper valley of the Balyando (a tributary of the Burdekin River), about eighty kilometres west of Clermont. The men decided that, as a last resort before their funds expired, they would investigate this site, despite its remoteness. On the way they came across a remarkably clear pool of water. Each immediately dropped his swag and dipped his pannikin deep. "We stood facing each other a thirsty trinity. We tasted and instantly restrained ourselves, we had all miscalculated; the water was as salt as brine, and we looked at each other in silence."[16]

The gold workings at Balyando were not promising, but appeared to be unusually organised. However there is a gap here in McKay's 'Fragments', and details about Balyando are missing. The manuscript resumes: "… and we were speedily supplied with gunny small sacks, capable of holding as much earth as a man might carry on his back."[17] Then they headed, with pick and shovel, into a likely looking gully, filled their sacks with a yellow clay 'wash', and lugged them back to the water hole, where the wash was panned out "for a very moderate reward indeed."[18] Once or twice they had a small find but they were earning barely enough to live on: "There

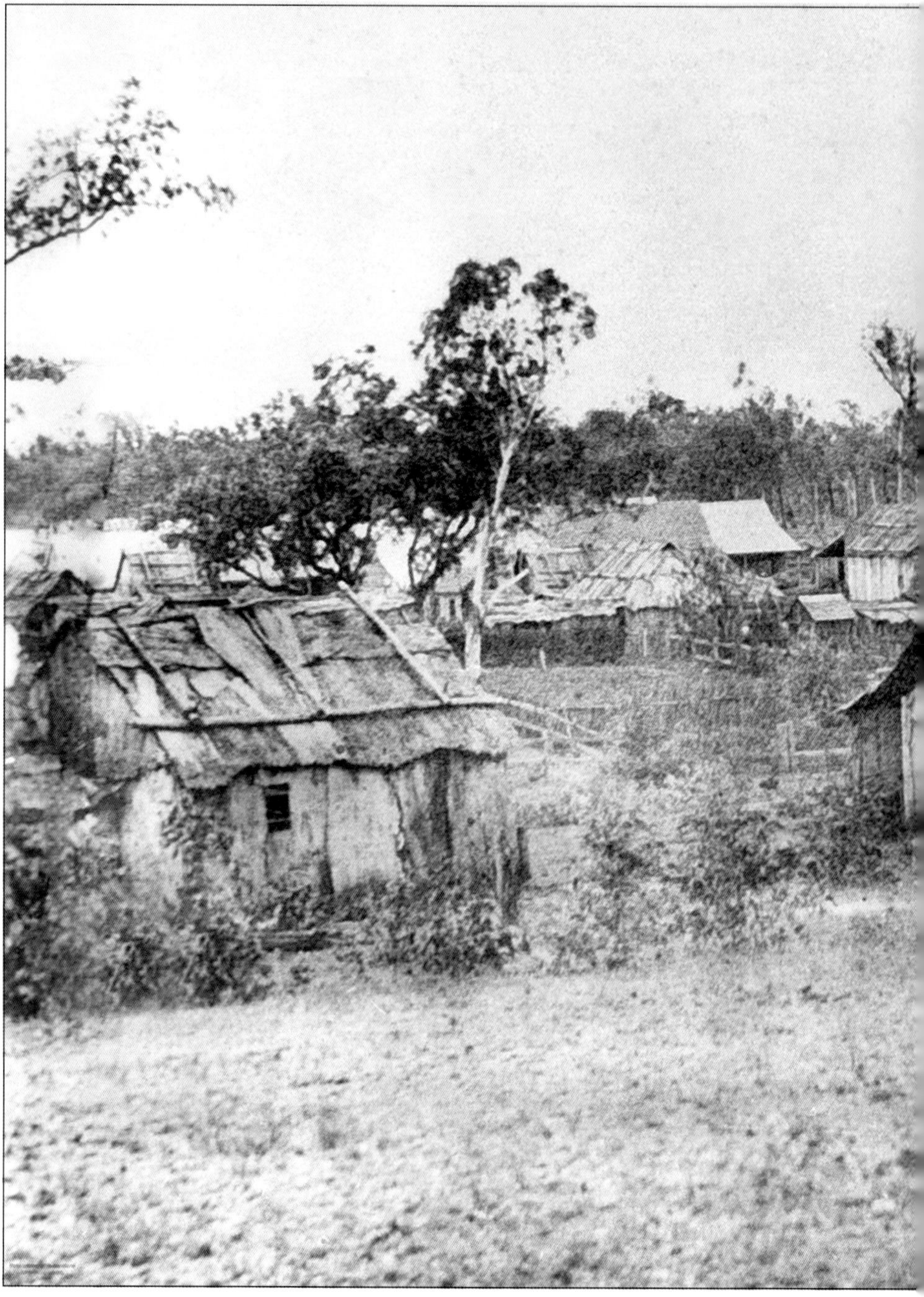

6. THE GRASS IS GREENER – AUSTRALIA   81

The shanty town of Clermont in central Queensland, seen here in about 1870, was a stark contrast to the bustling port of Dunedin (pages 66–67) that McKay had left behind in New Zealand. Today Clermont is a busy rural centre with a population of about 2000.
John Oxley Library, Brisbane

was no fortune making as far as we were concerned. Indeed there were no appearances of the kind amongst the others of the camp, who gained their living as we did."[19]

Malaria

It was overwhelmingly hot working down in the gullies. One day, while shouldering his bag of wash, McKay collapsed from what seemed to be heat-stroke. Soon it was pronounced that he was suffering from fever and ague.

> A week or two went past, and from mid-day till sundown I was good for nothing, and it was with great difficulty I could bring in a load in the forenoon part of the day. After sundown I recovered wonderfully and seemed quite well, and my two mates not quite understanding the nature of my disorder began to hint that I was tired of work, which was doubly galling to me, seeing that now my money was gone and I had to be in everything dependent on them. Yet what could I do? Only what I did do. While I was able I brought in my load of dirt in the morning, and in the afternoon I lay in the shadow of a gum tree and rolled round with the sun until it disappeared in the west.[20] We washed less dirt and thus our prospects of a fortune, even of a livelihood, waned, and I had sometimes rather melancholy reflections … And yet life was not all sadness. When there were gatherings round a common fire at night many tales were told that interested me not a little; for I was still a new chum, and life in the Australian Bush had its charms, even in this outlandish place. Its excitements, too, for sometimes there were differences of opinion leading to argument, and even to more dangerous results.
>
> One night there arose dispute between two men as to whether, when in the lion's den, Daniel smoked a meersham pipe or a church-warden. There had been some feeling between these men before, but that night it became so evident and hot that sheath knives were drawn, and bloody work was threatened. The common sense of the others prevailed, and if peace was not made at least the knives were replaced in their sheaths.[21]

A medical aquaintance, Dr Peter Strang, who has experience of tropical medicine, notes that McKay's description is consistent with malaria, which was endemic in Quensland at the time. It would have been many months before McKay recovered fully. The shallow billabong where they were camped may have provided a breeding-place for the mosquitoes carrying the disease.[22]

As time went on the water in the hole showed signs of diminishing, becoming more pulpy by the day. The waterhole was about 200 metres long, three or four metres wide, and in most parts not more than a metre deep. It supplied all the requirements of the camp for cooking, bathing, and the washing of clothes and it was continually being further polluted by the addition of the material they were washing for gold. Mcleod was now the only one of the three with any money remaining, and he decided, as director of their company, that they should return to Clermont and take fresh stock. The return journey was a nightmare for McKay and he remembered little of it until he awoke in a tent in Clermont.[23]

Mcleod then decided that he would go to Sydney (about 1300 kilometres distant) to get some horses, and that Mick O'Reilly, the Irishman, and McKay should find work on a station for the three months he expected to be gone. This was easier said than done and tempers became frayed as Mick and McKay trudged on in the heat. Finally they came to a station at Retro Creek, and here they were employed as shepherds at twenty-five shillings (about $180) per week, in anticipation of sheep which were yet to arrive. The squatter, Mr Brown, must have been an understanding employer: while Mick was immediately set to work to make a cabbage garden, McKay, who was still unwell, was left alone to rest for a week.[24]

September and October brought plagues, first of fleas, then of ants. In winter time snakes tended to move into the houses. On one occasion, McKay's work-mate noticed that his riding boot was unusually heavy. A two-metre long black snake had selected it as a suitable place for its winter hibernation, and filled the boot so tightly it could not be shaken free. "The boot had to be gently warmed at the fire which, reviving the snake, it quietly crawled out, and was killed before it became very active."[25]

Mcleod returned from Sydney, having purchased four horses and shipped them north to Rockhampton, but they had been killed or lamed when the steamer ran into a storm. He joined the other two men as a station-hand and there was no more talk of further expeditions to the north and west.

Tropical Storms

In November the heat increased and heavy thunderstorms ushered in the rainy season. The cyclonic storms were an almost daily occurrence, and some were of tremendous violence. On one occasion McKay was assisting a drover when ominous storm clouds made them dash for the shelter of a hut. They made it in the nick of time, as the force of the wind required the efforts of both of them to close and fasten the door:

> The fury of the storm was now upon us. It thundered and lightened most dreadfully, and the rain descended, without qualification, in sheets. It is needless to say it was dark as darkest night, and the wind with terrific force blew from every quarter of the compass, and took not more than a minute to be round and round every corner of the hut. The hut was formed of logs, strongly built, and with a log chimney. It seemed capable of resisting the greatest force

of any probable strength of the wind. The roof was iron, firmly nailed, and covered with a heavy frame of round saplins tied on the ridge and having a specially heavy saplin along the eaves. All this was in vain. There came one terrific blast that burst the fastenings of the door and carried away the roof. Ridges, iron, battens and rafters, as I suppose, all in one piece, but whether in one or a thousand pieces, I don't know.[26]

The roof was never seen again. Half an hour later the wind had ceased, and there was not a cloud in the sky: "After these storms, especially those that happened after midday, the country looked beautiful; this, however, was of short duration, as the morning sun ushered in the old thing over again. Intolerable heat and an unsteady flickering convection of an overheated atmosphere."[27]

By now it was December and the wanderlust was stirring once more in McKay. As the temperatures increased he began to long to drink the cool clear waters of New Zealand once more, but first he had to square up and dissolve the 'mateship' with O'Reilly and McLeod. He also had to await his employer's consent to his leaving his employment, as Mr Brown did not want him to go. And he had to find a travelling companion heading in the same direction, as it was considered too dangerous to travel alone.

McKay's departure from Retro Creek before he joined up with his travelling companion was not without drama. There was a hut in the valley of a small stream, near the peak of Peak Downs, an isolated hill rising about 300 metres above the surrounding country.[28] He had hoped to spend the first night in this hut but was disappointed: "The shepherds [occupying it] were new chums, and cared not to exercise hospitality to a vagrant like me."[29] McKay stretched his blanket from a fence to make a shelter but was woken in the night by yet another thunderstorm, more violent than any other he had experienced thus far. The peak

> presented an awful and alarming appearance. Great balls of fire seemed to be crossing round it at about mid-height as seen from where I lay, and these illuminations were nearly so continuous that it was but now and then that the mountain was lost sight of. When this did happen all was blackness till the next electrical discharge sent another succession of fire balls coursing round the mountain as before. The thunder was tremendously loud and continuous, the steady roar being continuously augmented and seldom lowered in volume of sound.
>
> I watched this tremendous display for some time, hardly in fear, for I delight in watching the lightning flash and listening to thunder peals. But this was to have an end in a tremendous downpour of rain, which proved a cloudburst, a waterspout, or something that would not play second fiddle to Noah's flood. Suddenly a tremendous volume of water was discharged along the creek bed below the terrace, and in the darkness I could hear the cries of the men in the

hut. These suddenly ceased and then things were all right again and like them I bethought myself of going to sleep.[30]

In the morning he saw that the hut had completely disappeared, apparently with its occupants, although the sheep were still in the yards. There was, however, a line of sixteen dead sheep close to the fence (beside which he had been sheltering). They had not been smothered or crushed, and McKay concluded that they had been killed by lightning. As he dried his blanket he was relieved to see the two men reappear. "They, however, did not approach me, and I went my way."[31]

McKay joined his travelling companion later in the day and they made what was almost a forced march to Rockhampton, walking in the cool of the night as often as possible, but frequently being caught in thunderstorms.[32] On one occasion they were able to find shelter in a roadside shanty. The ladies running it wished them to stay until morning, but this did not suit their plans and "nor was acceptance of the offer consistent with prudence …"[33] They made good progress, although McKay was clearly still unwell: "We did reach Yamba an hour or two before sundown, and learned that a boat was going down the river that night [to Rockhampton], but that a man was needed to assist in rowing the boat on the river. My mate bargained that if I got a free passage he would give the needed service."[34] From Rockhampton, McKay caught a steamer to Sydney, where he stayed for a week before returning to New Zealand.

A wood engraving of Wolfang Peak in southeast Queensland, where McKay witnessed a spectacular electrical storm. State Library of Victoria, A/S07/07/77/61

86 THE REAL MCKAY

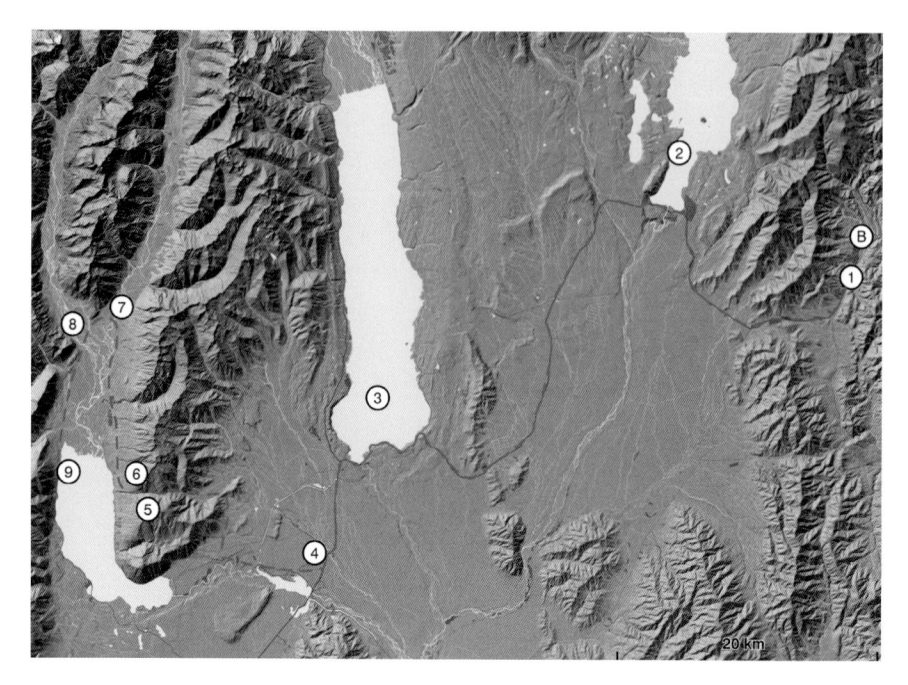

A digital terrain map of the Mackenzie Basin. McKay's route through the snow from Burkes Pass (B, at right) to Lake Ohau Station (9) is marked. Other locations: (1) assumed position of the Samaritan's house, (2) Lake Tekapo, (3) Lake Pukaki, (4) dunking in Irishman's Creek, (5) Flanagans Saddle, (6) shepherd's hut, (7) Dobson River, (8) Hopkins River, (9) Lake Ohau Station. Image: courtesy GeogaphX

The sight of the Southern Alps on the far side of the Mackenzie Basin drew McKay onwards like a magnet. Mount Cook is prominent centre left.

7. Lake Ohau – The Turning Point

While in Sydney, McKay took in some of its sights, including a race meeting at Randwick and, interestingly, a couple of visits to the Australian Museum. He then sailed for New Zealand. It was Christmas 1865. Once again the Tasman Sea provided a stormy crossing, this time on the SS *Claud Hamilton*. Landfall was at Hokitika, just as the SS *Bruce* was departing with the first consignment of miners for the South Westland gold rush. McKay, however, had paid his ticket through to Lyttelton and, perhaps recalling the Wakamarino fiasco, he stayed with the ship. The *Claud Hamilton* called briefly at Wellington, before he finally disembarked at Lyttelton.[1]

McKay soon located his brother farming a fifty-acre (twenty-hectare) block in partnership at Leeston, near Lake Ellesmere. He stayed several months, but the farm was unprofitable so in the autumn of 1866 he resolved to do something on his own account and turned his sights once more to the Otago goldfields. "My estate now was not a large one and was easily carried, and one afternoon I rolled the lot up, shouldered the 'bluey' and went."[2]

An Incredible Journey

His troubles began early. As dusk was falling he was confronted with a swampy backwater about five metres wide. Part way across he realised he was in danger of being mired in the mud, so he threw down his swag and by standing on it was able to reach the far bank. But there was no accommodation to be found and he was now wet through on a frosty night. Fortunately he found some firewood and soon had a fire going. But no matter how rapidly he rotated in front of it in search of sleep, one side was always chilled. He resolved the problem by lighting a second fire and lying between the two, which resulted in a "fairly comfortable" night.[3]

The next day he was ferried across the Rakaia River, but rather than face the dreary trudge down the plain to Ashburton, he decided to follow the river's south bank upstream. He meandered on, swinging gradually southward away from the Rakaia. At the Blue Gums accommodation house at Mt Somers, he discovered the landlady was acquainted with one of his Scottish aunts. He was heartened by this link with "home".[4] However, on the immediate front his prospects were not good. There was no work to be had anywhere, although a meal and lodging were often offered. He was almost penniless and had no blankets or change of clothes. It was early May, with summer well gone, yet he seemed to be inexorably drawn further and further into the foothills and the hostile mountain environment beyond. Eventually he found himself trudging up the slope to Burkes Pass.

It started to rain and by the time he reached the pass he was soaked to the skin. Still, there was worse to come, for then it started to snow:

> Shortly it was perfectly clear that a snow storm of some severity had set in, though for the time being it was no worse than the rain. At the western foot of the Pass the road altered to be more directly in the teeth of the wind, and it snowed more heavily as I proceeded on my way, so heavily indeed that I could see but a little distance ahead of me, nor was it long before I had some doubts as to what was road and what was not. By this time I had become so snowed at that I was now a huge shapeless snowball; in places I was occasionally relieved by avalanches from some part of my person, which for the moment relieved me of a growing weight.
>
> I know not that I was much concerned about my position in the midst of this snowstorm, or what the consequences might be. Yet without doubt my situation was serious. The snowfall was so thick that I could see hardly thirty feet ahead of me; the road was obliterated, and I had grown to be but a moving mass of snow. Unless something providential happened I must in the end make my bed in the snow, and in that case there was small chance of my seeing another morning.[5]

But Providence smiled and during a lull in the storm McKay was just able to make out the outline of a house.[6] Here he was met by a man who responded immediately to his plight and took him to a hut, supplied him with blankets, brushed the snow from him, helped him out of his cold wet clothes, put him to bed, and then brought him a bowl of hot beef stew.

The storm spent itself overnight and the next day was fine and clear. The 'good samaritan' brought him his dried clothes and provided a good breakfast.[7] On hearing of McKay's plans however, his benefactor strongly urged him to return to the low country, as it was virtually impossible to traverse the Mackenzie Country at that season of the year. McKay promised to follow his advice, but when he reached the road he reasoned with himself. "I could not better myself by returning upon my tracks of the previous day, and it were not easy to be made worse by going on."[8] As he stood there looking at the magnificence of the Southern Alps, dominated by Mount Cook, and with the Mackenzie Basin spread before him, he forgot his promise and turned once more to the west. It was a fateful decision: it was the turning point. He found there was no work at Tekapo Station, but he was not allowed to depart "without partaking of a more than ordinary good meal",[9] and received another warning against proceeding.

He paid for his stubbornness before the day was out, when he arrived at Irishmans Creek. The stream was running high as a result of the rain and snow of the day before. It was not wide, but deep and strong. Halfway across McKay was swept off his feet. Luckily for him, the current swept him against the far bank and he was able to scramble out. He trudged on, through snow that was now deep enough to slow his progress. For the second time in twenty-four hours he was wet through, again with no immediate prospect of food or shelter, and with a sharp frost settling. At least a full moon allowed him to continue moving.[10]

Providence smiled again. After crossing another stream he came to a hut at about nine in the evening, although he had to cross the stream again to reach it. He was taken in, the fire lit, the billy boiled, and some bedding found in a continuation of the astonishing tradition of high country hospitality.[11]

At Lake Pukaki he was pleased not only by the view once more of lake and mountains, but also by the arrival of two bullock drays which he had last seen on the eastern approach to Burkes Pass.[12] There was no punt at the lake outlet. Supplies for the station had to be offloaded into a boat and then loaded onto a bullock dray, which had been brought to the other side of the river from the station, alerted by smoke signals. By helping with the transfer of the load, McKay was able to earn himself a passage across the river.

The remaining obstacle in his path to Otago was the Ohau River. Below Lake Ohau the river could not be forded on foot, and no one was prepared to try on a horse. The only option was to go upstream. To do this he had to cross the Ben Ohau Range, then walk past the head of the lake and separately cross the two rivers that combined and flowed into it. The treeless slopes of the Ohau Range did not daunt him:

> I had been bred among mountains and I did not anticipate failure. All I had to do was to follow one mountain valley out till it ended on a saddle already stated, and follow down another valley and creek on the opposite side of the range, till close to a clump of trees more than half way down the slope to the east shore of Lake Ohau, I would see or have no difficulty in finding the hut where the shepherd lived.[13]

By mid-afternoon he had crossed the range by way of Darts Bush Stream and Flanagans Saddle (1225 m), and then down Darcy Stream. About halfway down the Ohau side he reached the hut to which he had been directed. He had an enjoyable evening with the shepherd occupying it (a Mr Cameron) and he was invited to stay a day or two and rest. But the drive to make a living was paramount, so McKay elected to continue his journey. Leaving the hut and without much trouble, he crossed the two large rivers, the Hopkins and the Dobson, which flowed into the head of the lake. He then got involved with a mob of frisky cattle that pushed him back up the valley towards Ram (Temple) Stream. It was dark by the time he splashed through Station Creek (Maitland Stream), "without making preparation and taking the precautions I should have done. The consequence was that when I arrived at the station I was suffering from the results of my indiscretion, but was soon put to rights by getting that change of clothing which I needed. A good meal followed, and again I began to think that life was worth living after all."[14] McKay had been on the road for ten days, in winter without a coat. He had walked nearly 500 km, been dunked in icy streams three times, crossed two high passes, and survived a blizzard. The experience was to be a turning point in his life.

On Burkes Pass there is now a monument, with a quotation from Michael John Burke, a graduate of Dublin University, who reached the pass in 1855. The inscription reads:

> O ye who enter the portals of the Mackenzie to found homes, take the word of a child of the misty gorges, and plant forest trees for your lives. So shall your mountain facings and river flats be preserved to your children's children and for evermore.

Although McKay did not settle permanently in the Mackenzie Country, he was to acquire land and plant trees at Lake Ohau, which was the first place in New Zealand where he was properly at home. The monument was placed on Burkes Pass in 1917, the year McKay died.

... and a Job ...

When McKay arrived at Lake Ohau, there were only two people living at the home station: the housekeeper, Mrs Cameron (presumably the wife of the shepherd with whom he had spent the previous night) and the overseer, Edmund Hodgkinson, the younger brother of George Hodgkinson, the owner. During the evening, on discovering McKay possessed some carpentry skills, Mrs Cameron persuaded the overseer of the need for a meat safe. This and other small jobs kept McKay busy for the next three days. His wages allowed him to buy a pair of boots – of which the station must have had a stock – and then he was ready to pursue his wandering towards Central Otago once again.

McKay was near Lake Middleton when he met the Hodgkinson brothers returning from Benmore Station with the mail. Shortly after they passed, the older man (George) turned and hailed him. He said he had been speaking with his brother, and if McKay liked to return to the Lake Ohau Station he would employ him for two weeks. Strangely, McKay did not immediately jump at this offer, but as he still "had needs other than a pair of boots …" (a blanket for one) reason soon prevailed and that evening he reappeared at the station.[15]

The next day he learned to row, a necessary skill on the station. The boat generally required three to handle it: two rowing, and one at the tiller. McKay came to enjoy the trips out on the lake, which was often like a sheet of glass with the mountains reflected so brilliantly it was hard to tell which way was up.[16]

He had no specific tasks. Edmund did the stock work, and in the main, McKay assisted the older brother with work around the station or in getting supplies of fencing material from nearby patches of bush. He worked hard and found he had "a good and indulgent master" and that they got on well.[17] Whenever the men had been out on the lake, and after the boat was secured, he was always offered a glass of whisky and advised to change his wet clothes as speedily as possible.[18] It came as no surprise at the end of the fortnight when it was suggested he stay on through the winter months, and this time he had no hesitation in accepting the offer. Although there were occasional severe storms and gales, he found the winter climate delightful and he longed for the coming summer so that he might explore the distant mountains.

At this point in his autobiography, 'Fragments', the story stops – just before his meeting with his future wife.

During the winter of 1866, station work would have consisted mainly of milling the timber needed for yards and outbuildings. A decision may have been made to build a jetty for the boat so that it did not have to be dragged in and out of the water each time it was wanted. At times the men would have worked at preparing the road, in anticipation of the time when a dray might eventually be brought through to the station. The tempo of work increased in the spring when the vagaries of the weather became more pronounced and a summer-like day might well be followed by a dump of snow, requiring all hands to be out snow-raking until the sheep were accounted for.

Lambing would have come early as the winter faded, as there were always ram lambs that had escaped docking[19] the year before, and the fresh crop of lambs would start to appear at unexpected times. Then there were musters to bring the sheep in for weaning and docking the lambs, then shearing, and selecting those for mutton or for sale. These were activities of which McKay had had previous experience, but it was probably the mustering he enjoyed the most. It is easy to imagine him volunteering for

The 'McKay' poplars (at right) on Lake Ohau Station. McKay apparently had title to this block of land, and probably planted the trees for fuel and shelter for a cottage that was never built.

the top beat, getting ever closer to the peaks and glaciers on which he was becoming fixated.

These were tough times, however, and the economics of farming were not good. When in the autumn McKay suggested taking some leave to do some exploration, George Hodgkinson was likely to have agreed readily.[20] He may have also suggested, perhaps as an inducement to hold Alex to the place, that he accept title to a plot of land, possibly in lieu of some of the wages he was owed. McKay selected a site that was partly sheltered from the south by a terrace edge, had a view of the mountains, and a supply of water.

… and a Wife …

Although he was happy, and becoming more and more involved with running the station, McKay's financial situation continued to decline. The wool cheque received by the Hodgkinsons for the last few years had been so low that there was little left for wages. At this time Lake Ohau was a very isolated station, accessible only by boat or a rough lakeside track. It was an unlikely setting for McKay to meet his future wife, but that is what he did.[21]

It may have come about because George was engaged and due to marry in a few months' time. It is unlikely that George envisaged his fiancee becoming the station cook, and much more likely that she would expect some domestic help. It was customary at the time for those settlers requiring

The head of Lake Ohau, the first view Susannah would have had of her new home. The station homestead is situated where the middle line of trees reaches the lake.

domestic assistance to meet incoming immigrant ships as they arrived at Port Chalmers, where the latest arrivals could be inspected and offered a domestic position.

Susannah Barnes was born in Chelmsford, Essex, England, on 22 April 1835. There is little else known about her, as her appearance, education and background remain a mystery. Her sister, Mary, may have emigrated with her.[22] Even the date of her arrival is uncertain; however, her *Intention to Marry* declaration states that at the time of marriage she had been resident in New Zealand for eighteen months, indicating an arrival in February 1867. On the 22 February 1867, the ship *Countess Russell*, out of London, berthed at Port Chalmers. Her passengers included 'Nine assisted domestic servants.'[23]

It is consistent with all known facts that either George or Edmund Hodgkinson met the *Countess Russell* and offered Susannah a position, explaining it as a cook/housekeeper/maid on a small sheep station beside a lake in the mountains and that she would be looking after his wife, and cooking for them as well as for a number of single men. The latter may have been an enticement, for Susannah was thirty-two, and acquiring a husband would have been one of her priorities.

It would have been a tiring journey of at least a week before the dray bounced over the last rise of the long and bumpy road[24] and Susannah finally saw the beautiful setting of her destination. For a young woman from the English low country it must have been a startling sight. The date was about the beginning of March 1867.

Three months later George Hodgkinson, the station owner, married. Their connubial bliss was short-lived however, for on 13 July 1867, less than a month after the marriage, George died of rheumatic fever.[25]

When the funeral cortege of George's widow, his brother Edmund, and the late lamented George disappeared out of sight, Susannah and Alexander were left alone. It was midwinter, close to the shortest day, and cold. There was little chance of any visitors. It was an ideal opportunity for the young couple to get to know each other and to discuss and plan the future.

Susannah may have confessed at this time that she didn't really like the high country – she may have felt frightened and oppressed by the mountains and the violence of the storms – and that she wanted to get back to somewhere more civilised and more populated. Alex expressed an interest in photography. They decided that they would stay put while they had food and accommodation and there was a little money to be earned, and that McKay would go on to Christchurch and learn the finer points of the art. Susannah would join him there later as a partner in a photographic business.

When Edmund Hodgkinson returned he was a worried man. Although George had died quite a wealthy man, with about £25,000 to his name, he had passed away without making a will. Now the station needed money for wages and supplies, George's widow claimed a share, and sundry debtors needed to be paid, but no one had the authority to do anything. There was no telling when he would be able to pay either of them wages, although he was happy to let them stay on at the station. He may have realised that if they left him now he would be unable to carry on and might have to walk off the land.

During the following year (1868), McKay was promoted to assistant manager.[26] Despite this responsibility, in the autumn he went to Christchurch for his lessons in wet-plate photography with Edmund Wheeler of E. Wheeler and Son, in Cathedral Square, for which he paid £5 (about $750 in today's terms).[27] He returned to Ohau in May.

In June, Susannah became pregnant. It was now important to organise their marriage quickly. The nearest minister was at Kurow, but understandably Susannah wanted her sister to be present at the wedding. For the marriage they required two witnesses, and had to complete an *Intention to Marry* declaration. This was officially required three days before the ceremony, but it was often possible to complete it on the same day if the minister was not too particular. Alex was sure he could find a co-operative minister, and either a shipmate or mining mate to act as the other witness, once they got to Dunedin where Susannah's sister lived.

The Hillside Manse of St Andrews Presbyterian Church where the marriage of Susannah Barnes and Alexander McKay took place on Monday 24 August 1868.

Hodgkinson would not have been surprised at McKay's plans. He may have suggested taking the two to Dunedin so that he could replenish the station stores. Perhaps he would try to find a married couple for the station at the same time. Looking further ahead, Edmund may have suggested that McKay might like to return for the next summer, as his knowledge of the station and its management was now extensive.

In Dunedin, inquiries revealed that the Reverend Robert Scrimgeour of St Andrews would marry them the next Monday at his Hillside Manse, and that he would not be concerned if the *Intention to Marry* declaration was completed immediately beforehand.

There are some curious aspects to Marriage Certificate No. 2105. The panel nominating Alexander McKay, of full age, Carpenter and Bachelor, and Susannah Barnes, also of full age, Spinster, as being married at the manse of St Andrews Church on the 24th day of August 1868, was filled in by the Rev. Scrimgeour and is perfectly clear and legible. However, when it comes to the individual signatures of Alex and Susannah, and their witnesses, Mary Barnes and J.F. Hedrass, Scrimgeour has signed for all except McKay. Furthermore, in the case of the two women, their surnames look more like 'Brown', and are quite different from the clearly written 'Barnes' in the panel above. The *Intention to Marry* declaration is even more odd: although the names are clear, Alex's age is given as twenty-three and Susannah's as twenty-five. In fact, McKay was twenty-seven and Susannah was thirty-three.

Scrimgeour had been inducted at St Andrews during the previous year, having arrived from Melbourne. Three years later "circumstances arose which led to a period of trial for the Church. The dissension which resulted was exceedingly prejudicial to church life and work …"[28] Scrimgeour retired on 7 June 1871.

Seven months after the wedding, William Alexander McKay was born on 20 March 1869. His birth was registered by Susannah, in Dunedin, on 3 June. In due course, the family arrived back on brother John's doorstep in Christchurch, somewhat to his surprise as he had no idea that Alex had acquired a wife, let alone a family.

These were difficult times. There was little work to be had anywhere. McKay decided the only option was for him to return to Lake Ohau for the summer and autumn, leaving his family in Christchurch. It took him a week to get there, probably retracing his original route over Burkes Pass and the Ben Ohau Range. Edmund, however, could offer work only until the end of autumn. There was also other news. The financial crisis facing the station had been resolved when a marriage was agreed between Duncan Sutherland, the manager of Omarama Station, and the prematurely widowed wife of the late George Hodgkinson. As part of the deal, Sutherland became a partner in Lake Ohau Station.[29]

By April McKay was ready to leave. Lake Ohau was no longer the place where he wanted to be. Once more he shouldered his swag, turned his back on the mountains, and set off on the long road to return to Christchurch and his wife and child. The next six months were hard going. Crowded quarters at John's lodgings near Wards Brewery, a fractious child, and little money for food and fuel to see them through the winter, taxed McKay's Scottish stoicism. But in spring he found a period of work with one of the region's more substantial farmers, a Mr Ayreton, near Kaiapoi. Susannah apparently obtained work with the same family.

Soon, however, Alex and John McKay were on the move again, although Susannah apparently stayed on at Kaiapoi, probably as a domestic. The men stopped first at the flax mill in Ashley Gorge, but in 1870–71 Alex, possibly accompanied by John, headed once more into the Mackenzie Country, on a prospecting trip that lasted about ten months.[30]

After this, he returned to Ashley Gorge, rejoining Susannah at the flax mill. There is a seam of coal at Ashley Gorge and McKay decided to evaluate whether it was workable, as fuel in the area was in short supply. The local stands of native timber were being depleted rapidly as the mills screamed to meet the demand for timber. Accordingly, he drove an 'adit' – a horizontal access tunnel – to test the continuity, thickness, and lie of the seam. It did not look encouraging. As he backed out into the daylight, and stood blinking in the bright light of day, he became aware of a man watching.

He knew the man as he had briefly worked for him in Christchurch, in 1868. He was Julius Haast (later, Julius von Haast),[31] the Canterbury provincial geologist. The two men, drawn together by their common interest in the coal seam, talked, and Haast, impressed by McKay's enthusiasm, knowledge, and ability, offered him employment as a general field assistant. This chance second encounter was to have a profound effect on the future of geological investigations in New Zealand.

Johann Franz Julius von Haast was born in Germany in 1822, emigrated to New Zealand in 1858 and became a British subject in 1861, about the same time as he became provincial geologist of Canterbury. He was to become a major figure in scientific and artistic circles, and received many awards and honours (which he actively solicited). The most notable of his achievements was the founding of Canterbury Museum. He died in 1887. Photo: Hay Collection, Canterbury Museum

8. The Door Opens

New Zealand's pioneering settlers found much to their liking in their new country – clean air and water, forests offering a seemingly inexhaustible supply of wood, land with high natural fertility and a bountiful sea. But it was gold that was seen as the immediate solution to the problem of how to obtain wealth, individually and nationally, and many provincial districts offered rewards for the discovery of an authentic goldfield. Gold had been discovered in Coromandel as early as 1852, and at Collingwood in northwest Nelson in 1857.[1] But it was not until 1861, when Gabriel Read found gold 'shining like the stars in Orion on a dark frosty night' near Lawrence in Central Otago, that the first reward of £500 was claimed.[2] A year later, Hartley and Reilly, two miners from California, collected a substantially larger sum (£2000) to encourage them to divulge the location of where they had recovered almost forty kilograms of gold from the bed of the Clutha River, a short distance downstream from Cromwell. Discoveries in other areas soon followed, particularly in the South Island, in Marlborough, Nelson, and Westland. Ironically the Coromandel area, where the first discovery was made, was the last to be exploited.

The Three 'Hs'

The gold rush achieved its purpose, but it also created new demands for other resources. Coal, a more efficient form of energy than wood, was needed to fuel the boilers of the ships, machines and trains of the increasingly mechanised and organised nation.

As a result, the opinions of geologists were treated with great respect. It was well deserved, for the 'Three Hs' – Hochstetter, Haast, and Hector – brought both energy and wisdom to the task of unravelling the geology of a complex and dynamic country. They didn't always get it right, but they covered the basics well and laid an excellent foundation for the future.

Ferdinand Hochstetter, the geologist on the scientific expedition of the Austrian naval frigate *Novara*, arrived in Auckland in 1858, just a day after Julius Haast. The two soon met, joined forces, and became life-long friends. Haast accompanied Hochstetter on most of his subsequent travels in New Zealand over the next two years. Although Haast was thirty-eight and Hochstetter only twenty-nine, the latter had more practical experience and it was Hochstetter who was soon engaged by the Auckland provincial government to examine the Drury coal field. The government was so impressed with his report that they persuaded him to stay on after the *Novara* sailed to make further surveys in Auckland and Nelson provinces.

Together Hochstetter and Haast travelled south to the Taupo Volcanic Zone; Hochstetter acted as mentor, and Haast was an apt and enthusiastic pupil. Later, they examined the Coromandel and other places of interest before sailing south to Nelson, with a brief stop in Taranaki on the way.

Hochstetter, who was later made a knight of both the Imperial Austrian Order of the Crown and the Royal Württemberg Order of the Crown, was an outstanding scientist. In his relatively brief time in New Zealand, he described and interpreted many important features of New Zealand geology. He recognised and named the Taupo Volcanic Zone and realised that Lake Taupo had been a major source of pumice. He described Auckland's volcanoes, and compared Tongariro with Vesuvius. He made important collections of fossils from Kawhia, the Waikato Heads, and Nelson, and also described the ultramafic 'mineral' belt of Nelson.

Haast benefited from his association with Hochstetter. When Hochstetter left Nelson to return to Auckland (and eventually Vienna), Haast stayed on, exploring the west and southwestern parts of the Nelson region, where he found abundant coal and traces of gold. He had already excavated some moa bones in the Aorere Valley and this had probably sowed the seed of one of the subsequent great passions of his life.

Haast was negotiating to extend his Nelson survey southwards into Canterbury when (fortuitously) the contractor on the tunnel between Lyttelton and Christchurch struck very hard rock and gave up. Haast was asked to examine the route of the proposed tunnel; he reported favourably and the tunnel was duly completed. He took up the post of Canterbury Provincial Geologist in 1861, and became a British subject at about the same time. He involved himself deeply in the development of arts and science in Canterbury, and founded the successful Philosophical Institute of Canterbury, which was a stepping-stone for his greatest ambition, a first-class museum in Christchurch.

Haast combined great energy with eclectic talent. He was a big man (100 kilograms), with a fine singing voice, and was an accomplished violinist. His scientific interests spanned the natural world. His ambition was rewarded when the Canterbury Museum opened in 1870, with Haast as founding director. He received many honours (which he actively solicited), including a hereditary knighthood from the Emperor of Austria, which entitled him to call himself von Haast, and an honorary degree of Doctor of Science from Cambridge University.

In 1861, the same year that Haast became Canterbury Provincial Geologist, a young Scotsman, James Hector, was appointed director of the Geological Survey of Otago. Hector had graduated in medicine from the University of Edinburgh in 1856. At the time of his appointment to Otago, he was thirty-two and had already established himself as a field geologist and natural scientist of note on Palliser's expedition to western Canada. Both he and Haast were intrepid and indefatigable explorers, but it was Hector's geological expertise and progress that attracted the attention of the new central government in Wellington. Hector proposed a national Geological Survey in conjunction with a museum and laboratory. His appointment in 1865 as Director of the New Zealand Geological Survey and Colonial Museum, at a salary of £800 ($120,000 in today's terms) was a tribute to his abilities as a planner and organiser. It was to his credit as an employer that Hector took with him to Wellington his original Dunedin staff, consisting of Skey, Gore, Buchanan and Rayer.

The Meteorological Office was later added to Hector's responsibilities and the following year he became manager of the New Zealand Institute (later the Royal Society of New Zealand), which gave him control of the dissemination of all scientific knowledge in the country. Hector was to edit the published proceedings and transactions of the Institute for the next thirty-five years. The only missing item in his empire was some field staff (other than himself); as Burton notes, 'When the Director was out in the field all office work stopped and, when he was in the office, the geological survey of the colony was suspended!'[3]

The wide-ranging achievements of a younger man may have rankled with the ambitious Haast (who was twelve years older than Hector, and still several years away from getting his museum!), although the two men maintained a professional cordiality.

These three men, in a very short space of time, had established the geologic framework of the country. There was a basement of 'greywacke' (as in the Southern Alps and the ranges of the North Island) or schist (as in Otago), with granite and other rocks further west. Overlying this basement was a sequence of cover strata which had many similarities in different regions of the country. Typically the oldest (or lowest) beds – those immediately above the basement – were white or yellow quartz gravel and conglomerate, and they commonly contained coal or sometimes gold. There might be mudstone (papa) above them, and higher up there was usually limestone. It was unusual for the whole sequence to be seen at any one place, and it was the task of the geologist to work out the sequence from the scattered rock outcrops in any one district. There were issues on a national scale, too. Was the limestone in Hawkes Bay the same as that in North Canterbury, or Oamaru, or Southland, or on the West Coast? Systematic geological mapping could provide the answer, but it was to be a century before a national survey was completed. At that time, the question for geologists was whether the various limestone manifestations, prominent around the country, might indicate the presence of coal or gold (or, today, oil or gas).

Fossils promised to provide some sort of answer – fossils that indicated the age of the rocks in which they were found.[4] But they were not easy to collect. First, they had to be found, then extracted from the rock in which they occurred, and later packed, crated and shipped back to Wellington for identification and storage. Collecting them was a time-consuming process and considerably restricted the amount of ground that could be covered by a field geologist. Fossils were heavy, too.

When Haast introduced Alex McKay to Hector and praised his collecting abilities, Hector's brain might well have gone into overdrive. Given McKay's lack of formal education, he could hardly appoint him to a position as a geologist, but McKay could certainly be a fossil collector. There were numerous areas needing systematic inspection, and if McKay turned out to be as good as Haast said he was, then Hector could promote him later.

But this was in the future. For McKay, it was Haast who first presented him with the opportunity to qualify in this geological fraternity.

The Fossil Collector

McKay's first assignment was as a general hand on a field trip to the Clent Hills, inland of Ashburton, to assist with the horses and other such duties.[5] Haast was a competent and experienced geologist, and McKay was a ready learner. He would have quickly grasped the identification of the main rock types, the sort of specific observations that were necessary, and the need for careful and accurate recording. Haast recognised his energy and intellect, and opened McKay's eyes to the rewards and satisfaction of a life of scientific investigation.

By the end of the Clent Hills trip, Haast apparently had enough confidence in McKay to allow him to search for moa bones on his own at Shag Point.[6] The success of these arrangements was such that Haast continued to employ McKay on 'menial work' at Canterbury Museum until the winter of 1872, when he sent him to the Waipara River for two months to collect saurian (reptile) fossils. River boulders containing teeth and bones had been found in the Waipara, and it was likely that a systematic search would yield better material. This time, not only was McKay his own boss,

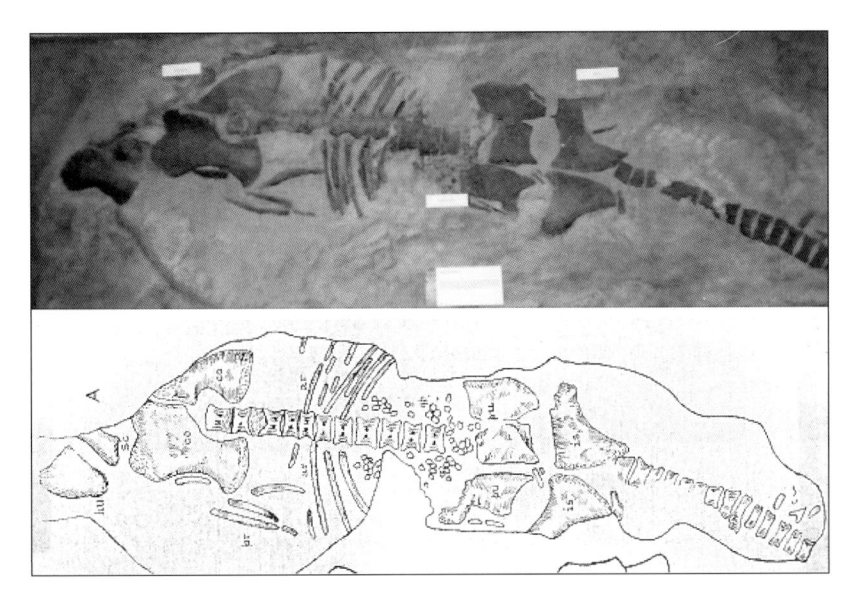

The slab of rock that McKay collected from Bobys Creek in 1872 contained the fossilised skeleton of a marine reptile, the mesosaur, Mauisaursis haasti, *which lived about 65 million years ago. It includes the main part of the body, with shoulders, ribs, vertebrae, pelvis and part of the tail represented. Missing are the long snake-like neck and head, and part of the tail. The remains are those of a juvenile; when fully grown its neck would have been about six metres in length and its body about fourteen metres (three times longer than a family car). The line drawing is from Hutton's scientific description of the specimen. An interesting detail is the presence in the abdominal cavity of gastroliths – rounded pebbles swallowed by the creature and retained in its stomach to act as a digestive aid, providing a mill-stone action to crush or pulverise its food.*

but he also had the authority to employ assistants.

Haast was now working hard on the development of the Canterbury Museum (including the acquisition of exhibits from both local sources and overseas)[7] and the arrival of six large cases of fossils two months later would have delighted him. The efforts of his efficient collector produced blocks of stone of several hundredweight, some of which included nearly complete skeletons. Haast was forewarned, however, as to what to expect, as McKay had written to him from Bobby's [Boby's] Creek Hut, in the Waipara, on 4 June 1872:

> This new slab is over 3 ft. 6 in. [one metre] long but is part of an immense block which cannot be less than 2 1/2 tons [about 2500 kilograms] and will take a long time to get, though I think I can get it safely.[8]

McKay would have had to excavate the fossil with great care and patience, chipping away the excess rock until the specimen was manageable. Then

McKay was still a relative novice at the art of fossil collecting. His achievement in separating the mesosaur slab from the surrounding rock, then bringing it down this waterfall in Boby's Creek and transporting it back to Christchurch without reducing it to a pile of meaningless rubble speaks of painstaking care and patience.

he probably built a crate around it for protection before lowering it down the waterfall. The specimen is now displayed in the Canterbury Museum.

Haast continued to employ McKay on further work around the museum until the end of the year, when he instructed him to excavate the Moa-bone Cave at Sumner. This excavation was the beginning of the 'Body in the Cave Affair', a protracted saga.

The Body in the Cave Affair

At Sumner, a northeastern suburb of Christchurch, the Avon and Heathcote Rivers converge to form a large estuary between the Canterbury Plains to the north and the volcanic hills and rocky coastline of Banks Peninsula to the south. Such intertidal estuarine areas, rich with nutrients from both land and sea, mixed and regulated by the ceaseless tides, are prolific sources of food, especially shellfish. The adjacent rocky open ocean coast of Banks Peninsula is also home to seals, penguins and paua, and provides good fishing spots. Add a large dry, three-roomed cave and the attraction of the area to nomadic Maori becomes clear. Early Europeans also made considerable use of the Sumner cave.[9] The presence of moa bones both in and around the cave, associated with charcoal and other fish and bird bones and stone implements, indicated that the cave could provide important information on when, and by whom, the great birds were exterminated.

This was a subject of considerable scientific interest in the 1860s and 70s, on which Haast had already published a series of papers. Accordingly, funds were eventually raised by subscription to assist with the cost of excavation, and in late 1872 the investigation of the Sumner cave began. It was to result in one of the most celebrated furores of nineteenth-century New Zealand science. It was debated in Parliament and even reached the pages of the international science journal *Nature*. The affair went on for over four years, from 1872 to 1876, and therefore needs to be examined in terms of other happenings of the period, including the delay between the writing and publication of various articles. It also spanned the period in which McKay graduated from being an itinerant labourer to a professional fossil collector and, finally, a fully-fledged staff member of the New Zealand Geological Survey.

Haast apparently had no reservations about McKay's ability when he instructed him to carry out the excavation of the cave, and directed him to employ another man (R. Lowman) to assist in making the excavations required.[10] Some time after the excavation, Haast claimed that McKay had asked him for permission to write up some notes of the results. This Haast 'encouraged him to do so, which notes, if I remember rightly, three

The Moa-bone cave at Sumner in Christchurch, a commodious and convenient shelter over the centuries, is now recognised as an historic place.

or four pages in quarto, after reading, I tore up as of no value to me'.[11] McKay, on the other hand, was to report that Haast ordered him to his study to supply him with the notes he had made, that they discussed the results and McKay expressed his interpretation of them. 'I told him that there could be no doubt but that the whole evidence proved that the moa-hunters possessed polished stone axes and other tools and ornaments. He replied, rather hotly, that he had no personal views to uphold, and that his object was truth.'[12] It was McKay's opinion that there was no evidence that the moa were exterminated by a previous culture, that it was possible that Maori had been in New Zealand for much longer than generally thought, and that they may have hunted the birds to extinction relatively soon after their arrival.

This incident was undoubtedly the crux of the contretemps which was to follow. Haast may have realised suddenly that his enthusiastic young protégé (McKay was thirty-three, while Haast was fifty), by way of his detailed and objective recording and logical interpretations, now posed a professional threat. One of Haast's cherished theories – that the moa-hunters were distinct and separate predecessors of the Maori – was under attack. Haast would have sensed the logic and the inevitable conclusion that followed but was unable to concede, and so pulled rank.

There was another issue too. McKay's notes undoubtedly referred to a body that had been dug up from the cave, and was now residing clandestinely in the museum. The last thing that Haast needed at this politically delicate

8. THE DOOR OPENS 107

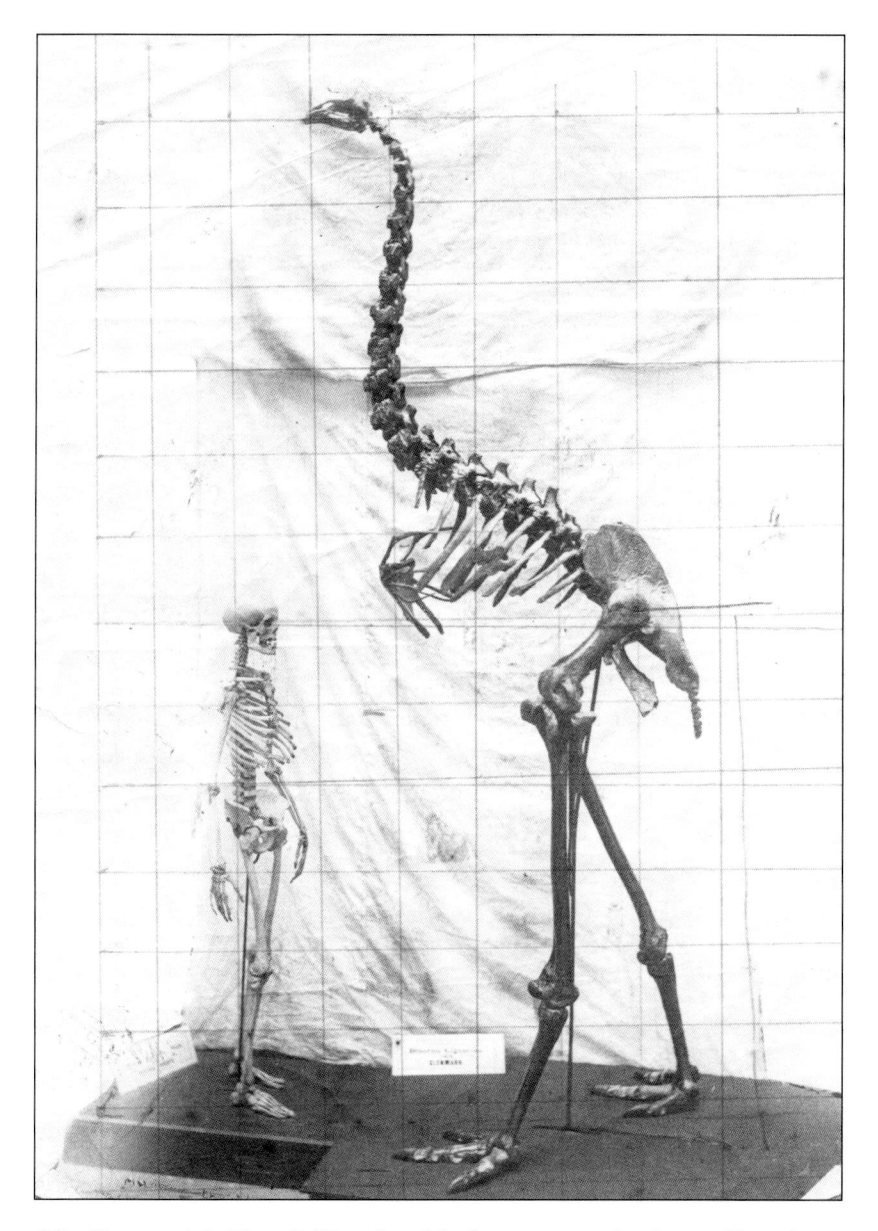

'The Hunter and the Hunted'. Haast hoped the Sumner cave exploration would reveal the identity of the humans who exterminated the moa. Were they Maori or were they an earlier race of moa-hunters? The discovery of a body during the cave excavations in 1872 complicated the issue. However, the date of Dr A.C. Barker's photograph of this display at Canterbury Museum – 1871 – excludes the possibility that the human skeleton in the display is from the body exhumed from the cave. Photo: Canterbury Museum

stage of the museum's development was awkward questions about how, when, and why it came to be there. So, in a simple, impulsive gesture of irritation, he shredded McKay's notes and sowed the seed of the row that followed.

McKay was certainly deeply hurt by Haast's actions, but apparently curbed his tongue and quietly resolved to make sure that the world would get to hear his interpretation of the information which he had retrieved from the Sumner cave, albeit under Haast's direction. The two men apparently remained on superficially cordial terms for another year or more, while McKay started work with the Geological Survey. Although he undertook an astonishing amount of field work and consequent report writing in this first year with the Survey, it did not deflect McKay from the belief that there was an important story of topical importance to tell from the Sumner Cave. He resolved to put forward his own interpretation. There seemed little likelihood of Haast ever publishing on the subject, especially given that the results of the excavation conflicted with his favoured theory.[13] And, given Haast's reaction to his original notes and views, it was little wonder he did not raise the matter directly with the museum director again.

And so McKay, finally 'Letting impatience outstrip his prudence',[14] again wrote down his interpretation of the observations at Sumner and on 8 August 1874, his paper 'On the identity of the Moa-hunters with the present Maori Race'[15] was read by Dr Hector before the Wellington Philosophical Society.[16] When Haast heard of the paper he was livid. His immediate reaction was to object, by telegram from Waimate,[17] and then to pen a beautifully illustrated thirty-two page paper to the Institute.[18]

An obvious objective of Haast's paper was to demonstrate that it was *he*, von Haast, who was the learned and able scientist. But he had a dilemma. McKay had scrupulously avoided the slightest reference to the disinterred body that now resided in the museum. But McKay and Lowman, Fuller (the museum taxidermist), Dr Barker (who analysed the stomach contents) and even the janitor all knew about it; it was only a matter of time before the word got out and the whole world would know. Even more troublesome was the appearance of the body, the state of which was more consistent with having been buried for only a matter of weeks, rather than for hundreds of years. So Haast went on the offensive. Not only did he submit his own paper to be published in the same volume as McKay's, but he had it printed privately and circulated as a pamphlet before it was formally published. A postscript to the paper was suppressed from the *Transactions* by Hector as being of 'an offensive nature', but it had already appeared in the public press.[19]

Meanwhile, the innocent centre of attention, the body, had been

8. THE DOOR OPENS 109

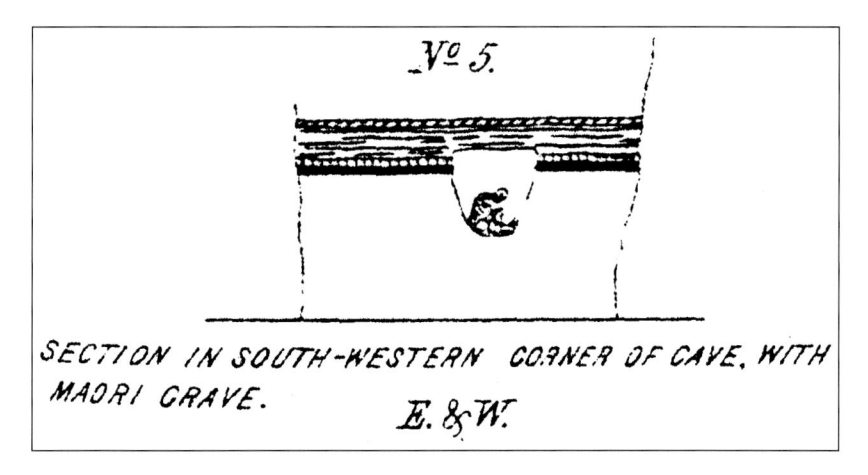

N°5.

SECTION IN SOUTH-WESTERN CORNER OF CAVE, WITH MAORI GRAVE. E. & W.

Von Haast's miniscule drawing of a section through the grave site at Sumner Cave showed the body had been interred before the deposition of the shell bed (top layer). 'It is thus evident the burial had taken place long before Europeans came to the cave ...' he concluded. McKay, however, was adamant that no shell bed was present at the grave site and there was no evidence at all that the body was of great age: 'the appearance of the Skeleton with the bones being covered by skin/the Stomach and Smaller intestine being still in place and not the least decomposed, with a grizzled beard about 3 inches long ... the body had been interred for no great length of time. In fact [initially] we doubted that was a Maorie at all ...'

macerated for three months. All traces of skin, hair, ligament, and internal organs were gone. It was then articulated by Fuller, and put to stand, nearly six feet tall, in plain view in the Museum.

Haast then set about denigrating and vilifying McKay both in public and in private. He referred to him as a servant, and an illiterate man who 'did not know the difference between the bones of a bird and of a mammal ...'[20]

McKay could give as good as he got:

> Some six months previous to the exploration of the Sumner cave, I was employed by Dr. Haast in searching for moa bones in Shag Valley, and as bullock bones are plentifully scattered about in that locality, I hope, for Dr. Haast's reputation, that he has not sent to foreign museums, as moa bones, any of the collections which I then made for him. If I was incompetent to distinguish a mammal from a bird bone, why did he employ me on this work? I leave him to answer.[21]

Although objecting to Haast's sneers at his menial status,[22] McKay reserved his strongest public rebuke in defence of his director and mentor, Dr Hector, who was at that stage overseas: 'Dr Hector's connection with the affair extends no further than, that, as a personal favor, he read [presented] my paper ... Dr Haast will, therefore, I hope, see fit to withdraw the last paragraph of his remarkable paper, in which he charges Dr. Hector with being the wilful abettor of my alleged dishonesty.'[23]

It was not McKay who was dishonest. His account forced Haast to counter with his own version. This in turn left Haast with no choice but to divulge the existence of the body, which he did in considerable detail, but he distorted relationships to make the body appear much older than it really was. His section no. 5 in particular, and the accompanying text, make it clear that the grave was excavated through the layers overlying the marine sands, but before the deposition of the upper shell layer.[24] McKay was emphatic that this was not so and that the grave had been dug in the marine sands in an area where the overlying layers were not present. If this was the case, then there is no stratigraphic evidence at all of the age of the body, and the condition of the lashings, skin, and internal organs assume much more significance.

McKay's reaction to Haast's paper was one of shock. It was he who had done the excavation and made the notes, and now his integrity was challenged. Haast himself had taught him the value of accurate and careful reporting of observations. McKay, in a remarkable letter (in what is indisputably his own unedited handwriting), wrote a detailed account of the relevant details, concluding that 'Dr Haast's paper which treats of this subject [is] eminently calculated to mislead, and [is] scarcely detailing the true facts of the case.' He also noted that 'So strongly was Dr Haast impressed that the skeleton had not been long there that he gave the strictest orders to have it conveyed to the Museum with the utmost secrecy least [sic] the Police should hear of the find and get us all into trouble …'[25] H.F. Haast noted 'Haast was full of fun, and one can well imagine him laughingly impressing on his workmen the necessity for secrecy, they knowing as well as he did that he was joking.'[26]

McKay's letter is undated and unaddressed. It is, however, annotated and countersigned by McKay's fellow worker, Lowman, who notes that he received the letter on 4 October 1875. Although he makes a number of minor suggestions, he clearly had no disagreement with the general tenor.

The letter ultimately reached Walter Mantell (humourist, former MP for Wallace and member of the Legislative Council) who tabled it in Parliament, although the resulting discussion was more flippant than serious. He raised the issue of the body by moving that an inquest be held on human remains found in the cave, 'as a body found under suspicious circumstances.'[27] The joke was eventually retailed in the topical international science magazine, *Nature*.[28] Haast's dismissive response, however, so embarrassed Mantell that he tried once again to have the matter debated seriously in Parliament.[29] The Members however persisted in regarding it as a joke. Colonel Brett

A facsimile of part of McKay's draft letter detailing the circumstances of the discovery of the body at Sumner Cave. The text reads 'So strongly was Dr Haast impressed that the Skeleton had not been long there that he gave the Strictest orders to have it conveyed to the Museum with the utmost Secrecy least the Police Should hear of the find and get us all into trouble

'From the above it will be Seen that My account does not agree with that given by Dr Haast and I cannot but regard that part of Dr Haasts paper which treats of this subject as eminently calculated to mislead And as Scarcely detailing the true facts of the Case.' The marginal comments and annotations appear to have been made by Lowman 'on railway near Rakaia'.

pointed out that the word 'body' was incorrect as it was a skeleton, not a body – an opinion that appears debatable in itself, given that the internal organs were remaining. The Premier, Dr Polen, concluded the matter by saying it was the best joke he had heard for a long time. However, McKay saw it as no joke and was affected deeply enough for it to show in his written work of the period.

Haast had defeated himself. Early in 1875, his resignation as President of the Canterbury Institute was accepted (having been earlier declined). However, his local *mana* resulted in his being reinstated in 1877.

It is only fair to note that Haast was under considerable stress at the time. He had put enormous effort into the stewardship and politicking necessary to keep the museum development on track, his wife had had a nervous breakdown and gone to Melbourne for hydropathic treatment, and now both his protégé and his colleague had apparently joined forces against him.[30] His responses became inappropriately derogatory and vindictive.

Hector, on the other hand, reacted with a statesmanlike silence, and his role in the affair remains speculative. Mantell referred to it as a 'silly business'[31] and von Haast's son and biographer commented that 'One can only regret that the friendly relationship of three such good men should have been severed by an incident that should never have occurred.'[32]

It was the illiterate servant who had the last word, however, and an unusual word it was too. For McKay wrote a poem. In fact he wrote two or possibly three poems, when, according to H.F. Haast, he was brooding over his wrongs in a lonely tent high above Lake Harris five years later (see page 137). The first poem consisted of thirty four-line stanzas describing the fierce storm that had trapped him for eight or nine days, in 'one of the wildest and yet most beautiful districts in New Zealand ...'[33] and he put his name to it. The second, published anonymously under the pseudonym '*Dinornis Sumnerensis*', was even more extraordinary. Again it had stanzas of four lines, but it continued for forty-three pages, to a total of 340 verses. It described the proud entry of the Savant (Haast) into the City of Christchurch astride a captured moa, only to have the giant bird break free and carry him off into the wilderness, neither of them ever to be seen again.[34] The poem's publication caused considerable interest in literary and scientific circles at the time, with much speculation as to the identity of the author. Despite the clue afforded by the pseudonym, the poem was originally attributed to W.T. Travers, and later to the Hon. W.D.B. Mantell, both of whom had impish wits and some insight into the subject matter. The secret was so well kept, however, that in 1909 the poem was wrongly ascribed, albeit tentatively, by Dr T.M. Hocken in his *Bibliography of the Literature Relating to New Zealand*, to William Miles Maskell. Hocken described it as 'A clever, good-humoured skit on Dr. Haast and his pet theories about the moa.'[35] It was not until 1936 that McKay's former colleague James Park, by then Emeritus Professor James Park, ended the enigma with a full explanation published as a letter in the *Otago Daily Times*.[36]

Both McKay's poems were printed in 1880 by John Hughes, Steam Printer, Lambton Quay, Wellington. An additional (unpublished and handwritten) poem was found in the Mantell family papers in the Alexander Turnbull Library.[37] The handwriting and subject matter indicate it was undoubtedly written by McKay. It also uses four-lined stanzas, fifteen of them in this case, and is similar in style and wit to the others, although more pointed. For instance:

>   […]
>   The world of Science does not seem
>   To be agreed about it
>   One says 'twas there before the Flood
>   Another says I doubt it
>   Now this looks grave and throws a doubt
>   On some ones observation
>   Which being so it is I confess
>   A serious accusation
>   […]

The poem is undated, so whether it was another product of McKay's enforced inactivity at Lake Harris is unknown.

Although McKay had died thirty years before, H.F. Haast in his biography could not let the second poem pass without critical comment. In somewhat more temperate but no less patronising tones than his father, Haast Junior admitted it was a bright little lampoon, humorous in conception and development, and 'gave even the son of Haast quite a hearty laugh'.[38] By the same token he did not refrain from suggesting it was 'corrected and refined' from its original 'crude doggerel' by McKay's colleagues.[39] It was once attributed to Maskell but 'No one, however, with any literary sense could imagine Maskell … guilty of perpetuating so crude a poem … fettered by the author's difficulty of expression, struggling to express a genuine love of Nature, but paying an unconscious tribute to his master's future reputation.'[40] The 'son of Haast' concluded with the astonishing claim that the Hector dossier of correspondence now in the Hocken Library in Dunedin was assembled by Hector's son 'not to enlighten readers upon the career of Hector as to cast discredit on Haast'.[41]

McKay wasn't brooding at Lake Harris. He was trapped by the weather. His body couldn't move but his mind could. He was using poetry to exorcise the hurt done to him by Haast. He was allowing the brain's astonishing recuperative powers to heal itself of the hurt done. Poetry is a concentrated expression of emotion and has been used as therapy for 2000 years. It was prescribed by Soranus, a Roman physician, as early as the first century AD.[42]

Five verses from *The Canterbury Gilpin* are quoted below.[43] A more comprehensive selection is given in Appendix 2.

>   COME, I have matter for your ear,
>   I have a tale to tell,
>   A song to sing, a race to ride,
>   And would acquit me well.

Speak of my effort what you may,
    But read it all the same, –
Read it, 'tis written to be read,
    Laughed at, and read again.

So much for my intent.
    I know that I shall not escape
The charge of being personal,
    And writing this in hate.

Yet there may be who do insist
    They see their portrait drawn;
And, in reply, I'm bound to say,
    "Thou art the very man."

This race began in Christchurch town,
    The reader will not doubt;
Though where it ended has not been
    So easy to make out.[44]

9. A Career is Born

Soon after the Sumner cave excavation had been completed, and before its aftermath of the total breakdown in communication between McKay and Haast, Sir James Hector, the Director of the Geological Survey and the Colonial Museum, came to Christchurch. Haast warmly recommended McKay to him, with the result that McKay was offered a position as fossil collector with the fledgling Geological Survey. Haast's motivation for this is unclear. He may have had McKay's interests genuinely at heart, being mindful of the difficulty of finding funds to employ him at an adequate wage, let alone provide a secure future. Alternatively, after the episode in which he tore up McKay's notes, he may have realised that McKay posed a potential embarrassment to his cherished theory about moa and moa hunters, and so passing him on to Hector was a way of diverting McKay's attention elsewhere.

Working for Hector

The two Scots, Hector and McKay, came from very different backgrounds but seemed to have formed an early close and complementary alliance. Indeed, it may have been more than that, for beneath the Victorian formality of their communication there are glimpses of a loyal friendship. Although in social standing Hector was a world apart, he was only seven years older than McKay, and quick to realise that McKay had the intelligence, power of observation, eye for detail, and persistence that were needed in a field geologist. He was soon promoting McKay's acceptance in the political-scientific circles of the times. Later he was to endorse, by publication, the freethinking McKay's conclusions, even when these were at variance with his own opinions.

McKay briefly had two masters in 1873, and made two collections from Amuri Bluff, one for Hector, the other for Haast, reporting frequently to both. He apologised to Haast for not following his instructions, having 'found it impossible to see and pass by a good specimen which was more than likely both new and rare.'[1] He also noted that he had 'forwarded the sledgehammer by the *Bee* [a coastal steamer] as it would have proved too much to carry it all the way [back to Christchurch] on horseback.'[2]

McKay received instructions from Hector on 18 February and started for Amuri Bluff on 22 April. Hector commissioned McKay to ship the Geological Survey's share of the collection from Amuri Bluff to Wellington and to accompany it personally. On 12 April, McKay replied to Hector from Christchurch, noting that he had consigned four boxes to Wellington at the first opportunity, and had received £15 ($2250) sent by Hector.[3] On 25 April, he mentioned to John Ingram that he had been in Wellington for about a fortnight, so he must have sailed north from Lyttelton on or about 15 April.[4] Susannah joined him a month later on Friday 16 May, and gave birth to their second son, Duncan, on Sunday the eighteenth.

According to H.F. Haast, Haast lent money to both McKay and Susannah for their fares. He also claimed that on 21 May 1873 McKay wrote to Haast, 'God knows how grateful I am to you for your substantial kindness to me and I acknowledge that I make you but a poor return.'[5] In a postscript McKay apparently added, 'My wife arrived here on Friday last, and on Saturday[6] was delivered of a son to my great consternation as I hoped she would have a few days at least to spare. Both are doing well.'

These sentences are out of character for McKay; it is the only known instance of him reporting personal details in a professional communication.[7] His communications with Haast at this time were professional and impersonal. He had been going to great lengths to collect the best material – as he noted in a letter to Haast, 'a saurian jaw in a boulder some ten or twelve foot in diameter and never wholly uncovered by the tide. I must get this jaw at all risks.'[8] He also wrote to a friend, 'I could not have stopped much longer as my wage was so small that I could not keep the wolf from the door …'[9] Fifteen years later, McKay's later colleague and friend, William Skey, Government Analyst, wrote a mock 'elegy' for Alexander McKay in which he also referred to the 'niggardly pay' McKay received from Haast.[10] There is no evidence that McKay considered himself beholden in any way to Haast.

Meanwhile McKay threw himself into his new career with New Zealand Geological Survey and within a year had completed major surveys in Otago, the West Coast and around East Cape. His enthusiasm and growing confidence in his abilities and opinions shows in his reports, which were produced with the accuracy and alacrity that were to become his trademark. 'If it's worth doing, it's worth writing it down' may well have been one if his dictums. However the 'Body in the Cave' affair (Chapter 8) was to have an aftermath lasting many years, which surfaced several times in the next decade.

McKay spent the winter of 1873 in Wellington, and it was not until early September that he sailed for Dunedin, for a stint of two months' fieldwork in the Catlins area of South Otago.[11] He spent the first week working near Dunedin, on Saddle Hill and at Boat Harbour (Brighton), before taking the coach south to Clutha Ferry (Balclutha), and then the steamer down river to Port Molyneux. Here, he was alarmed to hear that the existence of a reputed reptile skeleton at Bloody Jack's (now known as Tuhawaiki) Island was well known. McKay's innate collector's instincts surfaced: 'I determined to go there at once, for fear curiosity-hunters should injure it before I had the opportunity of seeing it.'[12] His concern was in fact ill founded as it was a case of mistaken identity, and the so-called skeleton turned out to be a few bits of the fossil wood which is common in the area.

The Catlins

The Catlins region is not renowned for its climate, and McKay, despite his enthusiasm and background, was not impervious to it: 'I persevered all day [unsuccessfully] in the rain.'[13] Even today the area is only slowly changing from a backwater of unsealed roads and isolated communities consisting largely of holiday houses. Much of the bush has been felled, both for timber and to clear land for farming. But the coastal scenery is superb, with bold rocky headlands, sheer cliffs, blowholes, caves, and wonderful sweeping beaches.

In McKay's time the area was even less developed. There were few roads worthy of the name, and the bush was to present him with a challenge that twice defeated him. Once he failed in an attempt to push through it to reach Tautuku Beach. On another occasion, night fell as he was trying to force a route from Cannibal Bay to Nugget Point: 'it was so hard to make progress that I was unable to reach Molyneux Bay that night. I however reached the Nuggets early next morning, and immediately commenced work in the cutting that leads up to the lighthouse.'[14] After an initial period of reconnaissance, he wisely decided to make the Nuggets area the site of his principal collection. He spent the next two weeks there, systematically collecting fossils from the sequence of rocks exposed in the region, looking for index fossils that he could relate to those found elsewhere, or which were described in reference books.

McKay, no stranger to walking, had employed an assistant to help carry his gear, which must have frequently included a tent and food for several days. He used the Old Mill (near Glenomaru) as a depot and returned there at intervals to pack his collections and arrange for them to be forwarded to Wellington. He did not confine his investigations entirely to the coast, for he walked inland some fifty kilometres, at least as far as the Popotuna [Kuriwao] Gorge.

Southeast Otago was an inspired choice by Hector as a place to start

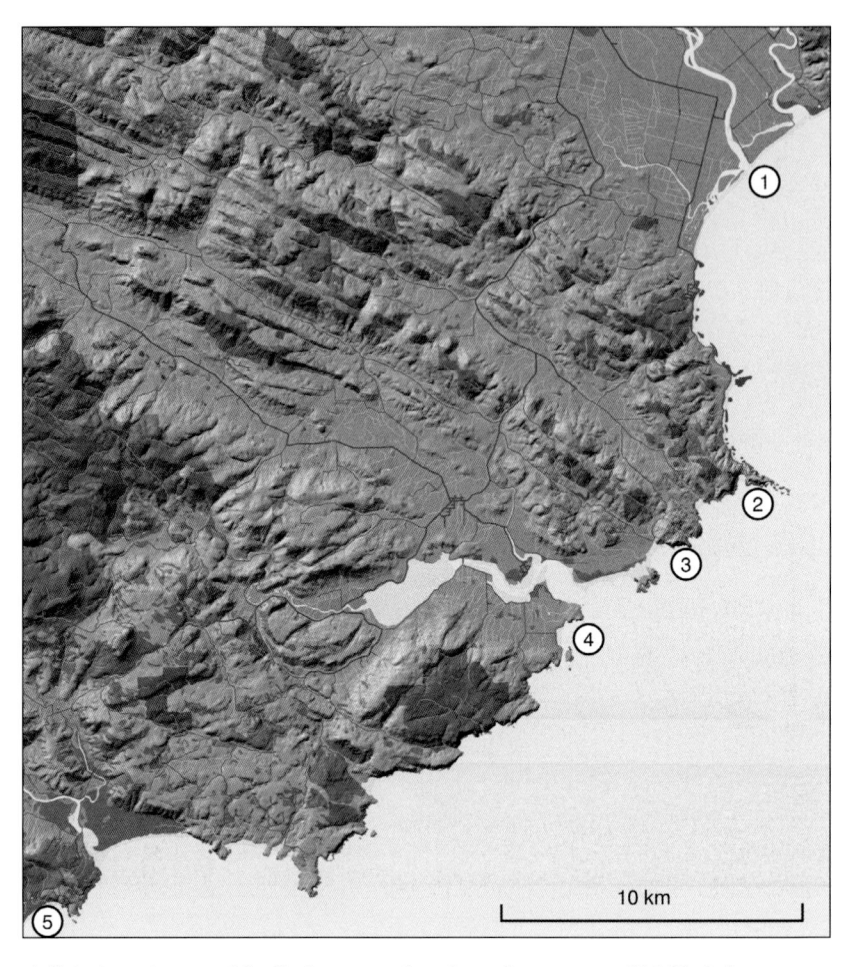

A digital terrain map of the Catlins coast of southeast Otago, scene of McKay's first assignment with NZ Geological Survey. (1) Clutha River, (2) Nugget Point, (3) Cannibal Bay, (4) Tuhawaiki Island. Image: courtesy GeographX

Mckay's career. The rocks are part of the 'basement' and are of Triassic to Jurassic age (230–140 million years old). They are generally clearly stratified and well exposed along the Catlins coast. The order of superposition is seldom in doubt,[15] and in places they contain numerous fossils.

McKay was working in what is now known as the Southland Syncline – a feature where the rock strata are folded into a structure like a canoe (but a canoe hundreds of kilometres long and tens of kilometres wide). Clearly visible on satellite photos, it is asymmetric. The strata on the south side are inclined at only moderate angles, but those on the north stand almost on end and form a dramatic set of parallel strike ridges. McKay's reports were usually very much to the point, but he was moved to eloquence by these

Nugget Point. On the left is Roaring Bay, a classic Triassic (200 million years ago) fossil locality where McKay reaped a rich harvest. The steeply inclined nature of the strata is clearly visible in the foreground 'Nuggets'. A walking track leads to the lighthouse (arrowed), which is a spectacular viewpoint.

ridges. 'I stood on the mountain-top and gazed wistfully after these beds, rising one on another, tier after tier, ridge upon ridge, til the eye failed to discern with precision, and the mind was lost in conjecture. But, descending this ridge and crossing the next stream to the north, the Waiwera …'[16]

There is now a road beside the Waiwera River. The geology is still the same but there are many other changes. The road passes the place where McKay crossed the river. It is easy to imagine him in his waistcoat and moleskin trousers held up by braces, with a long-handled hammer and a sugar bag with straps of twine as a daypack on his back.

But, conversely, McKay could not have imagined the changes that have occurred in the 130 years since he was there. There are wire fences to be

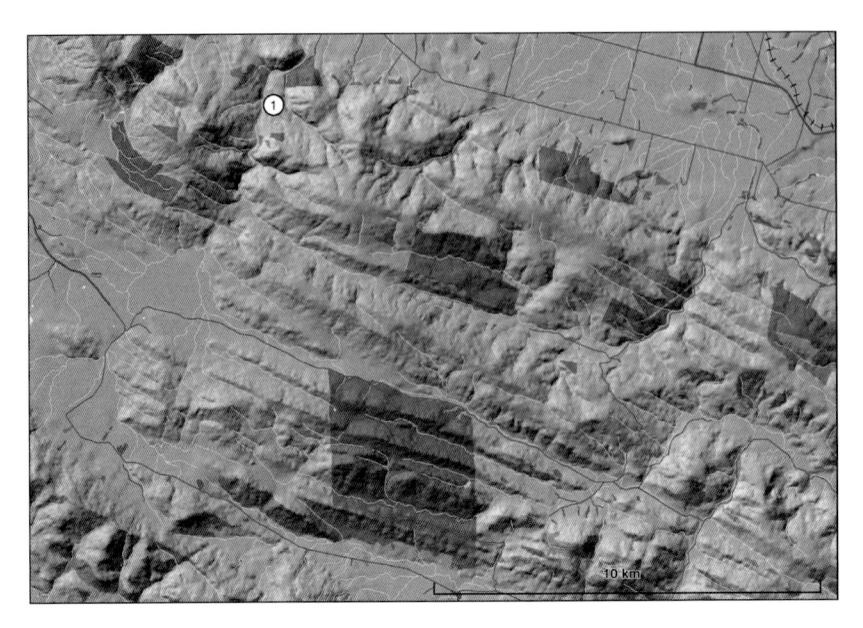

DTM detail of an area of the Kahiku Range southeast of the town of Clinton. The hard layers in the steeply dipping strata of the Southland Syncline form long parallel strike ridges 'rising one on another, tier upon tier, ridge upon ridge, until the eye failed to discern and the mind was lost to conjecture.'

climbed over now, with barbed wire or electricity. There would have been no pine trees, no gorse, no blackberry, no sheep or goats or cattle or bees. The natural cover of red tussock has been replaced by pasture grasses. The tuis and wood pigeons are now few. There are rabbits and hares, possums and stoats, and trout in the rivers where there were none before. Into this isolated valley, as in isolated valleys throughout the country, Europeans have introduced even rocks. The road is formed of gravel trucked in from Clutha River, which has already been swept downstream from its source hundreds of kilometres away, and is as exotic to the region as is the herd of goats that browse along it, or the magpies that roost in the pines beside it.

Did McKay camp beside the river, then crystal-clear but now clouded with erosion products and fertiliser run-off? Did he spend a night here, in this gentle, peaceful spot, with the river the only sound and the moon the only light, after a day of trudging through a strange and lovely land? Was it here he penned his evocative words? Did he have a tent? Was his mate with him? What did he have to eat? So many details remain unknown. But one thing is certain. For the first time in ten years he had a job that he enjoyed, and a regular income coming in. That would have been reason for considerable satisfaction, and a sound and peaceful sleep.

McKay returned to Wellington early in December and, with the efficiency which became his trademark, he commenced his report immediately. There are few extraneous details in his reports. He seldom mentions his accommodation, his companions or field assistants, or even how he travelled. Glimpses of his character emerge, however. In 1877, he wrote to Hector saying, 'But I confess that I was much too rash in writing to you in the dogmatic manner I did' (about the continuity of the rock sequence).[17]

On his Catlins trip, McKay did not recognise what we now call the Southland Syncline, but his analysis of the nature of the rocks, their fossil content, and their inclination (slope or attitude) was so accurate and objective that Hector correctly surmised its existence. By the time McKay wrote the second part of his Catlins report (28 December) he had had time to 'have carefully weighed the suggestion made by you [Dr Hector] with reference to the Nugget Point beds forming a synclinal trough … But there are some facts that look very favourable for the synclinal arrangement of the beds.'[18]

It appears that McKay wrote most of the first two parts of the Catlins report while on a succeeding field trip to the West Coast, such was the intensity of his field programme. The third part of the Catlins report had to wait until July of the following year. It is essentially a concluding statement, and is most notable for the wonderfully accurate and beautifully drawn cross-sections. These were probably the work of the artist and draftsman, John Buchanan, who was the Government Botanist and also worked for Geological Survey as a draughtsman. He is now remembered as a celebrated painter in his own right.

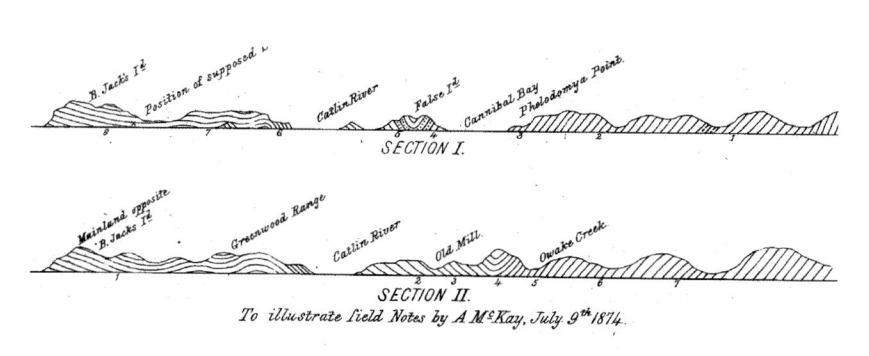

Cross-sections through the Southland Syncline, drawn by John Buchanan to illustrate McKay's report. The contrast between the steeply dipping strata of the northern limb with the more gentle inclined beds to the south is clearly seen.

West Coast

McKay was home from Otago for only a week before he complied with his next instructions 'to proceed to the West Coast of the South Island and join [Dr Hector] at Greymouth.'[19] Hector, however, was with him for only three days, showing McKay the localities he thought were important. Hector's extensive knowledge of where to go and what to look for, and why, was quite astounding. He would absorb information from McKay and other field staff and add it to his own store and produce a map of the result, building up a detailed, nation-wide picture in a remarkably short time.

It was ninety-two days before McKay returned to Wellington. This was his first visit to the West Coast. Although he had experienced the trials of virgin bush in the Catlins, most of his previous experience was in the relatively arid, open grassland areas of inland Canterbury and Central Otago.

The Coast is very different from dry tussock lands. It is dynamic raw country of dense forest, big rivers, and torrential rain, a narrow strip of land squeezed between the mountains and the sea. The rivers provided both routes and barriers to passage. Drowning was a common way of dying.

> There was a row of crosses
> on the bank
> where those who tried
> to cross a river too big
> didn't.
> Then the river swept the crosses out to sea.

The locals say if it isn't raining on the Coast, then it has just stopped, or is about to start. But there are times when the days sparkle as if freshly scrubbed and the special magic of the region can be savoured.

The geology of the West Coast is complex, and changes abruptly. McKay lacked the advantage of maps on which to record not only his notes, but also to display the spatial relationships of the rocks he was examining. Today maps are taken for granted, along with aerial and satellite photographs. Hand-held locator systems (GPS) have become commonplace and it is difficult to contemplate the problems of navigation and location in the days before maps and roads and signposts and the plethora of manmade features we take for granted.

McKay had no such aids. However, to a remarkable degree he managed to hold in his mind the three-dimensional arrangements of strata he saw at various localities. He was already attuned to the relationship between geology and topography: 'From the precipitous character of the country I guessed that the cherts [a hard siliceous rock, resistant to erosion] must continue for at least another mile …'[20] He identified numerous fossils and compared them and the rocks in which they occurred with others he had experienced on the east side of the island.

After a month or so in the Greymouth area, he arrived at Reefton, on New Year's Day 1874, to receive additional instructions from Hector:

> Take your time and examine the district well. …
> You will perceive the necessity for a careful collection from the different beds above referred to, as the section is one of the most important in the district. Take several days to it, as there are plenty of places to stay at and canoes to put you across the river at various points. The boats that go down the river will carry your collections down to Westport for you.[21]

The area around Reefton is rugged, difficult, bush-covered country: 'High granite ranges rise on either side, and sometimes confines [sic] the creek within deep, impassable guts, through which the water rushes with great force.'[22] It is not surprising that McKay had a field assistant, but only once, by a chance 'we' in his report, does he actually confirm the presence of a companion.[23]

His other companion was Lyell's *Principles of Geology*, the book that was to become his Bible. James Park – later Professor Park, and a colleague of McKay – records that McKay often carried Lyell's book in his pack and would read from it to his companions at night. *Principles of Geology* was first published in 1830 and ran to twelve editions by 1875.[24] It is interesting that McKay acquired his copy so early in his career, although it was not the first geological text that had attracted his interest: he notes buying Miller's *Testimony of the Rocks*[25] in Timaru, in 1864.

It is clear that McKay was referring to the book frequently, especially as he was working with rocks and fossils which, at 400 million years (Devonian), were almost twice as old as the Triassic rocks he had been collecting from Nugget Point. He noted, with undoubted satisfaction, when he successfully matched one with a description in Lyell. His avid enthusiasm for *Principles*, however, is also reflected in the rapid maturing of his grasp of geological concepts, even in the few weeks following his Otago fieldwork.

McKay's record of his activities and discoveries during this period is lucid, enthusiastic, and confident. Much of it was written up in the form of a daily diary, as if he couldn't wait to get his results down on paper.

He was back on the Coast a year later, this time to assist Herbert Cox.[26] They arrived at Reefton on 25 November 1875, with instructions to examine the geology of the area between Reefton and the Abbey Rocks (near Lake Paringa), a distance of about 320 kilometres, and also to investigate a report of coal at Jackson Bay. They first took a steamer south

The deep slow blackwater creeks, meandering through the West Coast bush and full of eels, could be more difficult to cross than fast water, especially for those who couldn't swim.

to Jackson Bay, and then, a few days later, back to the Abbey Rocks, thus avoiding having to cross some of the great rivers of South Westland. Once back at Abbey Rocks, they headed north on foot with occasional forays inland. Most of the time, however, they were forced to travel along the coast, as 'the country inland was so rough as to be utterly impassable.'[27]

The two men returned to Wellington on 26 February 1876 by steamer from Hokitika, after fourteen weeks. In the space of a year, McKay had spent nearly 200 days on the Coast. He was no longer a novice.

The bush-covered country south of Hokitika would have been tough in 1876. At least half of those 200 days would have been wet, some of them from dawn to dusk. There were few bridges, and when it rained even small streams would quickly become torrents, difficult to cross and requiring time to find a ford. There would have been times when there was no option but to pitch camp and wait overnight for the water to subside. Deep slow blackwater streams meandering through the bush were major problems for those who couldn't swim, and some of the swamps were interminable. McKay and company may have had oilskin coats (Macintoshes) but it is unlikely they had a change of clothes. They would have slept on damp ground, in their damp gear, wrapped in a damp blanket, with a fine spray coming through the tent. Keeping notebooks, maps, matches, and his precious copy of Lyell dry in those conditions would have required meticulous care.

The tent was probably a batwing affair, a simple square of calico or light canvas, pitched by spreading it over a rope or ridge pole: wide and flat if it wasn't raining, narrow and steep if it was. There was no floor, door, or end. A fly may have been used either to form a double layer, or to shelter one end and perhaps create a place for cooking. Fire was the only means of cooking, so the ability to light and maintain a fire in such conditions was critical. They probably ate and drank as opportunities arose – a chance encounter with a cave with some dry wood or a fallen tree offering a degree of shelter. There were few homesteads or huts, so they would have been constantly refining and improving their survival skills.

Cox mentions the difficulty they had in procuring provisions. Their staples would have been bacon, oatmeal and tea, some flour, and perhaps a few onions. Both eels and weka were plentiful and easily caught, and they would have stoned ducks and pigeons when the opportunity arose. The impact of ferrets, weasels, stoats, and rats may not yet have been fully felt in the area, and land- and sea-bird eggs may have been common enough to augment their diet.

There were one, or rather two, more trials they had to suffer: *te namu* (sandflies) by day, and the mosquito by night. *Te namu* bites through the skin and gorges on the blood beneath. Its presence poses a psychological test, as it wins only if you let it. Movement lessens the irritation, but there are times – such as when skinning fish or writing notes – when the annoyance level becomes intolerable.

The mosquito is arguably worse. It announces its presence to a recumbent victim on the edge of sleep with a high-pitched whine. Inevitably the mind follows it and tries to locate the sound until there is a sudden pause, when a wild slap does nothing more than spur the insect into further reconnaissance. The soft areas beneath the eyes are frequent targets, and may swell up considerably if bitten. Modern tents have bug screens and there are now scores of repellents, but for Cox and McKay there was no escape from the torments of these pestilential insects.

Poverty Bay

The cuts and bruises from the West Coast would have barely healed during McKay's two-week interlude at home in Wellington in February 1874 before he was away again – this time heading for the East Cape district of the North Island.[28]

Poverty Bay is an area of very challenging rocks and relationships, where folding and faulting have happened relatively recently in geological time: older rocks have been thrust over younger ones, resulting in a reversal of the normal sequence, and the intricacies of this have still to be resolved. Large-scale landsliding also complicates the issue in many regions. McKay noted 'From the effect of great slips up near the hot springs, these rocks get mixed in great confusion …'[29] No wonder he was puzzled. But there were fossils there and he was certainly enjoying himself: 'I was lucky enough to hit upon a fossil fish in a good state of preservation, the tail and pectoral fins being almost complete … [I will] content myself with saying that, as a specimen, it is indeed beautiful, and far excels anything of the kind I have as yet seen produced in New Zealand.'[30] At times, local Maori guided him to places of interest, incidentally testing his skill as a horseman: 'We left the river bed and galloped along the rough bush country at a round pace … despite the increasing difficulty of the road and the stony nature of the river bed, we rode on at a headlong pace, and reached Tuparoa, wet through, about dusk.'[31]

The year 1874 had been a watershed for McKay. He was now a professional geologist. He had completed three major field surveys for Hector, written up reports for publication on each, and had had two papers read, prior to publication, at the Philosophical Institute (the forerunner of New Zealand's Royal Society). He had progressed a long way in a short time from the world of an itinerant labourer. The career he so enthusiastically

'… *a fossil fish … it is indeed beautiful.*' Buchanan Collection, courtesy of NZ Institute of Geological and Nuclear Science

embraced after a decade in the wilderness was blossoming.

But October brought an unfortunate check when the 'Body in the Cave' affair exploded around him. Haast, initially supported by the Christchurch and Dunedin establishments, unleashed his tirade of invective. Despite his feisty responses, McKay was deeply affected and this most clearly shows in his Weka Pass report.[32]

In September 1874, a few weeks before the affair erupted, Hector had given McKay instructions to make 'a rapid examination of certain districts in the South Island' (Weka Pass, Waipara, Ashley, Rakaia, Broken River, and Buller) to establish the relationship between the 'cover' rocks of Tertiary age in Canterbury, with those of the same age on the West Coast.[33] This was a wonderful assignment, covering a vast expanse of country, and one which McKay, with his burgeoning confidence and knowledge, could have been expected to relish.

Hector's instructions were liberal but his expectations were unrealistic, and McKay was unable to fulfill all of them. That in itself was not a calamity, but there were other indications of a troubled mind. The exuberant McKay had disappeared and the report, although adequate, is dull and lifeless. Dates which are normally sprinkled freely through his reports, and which contribute significantly to the atmosphere of vitality and urgency, disappear. It is not even clear when he did the work, or how long he spent on it, other than that it was between the instructions of 21 September 1874 and the reporting date of 6 January 1875. I estimate it took at least six weeks. There is no sign of the man who a few months before had galloped furiously down a rocky river bed in the dusk, or who was lucky enough to hit on a fossil fish, 'indeed beautiful'.[34] In his place is a man on autopilot, still doing a capable job, but just doing a job. One forms an impression of a man for whom one day is very much like the last, or next, a man whose mental energy has plummeted.

Three more reports in the same flat mode followed, until finally, in July 1876, fully two years after the slanging match with Haast, the exuberant, enthusiastic Alexander McKay returned. He was on the Kaikoura coast. He knew what he was doing, and took pride in what he was doing. He blew up rocks with explosives to get the fossils out. On wet days he made up boxes and packed up his fossils. When he returned to Wellington after 119 days in the field, he brought with him 130 cases of specimens, as well as twenty-three blocks of stone containing saurian and other fossil remains, which were presumably too large to go in boxes. He was a man well satisfied.[35]

Hector was overseas at this time and McKay's instructions came from Mantell, the same Mantell who had tried to have the 'Body in the Cave' affair taken seriously in Parliament. His instructions were friendly, almost solicitous, as if Mantell realised McKay's involvement in the affair had contributed to his difficulties: 'It may be worth while to commence your collections at and to the north of Kaikoura, as, while doing this, you will be able to communicate with me, and receive replies, by telegram to that place.[36] Report your arrival there, and give me information of your movements from time to time.'[37]

10. Into His Stride

Field Geologist

In 1876, Alexander McKay was promoted to 'field geologist' at the New Zealand Geological Survey. He carried out new investigations all over the country, in Oamaru, Masterton, Wairarapa, Kawhia, Southland, Canterbury, Nelson, Wangapeka and Wakatipu. In ten years he produced sixty reports or publications,[1] most of them significant regional surveys in widely separated areas. His largest report in this period was sixty pages long, and five others were over forty. Few of these contain information of interest to the general reader, and although they are still consulted today even most geologists find his 'flowing Victorian verbosity'[2] heavy going. Detailed, accurate, invaluable records they undoubtedly are, but their entertainment value is minimal.

Commonly, McKay started his reports by quoting his 'Instructions' from Hector. These were generally terse and autocratic, in the style of the day: 'I wish you to proceed south to carry a section from South Canterbury to the West Coast'.[3] Sometimes McKay acted on the instructions on the day they were received. However, they may often have been essentially a formality. In 'Geology of the Waitaki Valley and parts of Vincent and Lake Counties', he makes it clear that Hector and he had discussed the objectives informally before the formal instructions were issued.[4] Sometimes, however, Hector became more specific, as in M017 where he instructed: 'You will proceed to the Wairarapa and East Coast, and spend ten days in the District between the Ruamahunga and the coast as far as the Cape Palliser. The following are important points to which your attention should be directed.'[5]

McKay responded to these unusually restrictive instructions with a rather precise account of how he spent his time. In the above scenario, he noted for instance that he had 'spent twelve days [not ten!] in the districts described in my instructions',[6] perhaps hinting that as Johnny on the Spot *he* was better placed to judge how many days were required. He makes a similar pointed comment in his report on Mt Potts: 'As such an investigation was not the first object of my visit to the district, and being further instructed to join Mr. Cox, in Southland, by the beginning of November, I had not time for this work, however desirous I might be to undertake it.'[7] Again, McKay was prickly in his Reefton narrative, commenting: '[I would] have risked further and more serious detention [delay by the weather] had I in this particular conformed to your orders …'.[8] However, he clearly heeded the general thrust of Hector's directions and the two men formed a productive and mutually beneficial relationship.

Occasionally chance details buried in his outpouring of technical information give glimpses of the man. In 1879, he was in the Wangapeka in West Nelson, where he spent ten days examining six miles of river.[9] This rate suggests a painstaking examination of every outcrop along the riverbanks, in addition to cracking open innumerable boulders from the bed of the stream. McKay certainly possessed an innate ability to find fossils, but it was an ability that was maintained with an enormously methodical and energetic devotion to the task.

All but a few of his reports involved extensive fieldwork. The longest field trip was 137 days in Vincent and Lake Counties,[10] closely followed by 130 days in the Rakaia district,[11] and 119 days spent on the Kaikoura coast.[12] Field trips were a summer activity and he seldom observed Christmas; it was only in 1880, seven years after he had joined the New Zealand Geological Survey, that he had his first Christmas at home.

Fossiliferous rocks are rare in the greywackes of the Southern Alps. In 1878 McKay was dispatched to collect from one of the few known localities, at Mt Potts in the Rangitata valley. The introduction to this report is one of his more readable narratives, and one that gives an idea of his writing style, the difficulties he faced in the field, and his resourcefulness, prudence, and priorities.[13] To this end, I have reproduced it here with minimal change.

Wellington, 1st June 1878

Having received instructions to make a collection from the *Spirifer*[14] *beds* on the western slopes of Mount Potts, in the Canterbury district, I left Wellington for this purpose on the 9th of October, arriving at Christchurch on the 10th.

From Christchurch I went to Ashburton by rail on the 11th, and thence by coach, to Mount Somers, on the following day.

From this place I hoped to hire a cart to take the tools and materials requisite for making and packing the collection, to Mount Potts, but as such could not at the time be got without considerable delay, I availed myself of the chance which a waggon afforded of getting as far as the Hakatere station; having decided to make the collection first and afterwards get the packing material by the same conveyance by which the collection would be brought down country.

Hakatere station being 24 miles [thirty-eight kilometres] from the place where the collection was to be made, encumbered with camp materials, tools &c., as I was I should have had some difficulty in getting there, but for the kindness of Mr. D. H. Potts, whose horses conveyed me to the end of my journey.

I was thus enabled to camp at the foot of Rocky Gully on the north-west face of Mount Potts, on the 16th of October, and without loss of time applied myself to the work of making the collection.[15]

For the first week all went well; the weather being fine for this season of the year, the spring floods having not yet set in. As a consequence of the retention of the past winter's snow on the ranges, all the creeks were very low, and the river bed of the Rangitata was dry, to the junction of the two main branches.

This state of things offered a rare opportunity of exploring the geology of the district along the western sources of the Rangitata ….

As such an investigation was not the first object of my visit to the district, and being further instructed to join Mr. Cox, in Southland, by the beginning of November, I had not time for this work, however desirous I might be to undertake it.

I therefore availed myself of the favourable conditions before mentioned, to collect from the bed of the creek in Rocky gully, specimens which could not have been reached when the volume of water was greater than it then was ….

After the 24th of October the weather became unsettled, and a considerable fresh took place, which, though having little effect on the main river, rendered the stream in Rocky Gully impassable, thus hindering the work there for a day or two.

This being the case, I left off the work of collecting and spent the next few days in examining the beds in the immediate neighbourhood, and during this time discovered the fossil ferns near the source of Tank Gully, in a position underlying the *Spirifer beds*.

Fearing that considerable difficulties would be encountered in getting the collections removed, if, as was shortly to be expected, the river should get flooded through the melting of the snow, I lost no time in getting the collection finished, and by the end of the month had got together all that could be obtained without an extravagant amount of labour.

My next care was to see them removed as speedily as possible, and for this purpose I came to Mount Somers on the 31st of October, whence I returned the following day with a two-horse dray and material wherewith to pack the collection. That night we reached the crossing of the Potts River, and hoped the next day would see the collection so far removed that the difficulties remaining would be of little consequence.

A north-west wind had been blowing during the day till late in the afternoon, but the evening was calm, and, save a mass of dense white clouds clinging to the south-east sides of the higher peaks of the main range, appearances seemed to favour the success of the undertaking.

Next morning all was changed: A tremendous north-wester was blowing, and though very little rain fell east of the Potts River, heavy rain-clouds filled all the gorges to the westward, above which appeared the higher peaks of the main and spur ranges, as yet but partially covered with clouds.

Appearances were not promising, as it was clear that a flood was impending, which, considering that the whole of the past winter's snows yet lay on the higher ranges, promised to be by no means a moderate one. Hoping still to be able to remove the collection before the river rose, we made a start, but soon found that the strength of the wind was such, that no progress could be made; added to which, the rain, driven by the force of the storm, so blinded both the driver and the horses, that, finding it impossible to proceed, we were glad to take shelter at Mr. Potts' outstation, still hoping that wind would prove our only impediment.

Between 10 and 11 a.m. the wind lulled considerably, but was followed by a heavy thunderstorm, during the continuance of which, heavy warm rains set in, which rendered any attempt to reach the place where the collections were lying, perfectly hopeless, seeing that the north branch of the Rangitata required to be crossed four or five times to do so; and, as in the event of a great flood, we were now on the wrong side of the Potts River, I considered it best to recross that and await the result.

For five days it rained in torrents with heavy thunderstorms, which generally began about dusk in the evening and lasted till considerably past midnight.

No hope now remained of being able to reach the collection with a dray for some time to come, as the rivers were in a high state of flood, and I was therefore compelled to send the dray down country without the collection. About the 8th of November the warm rains terminated, and were followed by a snowstorm, after which, the rivers fell rapidly. As soon as possible I made my way to Rocky Gully to ascertain what had become of the collections, which, though placed beyond the reach of an ordinary flood, might not, in this case, have altogether escaped. Fortunately, they proved to have been safe, and with some cases, which I carried from the Potts River, and others, which I obtained at Taylor's old station, I succeeded in getting all but the larger specimens packed, my chief anxiety being to see this done. This, and the removing of the specimens to a sufficient distance beyond the reach of the river, was all that under the circumstances could be done; and, seeing that the season during which the river is generally flooded had now most certainly begun, the probabilities were, that a second attempt to get them removed would not prove more successful than the first had done. I therefore decided to take no further steps until the rivers could be depended upon, which would not be before the end of February, or the beginning of March, so leaving the collections where they were, I left the district for Southland on the 12th of November, and joined

Mr. Cox, who was then camped at the lower end of the Otapiri Gorge, on the 20th of November.' [Three weeks later than instructed!][16]

During the following winter, that of 1879, McKay took an office break from writing reports. Continuing with the same pen, ink, and paper, he wrote a poem. The merit of the poem is debatable, and it was never published, but what is clear is that at the time life seemed pretty good:

[Long in the strife for worldly means]

Long in the strife for worldly means
The muse has been forgot
Amid the turmoil and the toil
Of what has been my lot

A time was when full oft my pen
Ran out the ready line
No greater pleasure then had I
For then my muse was young
Than thus to wile away an hour
Strange as the thing may seem
Long long did rust my pen devour
Oft I grieve the wasted time
And lost I know not why

Now with a will my pen I'll ply
And Heaven supply the theme
My helicon so long quite dry
Is now a powerful stream

Bravo for the hills and wood shall ring
Unto my joyous song
From Auckland's northern sunny clime
and in the south as far
my muse shall awake the echoes that
To woods to rocks belong
So seldom waked save by the storm
Or shouts of savage war [17]

(c. 1879)

The Routeburn and Hollyford

In early 1879 McKay was instructed to make an examination of the country to the west and north of Lake Wakatipu. He caught the steamer to Kinloch at the head of the lake on 9 February,[18] where he engaged a field assistant and probably also hired a packhorse, for even then there was a well-formed graded track up the Routeburn valley, and small groups of sightseers on horseback were being taken up there.[19] The Routeburn track climbs steadily until it reaches a point high above the river thundering down a narrow gorge, then it levels out to emerge at a splendid grassy clearing after two hours' travel.[20] In this clearing there were two small huts, and McKay and his mate would have spent the night in one of them.[21] They then headed up the track past Lake Harris and across Harris Saddle, and down to the bush line of the Hollyford Valley, on the Deadmans Track. 'Leaving the tent at this place, I took a trip to the northward, along the higher parts of the Lake Harris Range.'[22]

The Routeburn River is a tributary of the Dart River (1). The track climbs steadily from the road end (2) until high above the river, before sidling through the gorge (3) and coming out on to the grassy Routeburn flats (4) below Harris Saddle (5). McKay camped at the bushline in the Hollyford (6), not far below Harris Saddle. From there he worked north along the Main Divide to North Col (7) and then descended past Lake Nerine (8) into the valley of the Rockburn (9). Digital terrain map courtesy GeographX

This hut on the Routeburn Flats was built in the 1870s and used by McKay in 1880. When this photo was taken in 1957 it was still as sound as a bell, as it was when it was demolished in 1976 to make way for the new breed of DOC huts, after 100 years of providing safety and shelter.

He was probably initially intending to visit Serpentine Saddle, which he would have realised was an area where important rock relationships were likely to be exposed. The going was tough:[23]

> This trip in some respects proved a most unfortunate one, as the weather ... now broke, and it rained almost continuously for fourteen days. Besides the hardship which it entailed, this continuance of bad weather ruined in a great measure the expected results of this trip, as the small stock of provisions remaining would not warrant me in carrying out the plan I had intended to follow.
>
> After remaining for a week under such shelter as could be found at this place, the hopeless condition of the weather and failing provisions compelled a return to the camp at Lake Harris. This proved no easy task, as the ground which had to be passed over is exceptionally rough, for this district, and dense fogs prevented choice in the matter of selecting the best road.[24]

It is possible from McKay's observations to deduce the extent of his travels, which considering the weather, were impressive. The two men do not seem to have visited Serpentine Saddle, but they certainly reached North Col, and then continued north along the Main Divide, past Lake Nerine, to Park Pass. They then went down the Rockburn, probably as far as the start of the upper gorge. It is likely they used a prominent shelter rock in the Rockburn not far below Park Pass, which was later used by Park in 1886,[25] and again by members of the 1974 Alpine Rock Studies

Lake Harris after a fall of summer snow in December 1957. The snowfall that trapped McKay some seventy years earlier was probably two or three metres deeper at this point, and would have made the route around the bluffs above the lake difficult and dangerous.

Expedition.

The location of their base camp at Deadmans dictated that they then had to retrace their steps back to it across this difficult country, rather than take the easier and much more direct route from North Col down the North Branch of the Routeburn, which would have brought them back to the hut in a few hours. Thus they

> Arrived at Lake Harris, the weather did not in any respect improve, and the first opportunity of returning to the east side of the range had to be taken advantage of. It was not before the 6th of March that this opportunity arrived, on which day I returned to the hut in the upper part of the Route Burn Valley.[26]

They had remained trapped in their tent at the top of Deadmans for eight or nine days. During this time McKay wrote, 'I may say without any danger of being guilty of exaggeration, that while camped at Lake Harris, no fewer than 200 avalanches fell, there being during two particular days nothing but one continued roar.'[27] He was writing about avalanches taking place mostly in the Darran Mountains, on the far side of the Hollyford Valley 'so narrow that one might imagine a good rifle would send a bullet across it to the opposite mountains.'[28] The track past Lake Harris would have been threatened and at times impassable under these conditions. It is probable that the unseasonal snowfall which created the avalanche activity also brought snow down into the bush and surrounded their camp. Lighting or maintaining a fire may well have been impossible.

By the end of eight or nine days McKay and his companion would have exhausted their provisions. He was aware of Maori use of fern root as a food, and they may have supplemented their diet with that and any birds they could capture, shoot, or stone. There is no doubt that they would have been thoroughly wet, cold, and hungry, and living on the edge, where survival is by no means certain.[29] To pass the time McKay wrote two poems, *Lines Written on a Scene from Harris Saddle, West Coast, Middle Island*,[30] and *The Canterbury Gilpin*.[31]

The chance to break out finally arrived. In good conditions they could have reached the hut at Routeburn Flats in a little over two hours, but in waist-deep soft snow, with heavy loads of sodden gear, it may have taken more than twice as long. Even so it would have been a short day, and the shelter of the hut and warmth of a fire for the first time in nearly three weeks would have seemed like the end of a protracted nightmare. But there would have been little if any food in the hut to satisfy the empty ache in their bellies, and so early the next day they set out again to establish a new camp 'at the first crossing of the Route Burn',[32] probably in the clearing where the road now ends. Their first priority was to obtain fresh provisions from Routeburn Station, some five kilometres further down the valley. Baths and showers didn't rank highly as necessities in the 1880s.

Fieldwork continued from this camp for another three days, but the bad weather persisted and on the tenth of March they retreated to Kinloch. Two days later, McKay took the steamer down the lake to Queenstown. On the fourteenth he left Queenstown for the Von River, intending to cross the Livingstone Mountains to the Eglinton Valley, but almost immediately was recalled for undisclosed reasons. He stayed in the region, however, working mostly in the Richardson Mountains between the east side of the north arm of Lake Wakatipu and the Shotover River, until the sixth of April.[33] He arrived back in Wellington three or four days later, after an absence of eleven weeks.

In his discussion of the Routeburn rocks McKay notes:

> It is questionable if these [the foliated schists] be stratigraphically distinct. They cannot in section be shown to be so without calling to aid an enormous degree of faulting along certain lines, which requires to be again and again repeated, and which, although true in one particular instance, cannot be said to be proved in the other cases.[34]

Suggesting repeated movements on faults was radical thinking for the time, and is one of the first indications that McKay was wondering *how* certain processes could occur, rather than simply recording what he saw. In the Routeburn, McKay was working with low-grade metamorphic rocks – those that had been altered by heat and pressure, in much the same way as dough turns into bread (although flaky pastry might be a better analogy). New minerals grow like currants, and the mix changes colour and consistency. (The cooking time of about fifty million years at temperatures of three or four hundred degrees is a bit beyond the range of a normal oven.) The appearance of the rock is changed – it develops a flaky or schistose structure, and the original details, including fossils, are usually obliterated. These were very different rocks from any that McKay had worked with previously, but he handled them with aplomb, despite the atrocious weather.

Waitaki to the Matukituki

In 1880 Hector came up with what may have been the first stage of a Grand Plan. It undoubtedly arose partly from the unanswered questions arising from his own explorations in northwest Otago and south Westland in 1863. So he instructed his field men, McKay, Park, and Buchanan, to prepare a section from the mouth of the Waitaki River on the lower part of the east coast of the South Island: inland and westward by way of the Waitaki Valley and Wanaka, and over to the West Coast by the Haast Pass.[35] It was an ambitious concept, and in all probability would have been followed up with a similar traverse in the latitude of North Canterbury and the Lewis Pass. In the event, the plan was modified for reasons that remain unclear. The Haast Pass sector was abandoned, and an exploration of the Matukituki Valley substituted.

After the rigours of the Routeburn expedition the previous year, McKay may well have had some misgivings about another foray into the mountains of northwest Otago. The two expeditions, however, were as different as chalk and cheese, and whereas the Routeburn had become a survival exercise, the Matukituki sojourn was more like an extended, albeit energetic, picnic in wonderful surroundings, with benign weather and abundant food.

McKay produced his usual prosaic account of the rocks encountered with few other details, but this time he had two companions, both of whom left records, so an unusually complete account of this expedition can be constructed.[36] James Park was a young Englishman who had curtailed his education at Imperial College to emigrate to New Zealand at the age of seventeen. He was now twenty-four, but still the 'boy' of the party. McKay was forty, and the 'old man', John Buchanan, was sixty-two.

Buchanan[37] had been in the Matukituki with Hector in 1863, and was to provide minutiae of places, dates, times and weather, while Park supplied a romantic but valuable overview, although his account, written forty years later, is probably somewhat embellished with the passage of time. Park greatly respected McKay and later wrote, 'McKay was an epic poet of no mean order, and New Zealand's most distinguished field geologist.'[38] In turn, McKay would have appreciated Buchanan's previous experience of the area, and his botanical knowledge. McKay had collected samples for Buchanan on some of his previous trips. Park noted that Buchanan was 'the most genial of companions.'[39]

McKay, possibly with Park, left Wellington on 21 September 1880, travelling to Christchurch, and then on to Oxford and Malvern Hills.[40] He then returned to Christchurch and set out for South Canterbury on the fifth of October. Park may have joined him at this time for he notes that in November they walked over Elephant Hill to Kurow, and examined the exposures at Duntroon. McKay then left him for a few days to examine the limestone cliffs beside the main road at Maerewhenua, while he (McKay) was 'engaged elsewhere'. They then continued up the Waitaki to Omarama, where they were joined on 20 December by John Buchanan.[41]

According to McKay, 'December was spent amongst the mountains lying to the west of [Lake Ohau] and in the direction of the western sources of the Hopkins River.'[42] Park, however, says of this period:

> Together we walked to the head of Lake Ohau, [and] explored the mountains to the east and west of the Dobson and Hopkins Rivers. All the high peaks on the Ben Ohau Range, including Mount Hopkins, 8,800 ft [2682 m], and on the Neumann Range, lying between the Dobson and Hopkins rivers, were ascended and geologically examined; also Mount Huxley, 8229 ft [2508 m], and Mount Maitland, 7326 ft [2232 m], further to the south.[43] Buchanan … fairly revelled in the fine alpine vegetation.[44]

After returning to Omarama they crossed Lindis Pass on New Year's Eve and arrived at Pembroke (Wanaka) on 5 January. They camped amongst the wild Irishmen (*Aciphylla horrida*) at the site of the modern jetty. The next day Buchanan went to 3000 ft (914 m) on Roys Peak and then went up Mt Iron in the evening.

The men then made their way up the Matukituki Valley towards Mount Aspiring. On 8 January they crossed the river downstream of the junction of the East and West Branches and set up their camp near Hector's old campsite at the foot of the slopes of Mt Alta, in the lee of Round Hill, for shelter from the prevailing nor' west winds. Buchanan noted one day (the twelfth) spent on Mt Alta from 6 a.m. to 7 p.m., 'in a glory of alpine vegetation.'[45] The next day was a 'lay-to' for want of boots; they were apparently repaired on site, and saw Buchanan out for the rest of the trip. Meanwhile McKay had collected for him a sample of *Poa exigua*.[46]

After ten days the field workers moved from Round Hill to a new campsite at the top end of Cameron Flat, where the West Branch of the Matukituki issues from a short gorge. From this camp McKay (and presumably Park)[47] seem to have gone up the East Branch, probably as far as Kitchener Stream,[48] as he notes from the river shingle that the pink quartzites 'appear to pass along the eastern slopes of Mount Avalanche and Mount Aspiring.'[49] By this time Hugh Macpherson had built a homestead on the site of what was to become the 'Old Homestead' of Mount Aspiring Station, and no doubt the men called in to pay their regards.[50] It is recorded that Mrs Macpherson used to surprise her visitors by spreading butter on their scones with her thumb, a custom which would have endeared her to McKay.[51]

After a couple of days they were on the move again, up the valley of the West Branch for another twenty kilometres, to a new campsite at Cascade Creek, near the site of the present day Aspiring Hut. On 22 January they set out for Hector Col, but rain forced them to camp on a small flat (Pearl Flat) after about five kilometres. On the twenty-fourth the weather again forced them to 'make bed below a large rock.'[52] 'Rain rain, rain, up towards Col' continued the next day, but on the twenty-sixth they reached their goal.[53] McKay describes the geology of Hector Col and its approaches with his characteristic accuracy:

> At the far source of the river a thick band of compact green rock, dipping west at an angle of 45°, is overlaid by soft mica-slates which latter weathering rapidly leave the green rock as a smooth sloping face on one side of the approach to Hector's Col, while on the other hand the slates, as perfectly inaccessible precipices, admit of no other approach to the saddle than along the bottom of the narrow ravine thus formed.[54]

Buchanan's time was up and he had to return to Wellington. In two days he was back at Cameron Flat, and on Sunday 30 January he 'Started for Pembroke [Wanaka] early, walked 32 miles [fifty kilometres] to catch coach on Monday.'[55] For a sixty-two-year-old, it was a sterling effort. Buchanan's sketches subsequently illustrated McKay's map of the area.

Park and McKay proceeded down the valley at a more leisurely pace. Park claimed that they ascended all the high peaks to the south of Hector Col, specifically mentioning Mt Edward (8459 ft), Mt Tyndall (8116 ft), and Mt Ansted (8157 ft).[56] McKay's account, on the other hand, again does not corroborate Park's claims, although he does mention climbing to the conspicuous patch of red rock at about 6000 ft (1830 m) on Mt Tyndall.[57]

The upper Matukituki Valley and the approaches to Hectors Col. The shelter rock (arrowed) now known as Scott's Bivvy, is probably the same one used by McKay, Buchanan and Park. Photo: D.L. Homer, NZ Geological Survey

It is conceivable that Park went on to the summit of Tyndall and then crossed over to climb Mt Ansted on the same day.[58] A climb of Mt Edward, however, is a different matter. It would have required crossing the ridge between the Matukituki and the Dart valleys, crossing the Dart Glacier, and then making an ascent of a truly alpine, snow-covered mountain – a completely different exercise from the tussock and rock scrambles the men usually made. Park subsequently mentions ascending Fog Peak, Niger Peak and Black Peak, 'each of them a stiff climb from the floor of the Valley.'[59] McKay's report also mentions these ascents, and in addition mentions climbing the range between the West Matukituki and the Shotover River in three places to a height of 6500 feet (1980 metres).[60]

But Park's special contribution was to record the atmosphere and camaraderie of the trip. He wrote:

> We eventually returned to Wellington in March, 1881, after a summer of four months of glorious sunshine. The herds of wild cattle in the valleys of the Hopkins and Matukituki furnished us with an abundance of meat, and the runholders in the back Block stations sold us plentiful supplies of tea, sugar, flour, and oatmeal. … we preserved our wild beef by cutting it into thick slabs, which were smoked over a wood fire. The rare flavour of a juicy grill of smoked beef is one of the luxuries of life not often enjoyed by civilised man.[61]

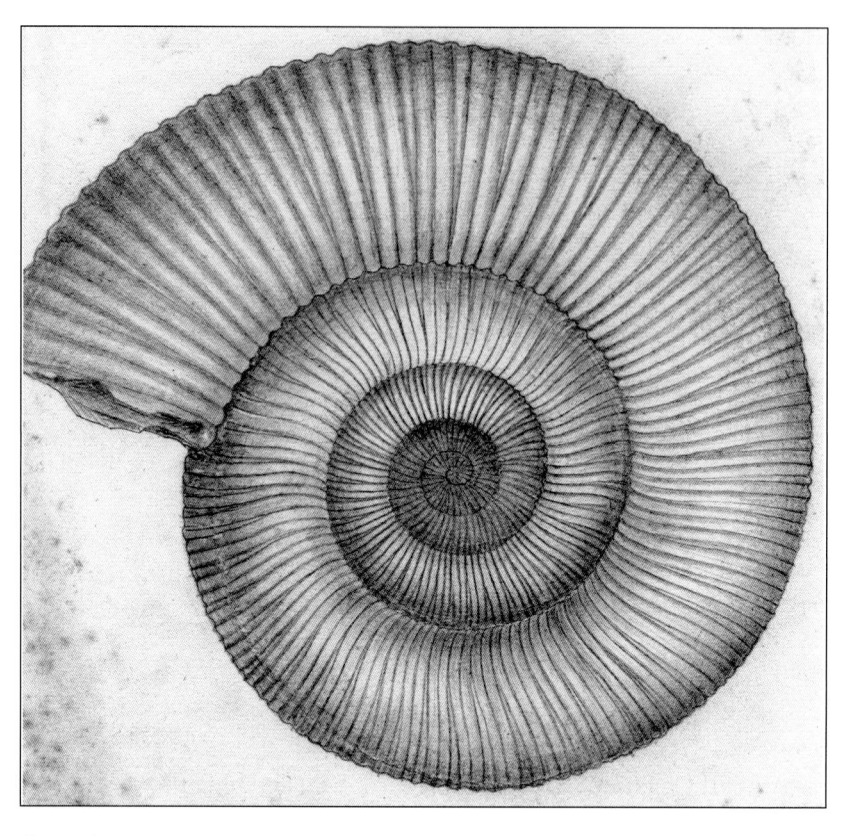

Ammonites are the shells of coiled squid-like animals that lived in the seas that covered New Zealand in Triassic, Jurassic and Cretaceous times (230–65 million years ago). Although this pencil drawing by John Buchanan is unlabelled, it is of a specimen of the genus Kawhiasphinctes *that was probably collected by McKay in 1884 from the vicinity of Puti and Motutara points on the northeastern side of Kawhia Harbour 'from whence a large series of ammonites were obtained.'* Image from the Buchanan Collection, courtesy NZ Institute of Geological and Nuclear Sciences

11. The Peak of His Powers

By 1885, McKay had far outstripped his initial role of fossil collector, although he had not lost his enthusiasm for collecting. He had covered the length and breadth of the country, from North Auckland to Stewart Island, and was competent with most types of rocks, of any age, and also with those economic aspects of geology that were important to the times – the prospects for coal, gold, and other minerals. His writing had become more lucid and less verbose, probably as a result of growing confidence. His horizons were steadily expanding, as he made deductions from his observations, which he now had the assurance to read to the Philosophical Society. He was no longer just looking and reporting, but questioning and thinking and starting to formulate hypotheses. From the terminology he was using, it is clear he was reading a wide variety of local and international geological reports.

An early report in the period is of special interest. It was 'On the Auriferous Quartz Drifts [gravels] at Clark's Diggings[1], Maniototo County', part of Central Otago.[2] The diggings are situated high on the flat-topped hills north of Naseby. Here McKay noted that some of the larger pebbles and small boulders were 'rounded imperfectly or in such a fashion as to show that a river or strong continuous current did the work, there being little approach to the effects produced by wave action',[3] and that similar deposits of quartz drifts in Otago

> show most conclusively that not merely has the country been elevated or depressed since their deposition, but that abrupt displacements, measured by thousands of feet in vertical height, that have taken place, so much so that the age during which such movements were taking place might be fittingly termed a 'mountain-making period'.[4]

These comments are notable for two reasons: first, that McKay was using the internal details of the deposit – in this case the shapes of the constituent pebbles – to deduce the environment in which the gravels were deposited, and second, that he recognised that the present distribution of such gravel deposits resulted from a period of faulting producing cumulative displacements which were sufficient to uplift the present-day mountain

144 THE REAL MCKAY

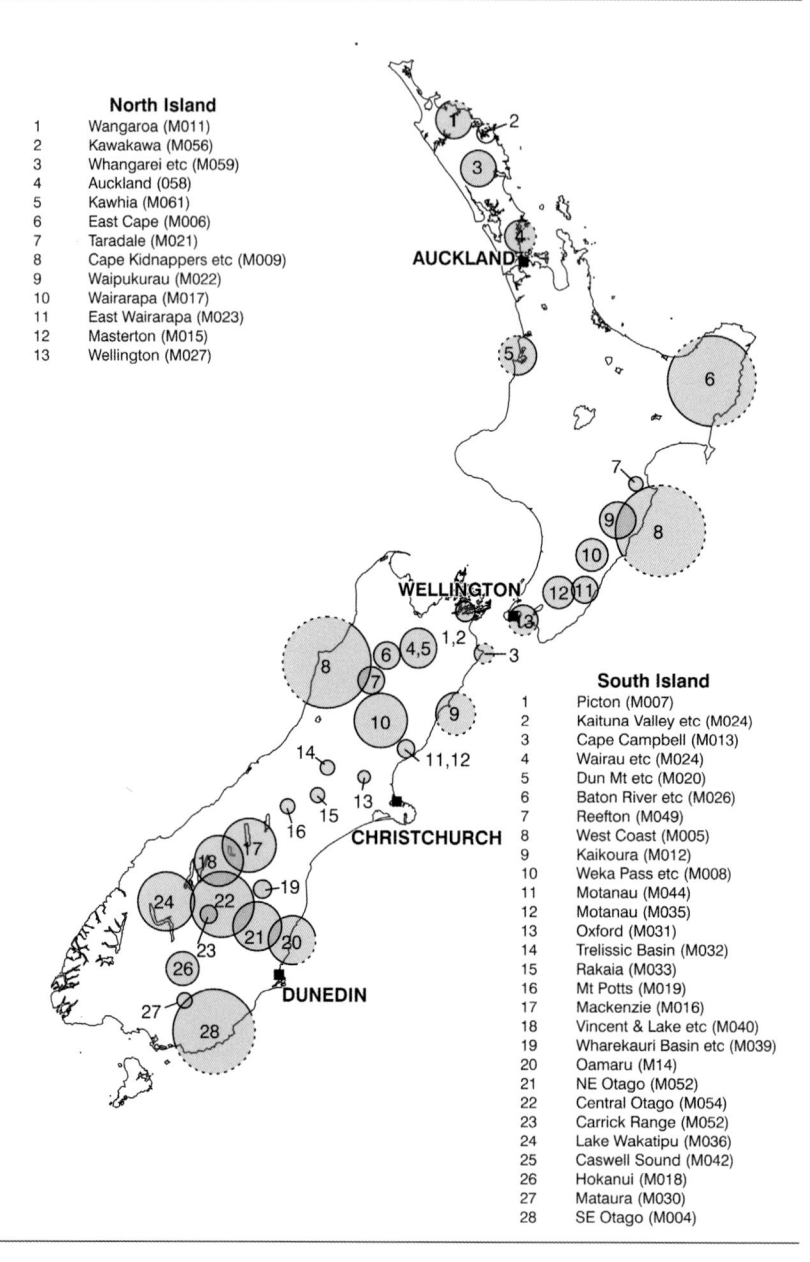

North Island

1. Wangaroa (M011)
2. Kawakawa (M056)
3. Whangarei etc (M059)
4. Auckland (058)
5. Kawhia (M061)
6. East Cape (M006)
7. Taradale (M021)
8. Cape Kidnappers etc (M009)
9. Waipukurau (M022)
10. Wairarapa (M017)
11. East Wairarapa (M023)
12. Masterton (M015)
13. Wellington (M027)

South Island

1. Picton (M007)
2. Kaituna Valley etc (M024)
3. Cape Campbell (M013)
4. Wairau etc (M024)
5. Dun Mt etc (M020)
6. Baton River etc (M026)
7. Reefton (M049)
8. West Coast (M005)
9. Kaikoura (M012)
10. Weka Pass etc (M008)
11. Motanau (M044)
12. Motanau (M035)
13. Oxford (M031)
14. Trelissic Basin (M032)
15. Rakaia (M033)
16. Mt Potts (M019)
17. Mackenzie (M016)
18. Vincent & Lake etc (M040)
19. Wharekauri Basin etc (M039)
20. Oamaru (M14)
21. NE Otago (M052)
22. Central Otago (M054)
23. Carrick Range (M052)
24. Lake Wakatipu (M036)
25. Caswell Sound (M042)
26. Hokanui (M018)
27. Mataura (M030)
28. SE Otago (M004)

Areas reported on by McKay during his first decade (to 1885) with New Zealand Geological Survey.

Gold-bearing quartz gravels generally occur at the foot of the mountain ranges of Central Otago. At Clark's (the Buster) Diggings, however, the white gravels occur on top of the flat-crested Ida Range, 1200 metres above sea level. McKay realised this called for a period of uplift and mountain-building in the comparatively recent past, geologically speaking. The seed of his interest in mountain-building was planted here. The tops of these upland ranges, although idyllic on a still summer evening, are snow-covered in winter and mining was possible for only a few months per year.

ranges and produce what is now known as the basin-and-range topography of Central Otago. McKay was developing in his mind a broad picture of the geological events that had led to the present-day configuration.

Marlborough

In 1885 McKay went to Marlborough. The result was a blockbuster paper, 'On the Geology of the Eastern Part of the Marlborough Provincial District', of 110 pages. It was profusely illustrated, and covered the 130 days he spent in the field there. But it was not only the blocks that got busted: 'when in consequence of a fall of rock I was disabled and my work interrupted, so that I returned to Wellington.'[5]

A month later he was back to resume his love affair with the region. In the preamble to his report he waxed lyrical about the deep limestone gorges of the Swale, the Meade, the Branch, the Dart, the Muzzle, and other streams:

> These gorges are a wholly unique feature in New Zealand scenery … The great cliffs rising from the deepest part of the gorge, yet high above in the sky these terminate in clear-cut pyramidal peaks, gables, and roofs, massive below, light and airy above. Architectural in aspect, these vertical walls and steep slopes, bearing just a due proportion of flowering plants and gorgeous shrubs, may be seen and admired, but are not easily described; and when a peep of sky dropping west from the zenith is seen, filled by the glistening snows

The gorge of the Meade River, Marlborough. A preliminary sketch for this engraving, which was published in 1886 as the frontispiece of Volume 17 of the Reports of Geological Exploration *series was found in a collection of drawings by John Buchanan held by the Institute of Geological and Nuclear Sciences at Gracefield. McKay also photographed the scene. Buchanan retired in 1885, so this may be one of his last works. It is unsigned.*

and jagged summits of Tapuaenuku, art may strive in vain to copy the beauty, the grandeur, and the majesty of the picture.[6]

He described the region with his customary thoroughness, but it was the faults that caught his attention. He had already realised their importance in shaping the landscape of Otago, but there the actual fault lines are commonly inconspicuous or obscured. Here in Marlborough they were obvious, so much so that he mentioned them separately.

McKay recognised that fault features were of central geological importance. He observed the earthquake rent along the line of the Awatere Fault – 'the result of one series of earthquake shocks which happened no longer ago than 1855'.[7] He noted that the line of the Clarence Fault takes it 'close to the City of Wellington, where evidences of a considerable amount of faulting within recent times are not difficult to discover'.[8] He further observed that earthquake rents attributable to the 1855 earthquake occur on the fault in several localities in the middle Clarence.[9]

The role of these faults in the development of the mountainous topography of the region was to become a focus of his developing ideas regarding mountain-building processes. McKay realised that the absence of detritus derived from land (pebbles and sand) in the Amuri limestone indicated that mountains did not exist nearby at the time when the limestone was deposited, about sixty million years ago, and that the mountains probably developed later, by repeated movements on the great faults. These movements commenced as recently as five million years ago, a mere yesterday in geological terms.[10] In his introductory pages to the relevant volume of *Reports of Geological Explorations*, Hector noted

> a very interesting report by Mr. A. McKay. … In the course of four months he geologised an area of 1,700 square miles [4440 square kilometres], including some of the most rugged and difficult country in New Zealand. During most of the time he worked either alone or with the aid only of a single companion. Some of the results which he reported from time to time appeared to me so novel and important that I thought it advisable to join him in the field, so that we might examine together a few of the most important sections on which he relied.[11]

Hector seems to have been convinced, even though McKay's thesis countered his own opinion. His comment appears essentially an expression of confidence in McKay.

Having finished the massive report resulting from this expedition, McKay laid down his pen briefly. He started on a topic of more immediate personal significance:

Wellington September 21st, 1885
The Director of the New Zealand Geol-Survey

Sir

On the 17th of April last I made application for the appointment of Assistant Geologist to the Geological Department and also for the Salary hitherto paid to the Assistant Geologist.

On the 30th of that month I had your memorandum stating as follow –. 'It is not intended to take any steps at present towards filling up the vacancy caused by the resignation of Mr Cox, but in view of the extra duty that will be required from you and your long and eminently satisfactory service to the Survey an increase of £45 to your Salary has been proposed to Government.'

In the Estimates for the current year I observe that my salary remains at £280, consequently the increase you were pleased to recommend has not been granted.[12]

I have been engaged in work connected with the Geological Survey of New Zealand since 1872, and considering the class of work which I have carried on since 1874, the many important results which have been arrived at due to my labours, and the energy with which, at all times, I have pushed the work of the Survey it will be admitted that my present Salary is not a sufficient remuneration; that it is less than is usually paid for the kind and amount of work done. I therefore beg to say that my Salary not being increased as proposed is not mearly [sic] disappointing, it is disheartening and not calculated to further the interests of the Survey under your direction.

I trust that some arrangement will be made whereby £50 may be added to my Salary commencing with the Current Financial Year as in the event of no action being taken in the matter I intend to apply for leave of absence for three months or such term as my years of service entitle me to.

I have the honour to be

Sir
Your most Obedient Servant
Alex. McKay[13]

He was promoted to Assistant Geologist before the year was done.[14]

McKay had a quixotic (and somewhat manic) sense of humour. Although it had not yet emerged in his published work, it surfaces in the following letter to Hector, written from the Empire Hotel in Palmerston. He had just completed fieldwork at Malvern Hills[15] and was about to start on the Moeraki–Kakanui coast.[16]

Blackley's Empire Hotel, Palmerston
January 26th 1886
The Director of the N.Z. Geol. Survey

Sir
I finished collections in the Malvern Hills on which day I left for Christchurch and yesterday

(Monday Jany 25th) I came by 'Express' to this place. I have already wired you that the Requisition form the Receipt at the foot of which I should sign, has been reposited from here in search of me but whether it was returned to the Treasury or posted to Palmerston North is uncertain, the Postmaster thinks the latter. It will be necessary to send it here once more as I shall have to sign the receipt.

I left my prismatic compas [sic] in the Fossil Room on the Table or on the gable shelf to right of fireplace, and my Aneroid at home.[17] Please send Big[18] up for the Barometer and post both to me here as I cannot very well get on without them.

I sent through Cuff & Graham, Lyttelton, two cases of fossils, from South Malvern on Saturday. The contents of these is about equal [to] 5 Brandy cases and is a valuable collection.[19]

Today I have had several matters to attend to and will get no fieldwork done. Tomorrow I begin in Shag Valley above Janets Peak where an outcrop of coal is seen in the Shag Riverbed and a bore has been put down on Mr Muir's land.

I have received and read V. Pikes Sixt. Article and dare scarcely express an opinion of it least I should be guilty of fulsome flattery.

I have the honour to be

Sir
Your most O.B.S.
Alex. McKay.[20]

McKay could also be tetchy if he felt his work was not being given its due. He was particularly hard on F.W. Hutton in his Waihao Forks paper.[21] When McKay read this paper at the Wellington Philosophical Society in July 1888, a 'Mr Park' (quite possibly James Park, who was not averse to questioning both Hector and McKay) commented that 'there was really no geology in this paper; it was merely an explanation of some personal differences between the author and Professor Hutton. He deplored the fact that personalities should find their way into scientific discussions, and thought it would be wise to exclude such papers from publication.'[22]

The year 1888, however, was to be momentous for McKay. His professional ability was publicly acknowledged with his election to the prestigious Geological Society of London. On 28 November 1887, Hector had nominated both McKay and James Park as Fellows of the Society. McKay was seconded by Mantell and James Crawford, both of whom were members of the elite band of Fellows already in New Zealand. His election to this august body was one of the high points of his career. Never again could anyone call him menial, illiterate, or uneducated. From the moment he was notified of his election, he proudly added the initials FGS after his name each and every time. His headstone was engraved, 'Alexander McKay FGS'.

Two fences on Glynn Wye station were displaced by 2.6 metres during the 1888 earthquake, providing the first record of sideways (transcurrent or strike-slip) movement. Prior to then, fault movements were assumed to be either up or down, but even with such compelling photographic evidence it was many years before the reality, and indeed the widespread occurrence, of transcurrent faulting was accepted. Photograph courtesy of Institute of Geological and Nuclear Sciences

Glynn Wye Earthquake

The next event in 1888 was even more significant for McKay, and secured him a place in the history of geological science. There was a major earthquake on the Hope Fault at Glynn Wye, near Lewis Pass, in the early hours of the morning of 1 September 1888. McKay was despatched from Wellington to investigate.[23] From Blenheim he walked or rode the full length of the Awatere Valley, then over Barefell Pass and down the Guide and the Acheron rivers to the Clarence. He crossed the Clarence River and then Jollies Pass to reach Hanmer, from where he headed towards Lewis Pass and the region where most damage had been reported. His report is an extraordinarily comprehensive account of the features resulting from the earthquake: ground rents, localised building damage and felt effects, broken and toppled trees, and secondary features such as slips and other forms of ground collapse and subsidence. He noted that, although a hotel was undamaged, 'the contents suffered severely.'[24]

It was on Glynn Wye Station, however, that McKay saw what had never been reported before. A fence which crossed the old earthquake rent had been broken, with one side displaced horizontally, 2.6 metres from the other. Two and a half kilometres away another fence was offset by a similar amount. McKay was able to show that the ground along at least thirteen kilometres of the fault line had been horizontally displaced by between 1.5 and 2.6 metres.[25] The reality of horizontal (strike-slip) faulting had been indisputably established for the first time. Contemporary theory allowed for only vertical displacements on faults. McKay's photograph of the offset fence would eventually appear in international textbooks, but it would still be some fifty years before the significance of strike-slip faulting was universally accepted.

However, there was more. The break had occurred on a fault-line that had moved in the not-too-distant past, perhaps only a few hundred years before. Suddenly geologists had an indication of the recurrence interval – a horizontal movement of perhaps 2.5 metres every 500 years. That equates to five kilometres every million years, or fifty kilometres in ten million years, more than enough to explain the present geological arrangement. And, as McKay was well aware, the horizontal movements were accompanied by some vertical displacement, say ten per cent of the total, which would be enough to explain the uplift of the mountains, too. Although McKay was certainly unaware of this at the time, the foundations of the new discipline of 'neo-tectonics' had been laid. It is a science of risk-assessment which becomes more significant as the population increasingly coalesces into concentrated communities on the Pacific 'rim of fire': Anchorage, Vancouver, San Francisco, Los Angeles, Lima, Wellington, Manila, Kobe, and Tokyo, to name a few. These cities have a vital interest in the neo-tectonics of their region. McKay not only initiated a new area of science, he gave New Zealand a head-start in earthquake engineering and in developing the appropriate expertise, which is now exported all over the world.

McKay's report was very impressive.[26] When he read the paper to the Wellington Philosophical Society on 14 November 1888, Hector publicly commented he 'considered that this paper, as a simply-told narrative of the observed facts, would become classical in the literature of earthquakes, and he complimented the author on its excellence.'[27] It was fitting that the 'Glynn Wye' report was the first of McKay's publications to bear the initials FGS.

The original version of the Glynn Wye report (M080) was not illustrated, although Hector, in his introduction refers to 'Mr McKay's observations [being] fully illustrated by photographs, which I hope to publish at an early date …'[28] A map of the fault at Glynn Wye appeared, almost as an afterthought, two years later in a separate report (M092), but it was not until 1902, when McKay reprinted the Glynn Wye report as part

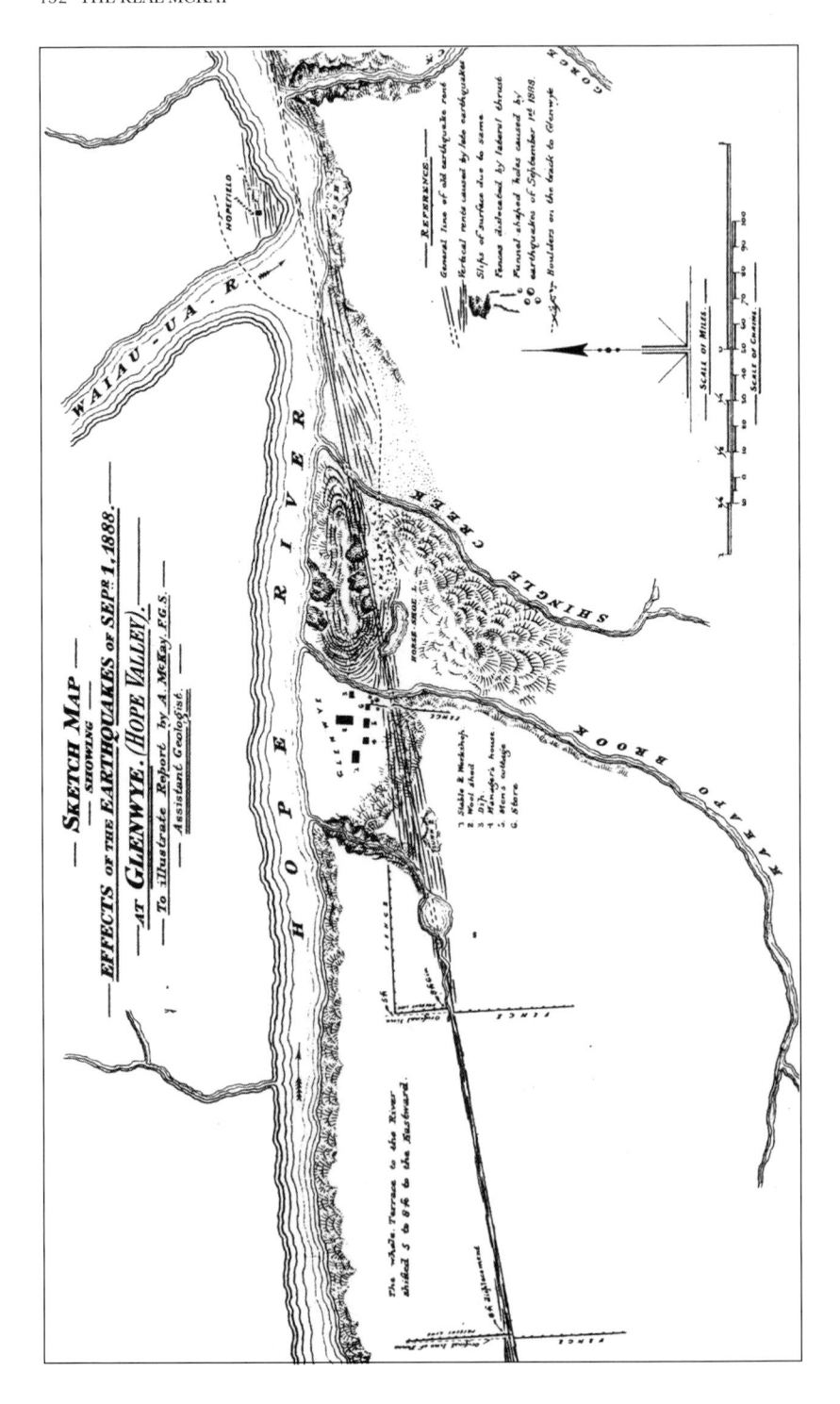

McKay's map of part of Glynn Wye Station, showing the position of the offset fences.

11. THE PEAK OF HIS POWERS 153

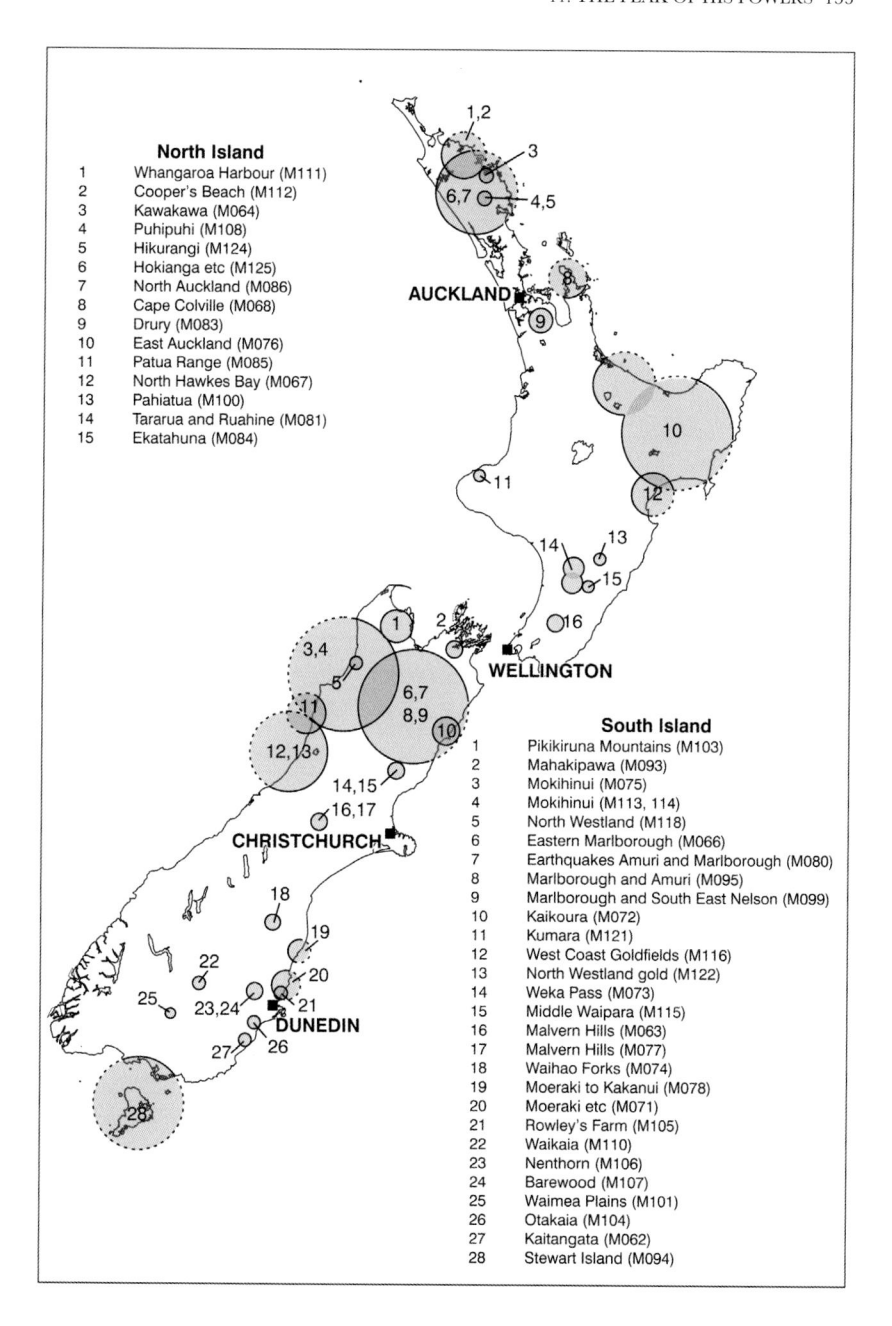

North Island
1. Whangaroa Harbour (M111)
2. Cooper's Beach (M112)
3. Kawakawa (M064)
4. Puhipuhi (M108)
5. Hikurangi (M124)
6. Hokianga etc (M125)
7. North Auckland (M086)
8. Cape Colville (M068)
9. Drury (M083)
10. East Auckland (M076)
11. Patua Range (M085)
12. North Hawkes Bay (M067)
13. Pahiatua (M100)
14. Tararua and Ruahine (M081)
15. Ekatahuna (M084)

South Island
1. Pikikiruna Mountains (M103)
2. Mahakipawa (M093)
3. Mokihinui (M075)
4. Mokihinui (M113, 114)
5. North Westland (M118)
6. Eastern Marlborough (M066)
7. Earthquakes Amuri and Marlborough (M080)
8. Marlborough and Amuri (M095)
9. Marlborough and South East Nelson (M099)
10. Kaikoura (M072)
11. Kumara (M121)
12. West Coast Goldfields (M116)
13. North Westland gold (M122)
14. Weka Pass (M073)
15. Middle Waipara (M115)
16. Malvern Hills (M063)
17. Malvern Hills (M077)
18. Waihao Forks (M074)
19. Moeraki to Kakanui (M078)
20. Moeraki etc (M071)
21. Rowley's Farm (M105)
22. Waikaia (M110)
23. Nenthorn (M106)
24. Barewood (M107)
25. Waimea Plains (M101)
26. Otakaia (M104)
27. Kaitangata (M062)
28. Stewart Island (M094)

Under Hector's direction, McKay continued to travel extensively, as demonstrated by this map of the areas reported on during his second decade (to 1895). Although many investigations had an economic focus (e.g. coal or gold) or were in response to natural events such as earthquakes, others were aimed at resolving the more esoteric scientific questions or conflicts of the day. McKay's own interests, especially in Marlborough, also appear to have become significant late in the period.

of a report on the 1901 earthquakes of the Cheviot district (M190), that the photographs were published.[29] The Glynn Wye report is also noteworthy in that in it McKay named two companions: Mr D. Rutherford of Leslie Hills Station, who seems to have been with McKay for several days, and 'Mr Thompson, manager of Glyn Wye Station, who accompanied us [in the Glynn Wye area] provided with an axe.'[30]

Marlborough continued to engross McKay, although his other routine investigations took him from the Bay of Islands to Stewart Island.[31] On Stewart Island his principal task was to investigate the tin deposits near Port Pegasus. Despite atrocious weather, he combined his observations with those of others to produce a map of the island which differs little from the version published seventy years later.

In 1890 he published 'On the Geology of Marlborough and the Amuri District of Nelson.' This was another hundred-page epic, especially notable both for a splendid foldout four-colour map, the first coloured map published by Geological Survey.[32] However it is the further twenty-eight pages of Part II, published in 1892, that is of greatest interest. In Part II McKay advances his reasoning for the uplift of the mountains commencing in the Pliocene (only five million years ago), claiming that the uplift came about primarily by movement on faults. He nominates the twelve major faults of the South Island, and their possible extensions into the North Island. Yet certain remarks made in passing are the most tantalising. For instance, he notes on page three that 'the abrupt slope of the west side of the Southern Alps … is largely due to the existence of a line of fault running along the base of the mountains',[33] and he remarks that 'it requires no great stretch of imagination to realise the probability of the connection of the crystalline rocks of the north-west of Nelson with those of western Otago …'[34] Unfortunately he was distracted by Edward Dobson's observation (as reported by Haast) that the major rivers of the South Island, and hence the major faults, appeared to radiate outwards from a point offshore of Hokitika.[35] McKay wondered if this seat of 'abyssological force' might have been responsible for the disappearance of the missing part of the western belt of rocks that were once continuous between Nelson and Otago.[36] He was to return to this problem later, not realising that – having established the reality of horizontal fault displacement, and the probable original continuity between Otago and Nelson, and knowing of the existence of a fault at the western base of the Southern Alps – the answer was at his fingertips. The missing sections of the Otago–Nelson belt had come about not because they had been sucked into the 'abyss' but because Nelson and Otago had become separated by large-scale *horizontal* displacement along the Alpine Fault.

Coal at Rowley's Farm

In 1890 McKay was to produce one of his most famous reports, which has endeared him to all with a shared disdain of the mediocrity of bureaucracy: 'On the Prospects of Finding Coal on Rowley's Farm, near Shag Point Railway-station'.[37] At the time this report was written, geological reports were presented to the General Assembly. To this end, it was suggested to McKay that he should limit his use of technical language. 'Rowley's Farm' is an audacious response.[38] First he defines the term 'breccia-conglomerate':

> which, being interpreted, in ordinary language signifies a regular, or irregular, higgledy-piggledy, pell-mell, and confused mixture of sharp-angled or partly rounded pieces of stone, mixed with sand, clay, mud or anything else that would fill up the spaces between the bigger pieces of stone.[39]

This led to a discussion of the angle at which the coal-beds lie:

> The seam [of coal] is not lying flat, neither is it straight-up and-down, nor is it exactly half-way between these two possible positions, but is a little under half-way between the mitre angle (45°) and vertical (90°), having an inclination to the horizon of 64°…[40]

He then felt required to describe a syncline – a down fold:

> To illustrate a syncline, and to better show what, in a geological sense, is meant by the term, an onion is required at least, this vegetable is very suitable for the purpose. Having procured a bulb one as round as it is possible to get cut it

In a syncline the rock strata are bent into a U-shaped fold. When an onion is halved and quartered, following McKay's instructions, the layers of the onion in the two quarters in the foreground ilustrate a synclinal fold. McKay's instructions were in response to a parliamentary suggestion that his reports were too technical.

vertically into two equal parts.[41]

Warming to his explanation, McKay carried on:

> Then, at right angles to the plane of the first intersection, and at any point between the equatorial and polar regions of the hemisphere selected, make a second cut in a latitudinal direction, and by carefully examining the section exposed by the last application of the knife the meaning of a syncline, and what is to be understood by it, will be apparent. This would be a regular syncline. Synclines are of various kinds, regular and irregular, and so are onions, especially shallot onions; and there is hardly any kind of syncline that may not be illustrated by some kind of onion.[42]

He reverted to his usual style a week later.

For the next year or two many reports were the result of short investigations into the mineral potential of various minor occurrences of gold, coal, or other minerals. One which is a little different from this run of applied work, however, was McKay's return visit in 1891 to the classic Weka Pass area,[43] where he went to recover a fossil saurian which he had seen in the river bed twenty years earlier. It turned out to be part of a jaw, extending about forty centimetres back from the muzzle, with eighteen well-preserved teeth.

As the second decade of his career ended, McKay was at the peak

McKay returned to a locality in middle Waipara in 1891, to recover a fossil saurian he had seen in the riverbed twenty years earlier. It turned out to be part of a jaw extending about 40 cm back from the muzzle with eighteen well-preserved teeth. This is not the same specimen but it was collected from the same locality and is now on display in the Canterbury Museum, next to the plesiosaur that McKay collected in 1872. It indicates the fearsome nature of these carnivorous reptiles.

of his powers. He was familiar with the geology of most of the country and had the enviable ability to recall with accuracy the details necessary to make country-wide comparisons. He had skill and confidence, was established and respected scientifically, and his standing in the broader community was recognised by his appointment on 2 May 1891, following the recommendation of the local policeman, as a Justice of the Peace.[44]

Photography

It was not only in geology, however, that McKay was breaking ground. During this period he was also expanding his interest in photography, in particular the taking of telescopic pictures. He maintained and expanded his interest in photography as his geological career consolidated. He noted in M190 that he had taken many photographs in Marlborough in 1886–87,[45] and again, as noted by Hector, at Glynn Wye in 1888.[46] In 1890 he presented a paper (M098) to the Wellington Philosophical Society on 'On some Means for increasing the Scale of Photographic Lenses and the Use of Telescopic Powers in Connection with an Ordinary Camera.'[47] In this he reported 'Some years ago I set myself the task of producing telescopic pictures …'[48] He went on to describe the technicalities of his solutions to the problems of getting enough light through the lens to enable the image to be focused and of eliminating the fuzziness caused by spherical and chromatic aberration.

McKay displayed not only some of the photographic prints he had taken, but also the most recent (lighter and most compact) camera and lens. Paper M098 is an unequivocal statement, published in the transactions of a learned society, that he had been taking telephoto pictures prior to 13 August 1890. In fact, at the meeting he displayed photographs taken in the Bay of Islands, New Plymouth, Central Otago, and of the recent earthquake effects in the Hanmer region. These localities suggest he was using his telephoto lens as early as 1883 or 1884.[49]

The oldest surviving dateable telephotograph, however, is from 1886, when McKay took a series of photographs looking eastwards across Thorndon from Lewisville Terrace, where he lived, using lenses of three different focal lengths. Some features are common to all three photographs, which were located and reproduced by W. Main in his book *Wellington through a Victorian Lens*.[50] The Shepherds' Arms Hotel (which McKay notes was five chains [100 m] distant) is prominent in the picture taken with the mid-power lens, and a framed copy of this print is mounted on the wall of the public bar of the hotel (now the Western Park Hotel). However, it is the photograph taken with the most powerful lens which is particularly impressive, both for its clarity and because it can be unequivocally dated.

The Russian warship Vjestnik *was anchored in Wellington Harbour from 23 May until 1 June 1886, which establishes this photograph as one of the first successful telephotos ever taken anywhere. The ship is approximately two and a half kilometres away. The house in the foreground, also in sharp focus, is only about 400 metres distant. The photo is one of a set of three that McKay took from his Lewisville Terrace house in 1886.* ATL¹/2-021856-F

The house in the lower right is about 400 metres from McKay's camera, but the ship in the centre, with its gun ports and rigging lines clearly visible, is the Russian warship *Vjestnik*,[51] which was anchored in Lambton Harbour, two to two and a half kilometres away. The *Vjestnik* was in port from 23 May until 1 June 1886.

McKay's address was greeted with great enthusiasm by the Society. One of the members, a Mr Travers, considered that it 'would completely revolutionize photography',[52] and Josiah Martin, editor of Sharland's *New Zealand Photographer*, hailed it as 'a world first'.[53] Dr Hector noted that McKay had 'perfected his invention after years of work and at great expense'.[54]

In London, however, the news was less enthusiastically received. This was despite the altruistic conclusion to McKay's address:

> in bringing them [my experiments and discoveries] and the instrument under the notice of the Society I do so with a view to their publication, so that others may have the opportunity of making improvements on what I have already effected, or of suggesting something entirely new in its place.[55]

Thomas Dallmeyer, whose prestigious firm made lenses and photographic equipment, was already working on a telephoto lens, and in 1890 or 1891 he patented a compound telephoto lens capable of a wide range of magnifications.[56] Controversy raged for some time, with Dallmeyer being accused of pirating McKay's invention.[57] It appears that as late as November 1894 Dallmeyer had still not seen McKay's published account.[58]

The *Cyclopaedia of New Zealand* (1897) includes a biographic entry for McKay which appears to have been written, or dictated, by him.[59] In it he clearly regards himself as the inventor of the telescopic lens, a claim which the evidence suggests is valid.[60] Considering his isolation from the state of the art internationally, and from a ready source of lenses, it was a major achievement.[61] The boy who once kept his feet warm on the back of a Galloway bull had come a long way.

Although the decade saw McKay at his peak, there were also indications that things were not always well. Scattered indications surface of brittle or unsettled periods. In 1883 his father died, unseen and unsung, on the other side of the world, twenty years after McKay had last seen him. In

The Shepherds' Arms Hotel in Tinakori Road, Thorndon, was about 100 metres from McKay's house. This photograph was probably taken the same day as the previous one. It is another measure of the success McKay had achieved with his telephoto techniques by 1886. A copy of the photograph is mounted on the wall of the public bar of the hotel, now the Western Park Hotel. ATL¹/2-021850-F

1886, McKay wrote a strange letter to Hector from Blackley's Hotel in Palmerston, in which he compared the volume of a collection of fossils with five brandy cases (pages 148–49). Later that same year, he was to make a vitriolic attack on Haast and Hutton, suggesting, amongst other things, that if they had done a bit more fieldwork, differences between them may never have arisen. As noted earlier, the paper was considered by some as 'merely an explanation of some personal differences between the author and Professor Hutton [and it was deplored] that personalities should find their way into scientific discussions.'[62] And then four years later came McKay's ultimate audacity, 'The Prospects of Coal on Rowley's Farm'. Politicians of the time disliked being mocked even less than they do now, and McKay was lucky he did not receive a stern rebuke. McKay's mother died in 1892, when he was fifty-one. Her death may have triggered the 'middle age' interest in spiritualism, reported by Burton, which irritated Hector, who suggested McKay was suffering from hysteria, and needed a holiday.[63] The information available is tenuous and incomplete, but there are indications of mood swings, and erratic, eccentric, and unsettled behaviour, which had not been evident earlier, and was not to be an issue later.

But the winds of change were blowing. His friend and colleague, James Park, had resigned in 1889 from the Geological Survey. In 1886, the staff of Geological Survey (Park, McKay, and Skey) had been transferred to the Mines Department, possibly as part of a systematic campaign by 'King Dick' Seddon to disempower Hector, but probably driven also by the need for economic reform in the public service. In 1892 McKay was appointed Mining Geologist to the Mines Department, and by 1893 Hector's empire had been reduced to a pitifully short-funded museum and a staff of one clerk. The unusual relationship between Hector and McKay, which had served New Zealand geology so well, was at an end.[64]

12. Government Geologist, FGS

In the third and last decade of his career as a field geologist, McKay worked alone. Since 1892 he had been Mining Geologist to the Mines Department. He was responsible to the Under-Secretary of Mines and the instructions which he received were brief and pragmatic ('Visit and report on the coal field at Puponga'). A lot of his work was *ad hoc* trivia – 'Can Mr McKay look at this', and so on. But he still averaged at least one major report each year and again covered the length and breadth of the country.

After some field investigations in this period, he would produce a relatively brief 'immediate' report and follow it up with a more extensive and discursive paper. One such couplet was a four-page report on the gold-bearing gravels near Kumara in Westland,[1] which was followed by the thirty-nine page paper 'On the Geology of the Northern Part of Westland'.[2] This in turn grew to 108 pages in the second edition, when he included the 'Southwest Part of Nelson'.[3] The paper is largely concerned with the origin of Westland gold. McKay argued that the amount of gold and the size of the particles was inconsistent with it having been derived from the rocks of the Southern Alps. Instead, the gold must have come from a high land lying not far west of the present coast.

But where was this land? Mckay was aware of the similarities between the rocks of Nelson and northwest Otago. He had previously acknowledged that 'the abrupt slope of the west side of the Southern Alps … is largely due to the existence of a line of fault running along the base of the mountains …'[4] He was revisiting the same arguments he had advanced five years before, but this time it seemed inevitable he would put all these facts together and realise the significance of the Alpine Fault, and that the missing source had been shifted sideways.

But the final flash of inspiration still eluded him. It was left to Harold Wellman in 1948, just over fifty years later, to postulate the now widely accepted thesis that the rocks of Nelson and north Westland had been shifted 480 kilometres along the Alpine Fault from their original position as part of Fiordland and northwest Otago.[5] As the gold-bearing rocks moved northward, gold-bearing gravel was washed out to the east, before the Southern Alps became elevated. Some of it was later washed back to the

162 THE REAL MCKAY

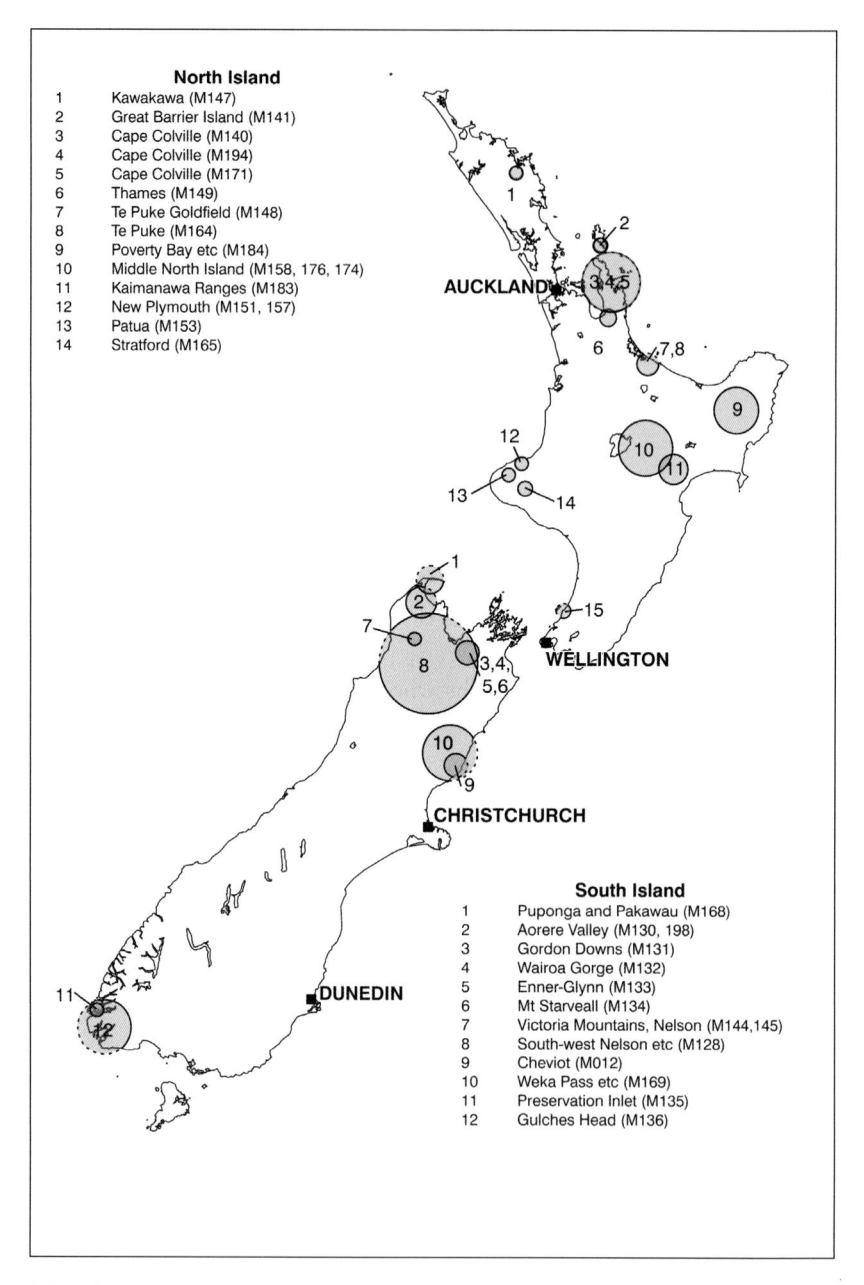

North Island
1. Kawakawa (M147)
2. Great Barrier Island (M141)
3. Cape Colville (M140)
4. Cape Colville (M194)
5. Cape Colville (M171)
6. Thames (M149)
7. Te Puke Goldfield (M148)
8. Te Puke (M164)
9. Poverty Bay etc (M184)
10. Middle North Island (M158, 176, 174)
11. Kaimanawa Ranges (M183)
12. New Plymouth (M151, 157)
13. Patua (M153)
14. Stratford (M165)

South Island
1. Puponga and Pakawau (M168)
2. Aorere Valley (M130, 198)
3. Gordon Downs (M131)
4. Wairoa Gorge (M132)
5. Enner-Glynn (M133)
6. Mt Starveall (M134)
7. Victoria Mountains, Nelson (M144, 145)
8. South-west Nelson etc (M128)
9. Cheviot (M012)
10. Weka Pass etc (M169)
11. Preservation Inlet (M135)
12. Gulches Head (M136)

Map of areas reported on during McKay's third decade (to 1905). In this, his last decade, his work was more directed to mineral resources, but once again he travelled the length and breadth of the country.

west to form the coastal plain as the uplift of the mountains commenced.

Gold continued to dominate much of McKay's work. A second edition of his report on the Central Otago goldfields was released.[6] He visited two equal and opposite fields, Aorangi Mine in northwest Nelson, and Preservation Inlet in southwest Fiordland, and found the same distinctive association of fossils, granite, shale and gold at both. He was struck by the coincidence, and once again he must have been only a whisker away from realising the explanation offered by the concept of horizontal displacement on the Alpine Fault.

The Crown's interest in potential mineral deposits remained keen. McKay's reports were presented to both houses of the General Assembly, 'By command of his Excellency'. This interest resulted in his going to Preservation Inlet and the south coast of Fiordland, in the far southwest corner of the South Island, to examine gold prospects there.

Fiordland

When he arrived at Cromarty in Preservation Inlet in 1896, a population of several hundred people was already present between Te Waewae Bay and Preservation Inlet. Even on the wild south coast there were groups of fossickers and a team of workers stringing a telegraph line through to the lighthouse at Puysegur Point. Toay the settlements of Cromarty and Te Oneroa and the mines and prospects have been long abandoned; steamers no longer call and the lighthouse is automated. Vegetation masks the exploitation of a hundred years ago, and there is a legacy of silence. Fishing boats and sometimes tourist vessels seeking safe anchorage in the sheltered waters of the inlet are the only visitors.

As usual, McKay left only a terse and prosaic report.[7] However on this occasion he was not alone. In addition to C.W. Linck, a scientific assistant to McKay with some botanical and geological abilities, he had with him as an assistant a capable, cheerful and observant bushman, George Biggar, who kept an uninhibited diary.[8] The quality of George's diary, and the additional insight it gives into this expedition, makes it a valuable account.

McKay left Wellington on 3 January 1896. He reported that he travelled on a steamer by way of

> the west coast of the Middle [South] Island, for Preservation Inlet, but, owing to the prevalence of excessively stormy weather, I was not landed at Cromarty[9] till the 16th of the month.[10] Here, again, owing to a continuance of the most excessive inclemency, practically no work could be done for the remainder of the month. Nor, with regard to the character of the weather, was the month of February in any respect an improvement on that which proceeded it, and it was not till the 20th March that any improvement in the state of the weather

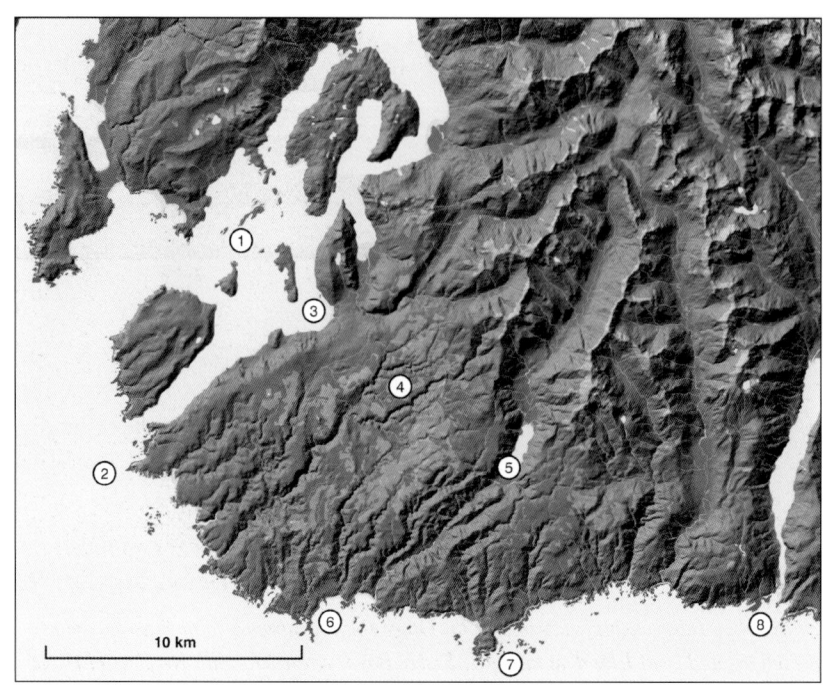

A digital terrain map of Preservation Inlet and southwestern Fiordland. Preservation Inlet (1), Puysegur Point (2), Cromarty (3), Wilson River (4), Lake Kiwi (5), Mouth of Coal Burn (6), Green Islets Peninsula (7), outlet of Lake Hakapoua (Big River) (8). Courtesy *GeographX*

> took place ... Throughout, high winds prevailed, and at frequent intervals storms of extreme violence occurred, blowing either from the north-west or south-west. Boating on the waters of the inlets was thus rendered unsafe ... Work was therefore pushed in a north-east and east direction, over the country surrounding the head of the Wilson River and Kiwi Burn, and along the coastline towards the mouth of Big River.[11]

A noteworthy detail is that McKay intended to make 'a number of trips, lightly laden with special provisions, into the rugged granite country around the sources of the Kiwi and Princess Burns' (the latter flows into the head of Lake Poteriteri).[12] George Biggar reports that they camped at the base of Bald Peaks, from the summit of which they had a fine view of the Solander Islands. McKay's mind could hardly have failed to slip back thirty-three years to that early morning on the *Helenslee* when, for a few minutes, his New Zealand experience seemed destined to begin and end on the rocky shores of the Solanders.

Their third camp was in the head of the Coal Burn, a bleak, almost flat area about 300 metres above sea level. Here there is little natural shelter from storms sweeping in from either the southwest or northwest. McKay

Preservation Inlet, looking southwest to the Otago Retreat entrance, with Puysegur Point on the top left and Coal Island on the right. Kisbee Bay is centre left, with Revolver Hill and Revolver Bay in the right foreground. The site of the settlement of Cromarty on the shore of Kisbee Bay is arrowed, as is the Morning Star mine, above Te Oneroa.

elected to stay at this camp while the other two blazed a track down to the coast at the mouth of the Kiwi Burn, as he was not feeling well.

Biggar and Linck set out with 'fairly heavy' swags[13] containing a tent and fly, blankets, and provisions for five days, leaving McKay with the main tent and a stock of provisions. When they left Cromarty the party must have been carrying awesome loads. Five days later, George got back to 'the chief':

> His three days solitary having reached five I found him in a very weak state, having been seized with that scourge of all explorers diarrhoea. However he recovered, he was a little better that day.
>
> He had a pitiful tale to tell of the previous day and night's rain, he having been flooded out. Although at dusk the day before it was raining heavy he had no fear of the water reaching the tent. However at nine o'clock at night he thought he felt something lifting the scrub of which his bunk was composed, and on striking a light found about a foot of water in the tent. He gathered everything together and tied them to the ridgepole and debated to himself whether he should remove everything to the Bush as the water was still rising. But on looking out he found that on either side was a stream of water that would have swept him off his legs. But as he was an old campaigner he decided to remain in the tent until he was washed out, at any rate. He therefore put an extra lashing on the biscuit box which he had tied to the ridgepole, and as the water

still kept rising he gathered his blankets around him and managed to scramble onto the biscuit box. Here he sat straddle legs with his body doubled up for several hours. From this point of vantage he had the melancholy satisfaction of seeing the bed in which he had lately lain being washed out of the tent and sailing towards the sea.[14]

At this point in the tale George could not contain his mirth: 'I raised his ire properly by breaking out into a hearty fit of laughter at the picture he drew …'[15]

Although McKay was still weak, they decided to make a start the next morning for the river (the Kiwi Burn), where they met up with a group of diggers and a survey party scouting out a route for the telegraph line from Orepuki to Puysegur Point. 'We were very glad to hear news of the outside world, as we had seen no one but members of our own party for over six weeks – not even a newspaper.'[16] About dusk they were also joined by Linck and a couple of men who had brought them some more supplies.[17] They then turned east and headed along the shore for Green Islets and Big River beyond. Apart from occasional sandy beaches, this coast is never easy travelling, being a mixture of steep boulder beaches and rocky reefs backed by high cliffs, and always with the unrelenting pounding surf of the southern ocean. Many promontories are passable at dead low water, but conditions change swiftly as the tide turns. And whatever the state of the tide, there comes, about once every twenty minutes, the 'big one' – a wave seven times the size of its predecessors.

The party had been encouraged to press on until a cave or 'blowhole' would allow them passage through the main point of land, which would save several hours of rough bush travel. After some difficult climbing they reached the mouth of the blowhole which was 'a fearsome looking place'.[18] By the light of a candle they made some eighty metres, before the cave walls closed in and they were forced to swim with their swags in the water that was surging through. The group retreated hurriedly, but not before cursing the sources of their information. However, it was too late and their line of retreat was cut by the incoming tide. After scrambling a metre or so clear of the waves, they waited 'squatting on our swags like so many penguins' and prepared for a long night on a narrow ledge. Successive waves were breaking ever higher, however, and as their position was becoming uncomfortably insecure, George[19] elected to scale the cliff above, bringing up the swags, the dog, and his companions with the aid of a rope. Their aneroids indicated that the cliff was ninety metres high, and it took them two and a half hours to climb it. At the top, 'With a prayer of thankfulness we lit our pipes and decided to have a short spell.'[20]

The men carried on through the bush at the top of the cliffs for an hour or two until it was prudent to return to the beach at the mouth of the Grace Burn, where they had dinner. In the dusk they then headed up the well-worn track in the bush over the neck of the peninsula, and down the cliffs to Boat Landing Bay at Green Islets. Dates they found carved on trees indicated that Europeans had been using the area since 1856; there was also evidence of earlier nomadic Maori occupation, both here and at many other places along the coast.

At daybreak they were woken by the sandflies. Continuing east along the coast, they reached the Cavendish River. From here the route was blocked by great granite cliffs falling sheerly into the sea. They headed inland, and climbed 600 metres to the top of the rounded hill between the Cavendish and Big Rivers, from where Biggar noted 'we were able to satisfy ourselves that the granite did reach as far as Big R[iver].'[21] They then moved about three kilometres north to a low saddle. This saddle is part of a belt of lower and less rugged country resulting from the presence of rocks much younger (Tertiary) and softer than the granite. Furthermore there are several outcrops of them on the saddle, but McKay did not see or record them. This oversight is surprising, and suggests that McKay's internal upsets had left him less on the ball than usual.

After camping overnight at the mouth of the Cavendish River, the party set off back along the coast. The next night, after a long day, they camped at the Grace Burn, feasting on local delicacies. As Biggar described:

> As our tinned meat was all consumed we made our supper from some kakapo and kiwis which our dog had caught, cooking them in Maori style in an umu or oven. To those who have never tasted fish or fowl cooked in this manner I must say they have missed a treat …
>
> Kakapos, Maori hens [wekas] and kiwis were very plentiful on our line of march, and we had to keep the dog[22] well in hand or he would have been killing them every few chains.[23]

Once they got back to Cromarty, McKay chartered the services of Captain Robertson and his cutter so that he could explore the different arms of the inlet and adjacent sounds (Isthmus Sound, Long Sound, Dark Cloud or Chalky Inlet, and Edwardson and Cunaris Sounds). There is a strong tidal flow through the Narrows between Preservation Inlet and Long Sound and they had to resort to the 'sweeps' (oars) when a fickle wind deserted them. They anchored that night in the wonderfully sheltered Jane Cove but had to beat up Long Sound against the wind the next day. On their return they stopped for lunch in the Narrows. While the billy was boiling, George and Captain Robertson baited some lines and soon had 'ten magnificent gropers each fully 70 lbs [thirty kilograms] in weight.'[24] From there they sailed across to Isthmus Sound, Cuttle Cove, and Gulches Head, inspecting the various mining claims and prospects, while the boat took Linck around into Chalky Inlet to survey the scene there.

McKay saved one of the geological highlights right to the end, possibly because it was accessible with relative ease on foot from Cromarty, and thus the journey was not dependent on the weather. The Morning Star gold mine at Te Oneroa lies about halfway between Cromarty and the Puysegur Lighthouse. In 1896, the Morning Star employed thirty men and operated on four levels. At the entrance to the mine McKay found graptolites – small stem-like serrate fossils with teeth like those of a saw, which are diagnostic of the age of the rock. He was struck by the geological similarities of the region – gold, graptolites, slate, and granite – with the Aorangi Mine area of northwest Nelson. He made recommendations to the mine manager on how best to proceed. Mr Hilton was sufficiently impressed to write to McKay a few months later, thanking him for his valuable advice and reporting a return of 233 ounces of gold (worth $81,550 at current prices).[25] Extensions were made the next year following these returns, and resulted in 1898 being the peak year, with a return of 2020 ounces of gold (worth $707,700).

A day or two later, on 18 April, McKay left to return to Wellington. The journey was made in only four days, compared with the two weeks it had taken to come down. In his diary, George Biggar implied he also left on the steamer, although perhaps only as far as Bluff (he lived at Croydon, near Gore). George finishes his account with a simple but telling statement: 'And so ended a trip of over three months which, if the work were sometimes arduous and dangerous was, owing to the ability and experience of our chief a pleasant one.'[26]

When McKay wrote his report on Preservation Inlet in July 1896, he was Mining Geologist, but in May 1897 when he wrote the subsequent Cape Colville (Coromandel) report his appellation had changed to Government Geologist. Like his FGS, the title of Government Geologist seemed to appeal to him, and he took it to the grave. It is not clear if this was a promotion, an administrative nicety, or a request from McKay that his broader responsibil-ities (other than mining) be recognised.

Family

On the domestic front, the dynamics of an evolving family were ringing in some changes. His sons William and Duncan were both now in the workforce, after completing their education. Their schooling had been initially at Mowbray Street School and subsequently at Wellington College. The older William was now a storeman and assistant to his father and Duncan was furthering his career as a clerk in Dannevirke. In 1896 William had already assisted his father during a lengthy period of fieldwork in Coromandel.

In 1897, at the age of twenty-eight, William[27] married May Matilda Maxton, and Duncan[28] (twenty-three) married Henrietta Earle (who was just sixteen). Henrietta's mother had been born a Maxton, too, and it is likely the two wives were cousins. Both young couples presented their parents with grandchildren the following year.[29]

That year, 1898, Alex and Susannah vacated the family home at 6 Lewisville Terrace, Thorndon, in favour of William and his young family. This ushered in a curious period as in 1899 Susannah unexpectedly turned up on the electoral roll at 7 Owen Street, on the other side of town, whereas McKay appeared on the roll to be living about a block away, in Coromandel Street. Number 7 Owen St was owned by Chas and Emma Hales, who was later listed as a boarding-housekeeper, although at a subsequent address. Chas Hales was a lithographer and was conceivably known to McKay.

This somewhat strange arrangement may have resulted from the McKays having taken temporary accommodation once they vacated the family home, until they found something more permanent. The enigma of Coromandel Street may have resulted from Susannah finding it unsatisfactory when Alex was absent on fieldwork, so she moved around the corner to the Hales' establishment. Possibly Mrs Hales entered Susannah on the electoral roll, as this was Susannah's only appearance on it. At this stage McKay was fifty-eight and Susannah was sixty-four. In 1902, they moved back to Thorndon, at 10 May Street (close to Tinakori Road), and possibly also briefly at 19 Hill St (near Parliament Buildings).

Meanwhile between 1899 and 1901 William, as an assistant geologist, published six papers, and in 1902 he accompanied his father to Marlborough. He was later employed at the Colonial Museum (later, Dominion) from about 1903 to about 1933 as a 'messenger and keeper'. Museum staff photos show William, at the age of thirty-seven and sixty-four, as having an oval face with a wide forehead and a narrow chin, and close-cropped hair and beard, white in the later photograph. There is not a strong resemblance to his father. William and May Matilda had four children: two girls and two boys.

Duncan was of a different bent from William. He spent several years in Dannevirke gaining clerical experience before setting up business as a Public Accountant in Wellington. His office address, at 153–55 Featherston Street, was in the heart of the financial district. He left notebooks and ledgers filled with minutiae (4/6 for a dress for his daughter) and it is apparent that at times he borrowed investment money from both his father and his brother.

He appears as a fine-boned, slim, good-looking young man with a sense of style and an attractive wife. Duncan was an enthusiastic athlete and won many trophies for long-distance running. He later became President of the Accountants and Auditors Society, and the Clan McKay Society. He also had a long association with the Wellington Trotting Club. Duncan and Henrietta had one daughter, Rosa.

Coromandel

McKay had barely returned from Fiordland in 1896 when he was directed by the Minister of Mines to commence a geological survey of the Coromandel region. This was to become a major focus of the rest of his career, but in the meantime interest was developing in new directions: petroleum, iron sands, glass sands, pumice (for light-weight concrete), and earthquakes. To each he turned his attention, maintaining his exceptional output.

He had previously worked in the Coromandel in 1883, as part of the directive at that time to locate more supplies of coal, so he was already familiar with the area. Between September 1896 and May 1897, on receipt of the ministerial directive, McKay and his son William (now twenty-eight, while McKay was fifty-five) carried out a prodigious amount of fieldwork southward from Cape Colville, to Te Aroha and Katikati. In addition, after further instructions from the Minister in January 1897, he visited and reported on the geology and gold and silver lodes of Great Barrier Island.

His report ran to eighty-one pages and included a comprehensive review of all previous work. Typically, he reacted with highly detailed rebuttals of previous work with which he disagreed. On a more positive note, he recognised that the alteration of the rocks and the gold-bearing quartz reefs and veins were of hydrothermal origin – the result of hot thermal waters permeating through the rocks. Once again, his acute observations and free-thinking had led him to an advanced conclusion.[30]

By the end of 1898, over 3000 rock samples from Coromandel were in the collections of the New Zealand Geological Survey. McKay selected 405 of these and sent them to Professor W.J. Sollas at Cambridge, in England. He accompanied many of them with full-page photomicrographs of outstanding quality. The result was the comprehensive, two-volume book *Rocks of the Cape Colville Peninsula, New Zealand*. It is a handsome publication for its time.[31]

Cheviot Earthquake

In November 1901, a swarm of earthquakes commenced in the Cheviot district in North Canterbury. During the nineteenth century, New Zealand

A photo taken down a microscope of a thin slice of rock, a 'pyroxene dacite' from Coromandel. The large striped (twinned) crystal is feldspar. To the naked eye it would have appeared about the size of a grain of sugar. The matrix of the rock consists of minute crystals and opaque glassy material.

experienced a number of strong earthquakes which, boosted by the eruption of Tarawera in 1886, had earned the country the not-undeserved reputation of being 'The Shaky Isles'; people had become a little apprehensive about earthquakes and volcanic eruptions.[32] The first shock at Cheviot was on 16 November. McKay left Wellington for Christchurch on the twentieth, with his son William as assistant. He noted there had been a slight shift of the spire of Christchurch Cathedral. He then took the train to the railhead at Amberley, and continued on by coach to the 'stricken Cheviot' (then commonly known as McKenzie).[33]

The damage in Cheviot was not overwhelming, although almost every chimney had been toppled, in many cases falling through the roof. This of course meant that the inhabitants were left with no means of heating or cooking, and many had pitched tents and harnessed buggies in case retreat was deemed necessary.[34] Aftershocks continued to be felt for about eighty days and did nothing for the equanimity of the residents. McKay describes one aftershock, on 2 December:

> I wrote … till about 1 a.m., and retired to bed at that time. I did not go to sleep for an hour …
>
> Shortly before 2 a.m. a sharp report was heard. This was much louder than the crack of a rifle and less than that of a cannon. It was of the nature of a double sound, and is best rendered in writing by the word '*rat-tat*'. I was

convinced that the report originated in the atmosphere not greatly but at some distance from the ground, and north of where I heard it, perhaps a quarter of a mile [400 metres]. A few minutes after hearing the report a series of gentle undulations of the ground began. The motion was a long swing, and if an earthquake can at all be a pleasing thing this was not unpleasant; and to tell the truth I enjoyed the rocking motion. There were three distinct movements in this the first shock. After a pause of a few seconds a second shock exactly like the first was experienced, and after a like interval a third that in no way differed from the other two. After this all seemed to be quiet, and I composed myself for some needed rest. Shortly before 4 a.m. I awoke, and though the wind had risen before I went to sleep it was now calm. I noticed the calm, but did not anticipate what was about to follow. At 3.59 am. there occurred what by many is considered the heaviest shock of earthquake that has been experienced since the 16th November. This was the shock of Monday, the 2nd December. I rose to note the time, and had just done so when a dull thud and a booming sound proceeded from the earth, as I judged at some distance to the north of where I was. This sound was quite different from that which preceded the earlier gentle shocks that occurred at 2 a.m., and which seemed to be in the atmosphere.[35]

It is unlikely that any of the local residents viewed the events of the night with the same dispassionate interest as McKay.

He also made some astute comments on the effects of earthquakes on humans and animals:

Violent earthquakes in all cases produce a sense of terror in both men and animals, and though in this connection there may be nothing new to tell, there are still some things that are worth being recorded. With respect to man, during the recent disturbances in the Cheviot and Amuri districts the first impulse was to flee the danger, and there was consequently an indiscriminate rush from houses into the open street or field. In many cases this could but barely be effected; many were thrown down, and, finding it difficult or impossible to get on their feet again, the will to make the attempt left them, and they remained in a semi-paralysed condition till the greater force of the shock was over. Many have expressed to me the opinion that they could not move, not so much on account of the agitation of the ground, but that they seemed to be spellbound.[36]

McKay concludes his report with an account of how Mr Sloss's horse came to die:

Mr Sloss at the time of the great shock was in the field, and rode the horse in question. Becoming aware that an earthquake of unusual violence had taken place, he returned to the house to ascertain what had taken place, and how it fared with the family. Arrived at the farm-steading, Mr. Sloss, on putting the horse in the stable, noticed that it trembled considerably, but of this he took little heed, more important concerns engaging his attention … in about an hour it [the horse] was attended to, when it was found bathed in a cold sweat, due to the continuation of violent shocks. The animal was turned out and put in a paddock ... the horse went no farther than a chain or two [40 m] into the paddock when it lay down and died instantly. It is surmised that had the horse been turned out at once, where it could have had the companionship of the other horses in the paddock, it would not have been so stricken with fear ...[37]

The report is again lacking in general details that allow McKay's day-to-day movements to be tracked.

There are however two additional forms of insight. These are the photographs he took, several of which include people, and a letter he wrote, presumably to his host at Glenkens, the homestead where he made his base:[38]

No 10 May Street, Wellington,

February 15th 1902.

Dear Sir. – You will possibly have expected to hear from me before this date. I did myself intend to write to you earlier but since my return I have had no end of writing and have otherwise been busy enough with reports photographic work etc. In any case I can count on it that you will excuse me since now at last I have taken pen in hand to tell you of my doings since last I saw you. On leaving Glenkens and Cheviot I went to Amberly and Leithfield where I staid [sic] a night at Mrs. Robert McAdams ... On xmas morning I reached Wellington and have been here ever since. My report is now in the hands of the Minister. It is rather a bulky affair extending to 150 of the page on which I write this [foolscap]. It will be illustrated by 18 photographic process prints. The frontispiece will be a view of Glenkens house taken from the crossing of the creek. [He goes on to detail many of the other photographs.] *On issue of the report you may expect a couple of copies at least and I think you will find them readable. The report proper occupies about one third of the whole. The rest is taken up by a reprint of the Glen Wye [sic] Report.*[39] *The report ... closes with a pathetic recital as to how Mr Sloss' horse came to die. In all I took 76 photographs and the greater part of them are very good.... Tell Maggie*[40] *that I make her a present of yourself surrounded by your dogs ...*[41] *I have printed 250 copies of these photographs and I shall probably have to print as many more before I can send out all that I have promised ... Tell Mary that at one time I meant to put her picture in the book but on reconsideration both her and the big stone has [sic] been left out. I made the enlargement however and will send it to her ... I hold in constant remembrance your kindness to us*[42] *when I was in the Cheviot District and I hope once more to pay you a visit ere all my years I shall know be past. Remember me to all inquiring friends and with well wishing I shall conclude this letter trusting that long years of prosperity are in store for you.*

I remain yours truly, Alex McKay[43]

McKay's wish to return one day was not to be granted. This was his last field trip.

Ill Health

The year 1902 did not start well for McKay. He felt tired and listless, and even the gentle gradient up Molesworth Street on his way from the office to his home in May Street would have become a major challenge for his heavy legs. On Friday 14 March he saw Dr C.D. Henry, MB. BC. Dr Henry's report was brief and to the point.

> I have this day seen and examined Mr McKay, Govt. Geologist, and [report] that I consider that he is not in a fit state at present to travel or to do any active work, owing to a degenerative condition of his Cardiac Muscles.[44]

The swiftness of the bureaucratic response was testimony to McKay's standing. The next day, 15 March, Mr Eliott, the Under-Secretary for Mines wrote:

> The Hon. Minister of Mines,
>
> Referring to the attached medical certificate I recommend that as Mr McKay will probably be unfit to again undertake field work, he should place on record in narrative form the geological knowledge he has accumulated during many years past. To enable this to be done a shorthand reporter should be engaged – probably one of the Hansard staff. I have already spoken to Mr McKay on the subject and he understands the proposal.

The following Wednesday (the nineteenth) the letter was endorsed by the Minister, James McGowan: 'Appoint Mr Berry as reporter to take the notes referred to.'[45]

There was a positive aspect to this curtailment of his field work. Although McKay would miss the delights and stimulation of new places, new rock outcrops, and new information to stimulate the tremendous store he had contained within him, his mind was still clear and active. Second only to the love of rocks and fossils was his love of writing, and now there would be ample time for that.

He wasted no time in getting started, and four months later Berry reported to the Under-Secretary: 'the work in connection with Mr McKay's book on "The Geology of New Zealand" is progressing steadily. Up to date 670 folios [probably double-sided foolscap] have been completed – ready for final consultation before printing.'[46] According to the annual reports of the Minister of Mines, the work went on for another two years and if the early enthusiasm was maintained it would have resulted in a manuscript of thousands of pages.

But on 31 May 1904 McKay wrote in his annual report 'I have been unable to prosecute geological examinations in the field, due to the continuance of the disability under which I labour.'[47] It was perhaps a hint that his desk-bound existence was beginning to pall. Of the manuscript of 'The Geology of New Zealand' by Alexander McKay there is now no trace, despite extensive enquiries by Alan Mason of the Historical Studies Group of the Geological Society of New Zealand.

McKay was adroit at republishing his major works in several versions. The year 1902 was to see the fourth and most comprehensive edition of one of the earliest of his landmark papers, 'The Older Auriferous Drifts of Central Otago', although no new fieldwork had been undertaken, and he was simply drawing on his notes and memory. Several other major reports from his career ran to several parts and at least two editions.

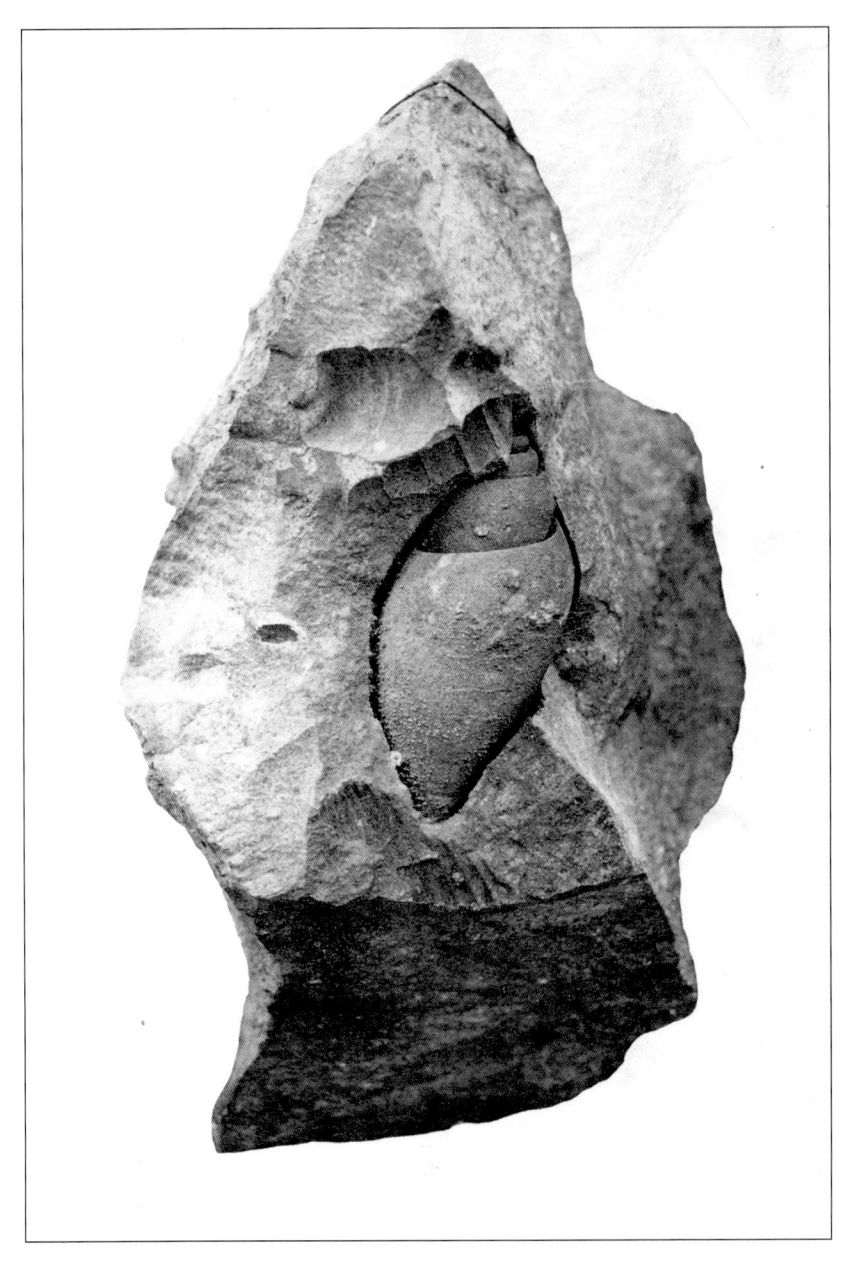

Several unlabelled photographs of fossils are present in the Buchanan Collection at the Institute of Geological and Nuclear Sciences, which appear to be examples of McKay's 'shadowless technique'. This may have involved holding the specimens in the fumes of ammonium chloride, *so that a thin white coating formed on the fossil. This sublimate reflected light evenly and reduced the contrast between light and shade. This fossil gastropod, still partly enclosed in the rock matrix in which it was found, is thought to be an example of the results he achieved.* Image from the Buchanan Collection, courtesy of New Zealand Institute of Geological and Nuclear Sciences

13. Winding Down

In 1904, McKay's son Duncan, his wife Henrietta and daughter Rosa returned to Wellington from Dannevirke, moving into 155 Tinakori Road, just around the corner from May Street. Perhaps motivated by their failing health, Alex and Susannah also moved, into 155A (which was possibly either a semi-detached dwelling or the house next door). Duncan and Henrietta appear to have taken on the role of providing domestic care for Alex and Susannah, with William helping Alex during the day.

In 1906, on 30 June, Susannah died at 155A Tinakori Road, at the age of seventy-one, thirty-nine years after she first arrived in New Zealand. She was buried in Karori Cemetery.[1] As mentioned earlier, almost nothing is known about Susannah – her build, her appearance, background, family, or education. She was in her early thirties when she landed in New Zealand, and had been in New Zealand for only about eighteen months before she married McKay.

Susannah too had an enterprising life. She was born in Chelmsford, Essex, England on 22 April 1835. Emigration, probably with her sister Mary, may have been a decision born of desperation, but it was to open for her a future the like of which was impossible in England at that time. On arriving at Port Chalmers, she was doubtless unaware of how far she was removing herself from the mainstream by going to Lake Ohau. And then along came one Alexander McKay, a young man going places, who needed a supportive wife. And she proved just that, through the tough times in Christchurch to their progressively more comfortable and secure existence in Wellington. Coping with the needs of two small children and the general demands of running a household during McKay's protracted absences required a resourceful woman. She had every reason to take pride in her husband's success, in the successes of their children, and in her own contribution to these.[2]

Still, Susannah remained a shadowy figure in the background. She is mentioned only once in surviving correspondence – when she was delivered of her second son, Duncan, a day after having arrived in Wellington. Her name scarcely survives even in administrative records. Other than her marriage registration and death certificate, she appears on such lists only with the birth of their first son, William, in 1869,[3] and, unexpectedly, on the 1899 electoral roll. Given the discrepancies on her marriage certificate and that her name has been entered by the Registrar in the signature panel on William's birth certificate, it is likely that she was illiterate.

Mortality was also in the air at the office. In the same year, the Minister enlisted the help of McKay and the new government analyst, J.S. Maclaurin, to find a replacement for McKay himself. There were fifty-seven applicants, from which they produced a short list of nine. McKay and Maclaurin were then asked to further consider the testimonials of three candidates: Skeats, Parkes, and Bell.[4] In a memorandum to the Under-Secretary of Mines dated 22 November 1904, the two reported that they thought that Skeats lacked the experience in rough field work that would be required in New Zealand. Of the other two they thought Parkes better suited if the emphasis was to be on structural[5] geology, whereas they thought Bell was more suited if the emphasis was to be on exploration and economic aspects.

James Macintosh Bell of Canada arrived in New Zealand early in 1905 to take up the position of 'Geologist to the Department of Mines of the Colony of New Zealand'.[6] Bell must have been a smooth talker, for within two months he had renegotiated his title to 'Director of the Geological Survey of New Zealand'. He had also negotiated funds to allow him to employ staff. A list of eight staff was released on 1 September 1906. Heading the list was 'Alexander McKay, Geologist and Palaeontologist'.[7]

McKay and Bell did not hit it off. Both were men of strong opinion, but McKay was sixty-five, in less than optimum health, and his wife was not long dead. At twenty-eight, Bell was in the prime of life, and younger than both of McKay's sons. The latter resolved the differences swiftly by having McKay transferred from Geological Survey to direct control of the Mines Department before the end of September. From then on, Bell completely ignored McKay in his annual reports. However, in a letter to the ministry, he objected that

> [McKay's] salary, the wages of his two men, and the cost of the material used by them at the museum have been charged to the Geological Survey vote. It is not altogether the paying of Mr. McKay and his men out of our vote to which I take exception, but I consider that no expenditure should be charged against the Geological Survey vote unless the vouchers are certified by myself or an officer authorised by me.[8]

There is no evidence that McKay harboured a grudge, but at the Christchurch International Exhibition, which opened a month later, there were two separate displays in the Minerals Court, one organised by Bell as Director of the Geological Survey, the other by McKay as Government

Geologist. McKay's Mines Department display was by far the larger of the two:

> The Government Geologist [McKay] has catalogued and packed eighty cases of rocks and mineral – He has selected specimens …. 817 hand-specimens of rocks and minerals from all parts of the colony; these will be shown in glass cases. The balance of the exhibits will consist of bulk-specimens in one or more pieces, which will be placed on stands in different parts of the Minerals Court.[9]

The Minerals Court was described in detail in a later issue of the *Mines Record*. In comparison, Bell's Geological Survey display received little more than a passing mention.[10] McKay would undoubtedly have gained further personal satisfaction that it was he, not Bell, who was on the panel to select the best essay on the 'Mineral Resources of New Zealand'.[11] Clearly McKay still had friends in the right places.

McKay's enthusiasm for 'The Geology of New Zealand' seems to have lapsed in about 1904, when he began the enormous task of sorting and cataloguing the fossils that had been collected, many of them by himself. He had the services of two assistants. One them was probably his son William. McKay himself regarded his collections of fossils as his most significant contribution to New Zealand geology. Although they belonged to the Geological Survey, in his annual reports Bell continued to ignore the very significant work that McKay and his two assistants were doing.

McKay did not overlook the application of new photographic techniques to his beloved fossils. He wrote of

> a style of photograph which has not previously been successfully accomplished. Hitherto the photographing of natural objects, such as rocks and fossils, has, in comparison with drawings, laboured under the disability of being accompanied by shadows that, seemingly unavoidable in connection with the photograph, are not necessarily a part of the drawing … I know not whether I should claim for my achievement the rank of a discovery, but it … enables the production of process-blocks equal to those from drawings, and at a much less cost.[12]

Just what his technique involved is not explained, but it may have involved coating the fossil with a sublimate of ammonium chloride so that strong contrasts were eliminated (see page 176).

The passion and determination which McKay had shown in his geological work is equally apparent in his photographic achievements. Some of his photographs are preserved in the holdings of the Alexander Turnbull Library, Wellington, and copies of many are also held at the Institute of Geological and Nuclear Sciences (formerly the New Zealand Geological Survey), at Gracefield. Many can be related to his reports;

replicating them with modern equipment would be a revealing exercise, not only of McKay's ability, but also of the environmental change since the photographs were taken in the late 1880s.

Retirement & Remarriage

On 30 June 1908, McKay wrote to the Secretary of the Government Superannuation Board with formal advice of his intention to retire from the Public Service from the thirtieth of September. And he did something that adds a new dimension to his image, as he paid the fare to New Zealand for Peter Shankland, the son of his elder sister Kate, who almost fifty years earlier had farewelled him at the Broomielaw in Glasgow. Peter arrived on the SS *Ruapehu* in 1909. McKay had hoped that he would take up farming, but instead Peter was drawn to photography and took at least one of the well-known pictures of his uncle.

The bureaucracy would not let McKay go completely. On 13 January 1909, the Under-Secretary of Mines wrote to the Minister recommending that 'he be retained as Consulting Geologist at a small salary, say £100 per annum.'[13] The Solicitor-General approved the deal and McKay's career inched onwards. But it was not for long. On 18 October he was advised that the arrangement would be terminated on 30 November 1909.[14] And so on that day, when he was sixty-eight, the prodigious career of Alexander McKay FGS came to an end.

In 1907 Alex had remarried, less than a year after Susannah died. The wedding of Alexander McKay, civil servant, and Adelaide Dootson, domestic duties, was held in St Peter's Church, Mersey Street, Island Bay, Wellington, on Monday 3 June 1907. Witnesses to the ceremony were John Dootson, brick-maker (father or brother), and Thomas J. Lark, bricklayer. The McKay family were conspicuously absent from the official party, inviting speculation that the union was being encouraged by the Dootsons, but did not have the approval of the second-generation McKays.

If Susannah was a shadowy figure, there is little more substance to Adelaide. She was born in Bolton, Lancashire, England, in 1861 and came to New Zealand in 1886 at the age of twenty-five. When she married McKay, she was forty-five.[15]

Who was Adelaide, and how did McKay come to meet her? With his heart condition and the immediate demands of his job he was unlikely to be involved in heavy socialising, and opportunities to meet single women would be few. In 1902, when McKay was diagnosed with a heart problem, he was sixty-one and Susannah was sixty-seven. This seems a likely period for Adelaide to have come into the picture, as a maid to do the general cooking, shopping, and cleaning. When Susannah died in 1906, Adelaide may already have been established as an indispensable part of the family support system. Susannah's death, however, created a social dilemma. A single woman could not cohabit with a widower in the social climate of the times, no matter how pressing his needs. Meanwhile, Alex, either with or without Adelaide, continued to live with Duncan and Henrietta, at 155/155A Tinakori Rd.[16]

McKay would have been fully taxed by his working life, despite its being office-based, and in fact in 1907 was contemplating retirement. He would have been quick to realise the advantages of marrying Adelaide, and the 'indecent' haste is evidence that he already knew and approved of her. However the absence of his family in the official wedding party suggests that the wedding may have been a private affair. This thesis is supported by the fact that in 1908 McKay was still recorded as living with Duncan and Henrietta, at 155 Tinakori Road, whereas Adelaide McKay (married) lived at number 275, in the same street, perhaps a kilometre away.[17]

All must have been resolved, for later in the year Alex and Adelaide were both recorded as residing at 275 Tinakori Road. Number 275 was immediately adjacent to the Shepherd's Arms Hotel. Alex and Adelaide may have found the proximity to the hotel disturbing, for the next year they had a new address in Ribble Street, Island Bay.

The marriage of Alex and Adelaide was probably pragmatic, but it seems to have worked quite well. Soon after they moved into 135 Upland Road, in Kelburn, they hosted the wedding of his nephew Peter to Christina McDougall Tait, inviting guests to their house, 'Drumness' (Drumness was the property adjacent to Braidenoch, where he spent his infancy). In 1912, Alex signed a letter of condolence 'A. and A. McKay'.

Adelaide was to make one particularly important contribution to the life of Alexander McKay, in much the same unsung way as her predecessor, Susannah. She established and maintained an environment in which McKay could write, not about geology, for he had gone from there, but about his life. She supported him while he wrote the first twenty-five years of his story, the 'Fragments' that early chapters of this book draw on. Without that, his early life, both in Scotland and New Zealand, would have remained a blank, and the factors which shaped the man would have been purely conjecture.

Consequent on their move to 'Drumness', there would have been an effect that Alex may not have fully anticipated, for suddenly he was isolated from his colleagues and his rock, fossil, and mineral collections. In October 1915 he grizzled to his nephew, 'A trip to town costs me two or three days for recovery, after which I must keep my chair and amuse myself writing.'[18] He amused himself well. Geology was not entirely forgotten and he wrote

Alexander and Adelaide moved into 135 Upland Road, Kelburn, Wellington, in 1910 or 1911. He named it 'Drumness', after a farm near his childhood home of Braidenoch. It was here he wrote his uncompleted autobiography, describing with his customary accuracy and detail places half a world, and a lifetime, away.

an impassioned plea to the Minister of Mines for better storage for the 130,000 specimens collected since 1862. The concluding paragraph reads:

> *New Zealand stands high in the estimation of the world for her appreciation of arts and sciences, and many of her sons in these walks of life have been distinguished. May it not be said that the Government of today are less enlightened in this respect than the rank and file of the people. Rather be it they are approved as leaders in this respect.*
>
> *Such is the prayer of your humble servant.*
>
> *Alex McKay*[19]

The appeal was fruitless.

Despite the effort involved in going to town, McKay would arrive at the Geological Survey office soon after the publication of a new report or bulletin in 'formality and style'.[20] Seated opposite the author, with his hands wrapped around his knob-head cane he would cross-examine the unfortunate author on the following lines:

'Did ye go up Waikiekie Creek?'

'No'

'Well if ye had, ye'd ha' seen the unconformity.'[21]

He had other interests, too. Amongst his papers there are notes for a cantata, 'The Jolly Beggars'.[22] A late interest in music, or family entertainment perhaps? He had commented previously to his nephew on the lack of musical ability in the McKay clan, but in his will he bequeathed his musical instruments to his wife, Adelaide.[23] The instruments may have been the new-fangled phonographs and gramophones, which were becoming popular then. He apparently also acquired a typewriter about this time.

McKay notes that his sister-in-law, Mrs Earle, was both a friend and a source of information.[24] In the same letter to Peter he mentions 'I take up too big subjects and fail in carrying them to a finish.'[25] He may well have been referring to two uncompleted manuscripts, one on the 'Antiquities of Kirkudbrightshire', and the other on 'Place-names in Galloway'.[26] Both seem to consist largely of information extracted from reference books. But the *magnum opus* of his retirement was his autobiography. He indicates he was writing it at the age of seventy-one, but how long he was engaged on it, or whether its premature end was brought about by his own failing health, is a matter for conjecture.

The End of the Road

On 8 July 1917 Alexander McKay, in a state of 'extreme exhaustion' as his body struggled to function, slipped into a coma from which there would be no awakening.

Tributes came quickly.[27] The *Evening Post* published a comprehensive obituary the next day, noting that 'as a geologist he had a reputation which extended far beyond the confines of New Zealand',[28] and both the *New Zealand Times* and the *Dominion* followed suit with their versions on Tuesday the tenth. The *Evening Post* followed with further articles of appreciation on the tenth and eleventh. And finally in 1919 the *Quarterly Journal of the Geological Society of London* published the obituary of one of its Fellows, Alexander McKay.

OBITUARY (*Evening Post*, Monday 9 July 1917)

MR ALEXANDER M'KAY

Mr Alexander M'Kay F.G.S., formerly geologist to the Mines Department passed away last night at his residence. Kelburn. The late Mr M'Kay was a prominent and picturesque figure in the public life of New Zealand for very many years, and as a geologist he had a reputation which extended far beyond the confines of New Zealand. He was born in Kirkcudbrightshire, Scotland, and came to New Zealand in 1863, landing at the Bluff from the ship 'Helenslee'. For some time he followed the occupation of a goldminer in Otago and Wakamarino, after which he went over to Australia and worked on the New South Wales and Queensland diggings. In 1866 he returned to New Zealand and for the next four years was engaged in exploring and prospecting the southwest part of the Mackenzie Country on the borders of Canterbury and Otago. There he conducted explorations alone and at all seasons of the year, and was known as "the wild man of the Mackenzie Country." Incidentally he claimed to be the first man who refrigerated meat in New Zealand, having in this manner preserved for long periods both mutton and game in the glaciers of the Southern Alps. In 1868 he became acquainted with Dr. (afterwards Sir Julius) von Haast who was then founding the Canterbury Museum, and contributed largely to its enrichment. In 1870 he was prospecting for coal at Ashley Gorge, Canterbury where he again met Dr. von Haast, who engaged him as his assistant in prosecuting some geological surveys he was carrying out for the New Zealand Government. After exploring the central mountain region of Canterbury and the Shag Point coal fields, the expedition returned to Christchurch and later Mr M'Kay explored and made large collections from the saurian (reptile) beds in the middle Waipara district, North Canterbury. In 1872 he explored and excavated the "Moa Bone Cave," near Sumner, Canterbury. At the end of the year the late Dr. (afterwards Sir James) Hector was in Christchurch and noting the additions to the Museum of the fossil saurians from Waipara he engaged Mr M'Kay to make a collection, at Amuri Bluff, of similar remains for the Geological Survey. This work he finished in March 1873 and brought back to Wellington a very large collection of rare and valuable fossils that are now one of the most interesting features of the Dominion Museum. Also in the end of 1873 he made a geological survey of the southern part of Otago, of many of the West Coast goldfields, beside accompanying Dr Hector to the East Coast of Auckland Province, and examining the country from Gisborne to the mouth of the Waipao River. Then he was appointed a permanent officer of the geological department and published full details of the results of surveys of many districts. In 1892 he was appointed Mining Geologist, which position he held up to his retirement some years ago. The late Mr M'Kay was a fellow of the Royal Geographical Society and of several other learned societies. He contributed many valuable papers to the Transactions of the New Zealand Institute. The late Mr M'Kay was a keen student of photography, and to him science is indebted for the invention of the telephoto lens, which is considered to be one of the most important discoveries made in connection with photography.

Mr M'Kay, who was 76 years of age, leaves a widow and two sons, – Mr Duncan M'Kay, F.N.Z.A.A., Wellington, and Mr William M'Kay, of the Dominion Museum staff. He was twice married.

McKay was cremated, a procedure unusual for the period, and his ashes added to the grave of Susannah. At the same time, a rough marble headstone was erected. The inscription reads:

Sacred

to the Memory of

SUSANNAH M[C]KAY

BORN APRIL 22ND, 1835 DIED MAY 14TH 1906

AND ALEXANDER M[C]KAY, F.G.S.

LATE GOVERNMENT GEOLOGIST

BORN APRIL 11TH 1841 DIED JULY 8TH 1917

Last Will and Testament

McKay signed his will on 13 October 1916, nine months before he died. It is a thoughtful document and brings a little extra enlightenment about his last few years, and his relationships, possessions, values, and priorities. To Adelaide he left not only his musical instruments, but also pictures, china, household goods, furniture, personal effects and the photographs of her choice. He also specified that she was to have an income for life from the trusts he had established, and was to be able to stay on at 'Drumness' on Upland Road for six months free of any charge or payment whatsoever.[29]

McKay as he appeared in the Cyclopaedia of New Zealand. *He was fifty-six when it was published in 1897, but the photo may have been taken some years earlier. In the* Cyclopaedia *he described himself as 'the inventor of the telephoto lens, and [with tongue in cheek] of the frozen meat industry.'* Image courtesy of the NZ Institute of Geological and Nuclear Sciences

William, the elder son, inherited this house and all of McKay's photographic apparatus and negatives. His younger son Duncan, already a successful Wellington accountant, had his debt to McKay of £13,210 (equivalent to about $200,000) wiped, and he also inherited his father's microscope and other non-photographic optical instruments.

14. The Legend & The Real McKay

His Achievements

The achievements of Alexander McKay were astonishing. He arrived in New Zealand at the age of twenty-two with barely two full years of formal schooling. He spent the next ten years leading a hand-to-mouth existence until he got the break he needed. From that moment on, there was no stopping him. In a few years he became proficient with rocks of all types and ages, and with all facets of geology in general. He brought to his new career an enormous energy and enthusiasm. Within ten years he carried out investigations over the length and breadth of the country, a coverage he was to repeat in both the next two decades. The travel required alone – by coastal steamer, railway, coach, horse, and ultimately on foot – must have been demanding, in an age when the speed and convenience of cars and flying machines was still unimaginable. The luxury of going back for another look was not taken lightly. And then McKay described what he had seen or deduced in some 200 published reports, which are still valued reference documents. As a sideline, he mastered sufficient optical physics to overcome the problems of developing a telephoto lens, taking photomicrographs, and of pioneering other photographic developments.

McKay himself regarded his fossil collections, which numbered close to 100,000, as his greatest contribution to New Zealand geology, and certainly they were of incalculable value in resolving the complexities of local geology and establishing the framework we know today. His documentation of horizontal movement during the Glynn Wye earthquake of 1888 (page 149), graphically illustrated by his photograph of an offset fence, won him a place in geological history.

It was McKay's ideas on the nature and timing of mountain-building in Marlborough, however, that had the most significant effect on the development of earth science in New Zealand. It laid a cornerstone of advanced thinking that was to be brilliantly exploited by the next generation of geologists, such as Charles Cotton and Harold Wellman. Their students in turn took the concepts still further and demonstrated their validity. The new discipline of neo-tectonics – the nature, rate, and scale of dynamic earth processes operating today – was born, firmly rooted in the observations and theories of Alexander McKay. The significance of his legacy is outstanding; he was the key figure in providing the basis for the eminent reputation that New Zealand geological science enjoys today.

McKay's contribution to photography was almost as astounding, given that it was not his primary activity, although he was undoubtedly drawn to it by the advantage of illustrating his work. It is, however, a further example of how his mind was always probing and exploring, and of his determination to track down the best solution. In noting his success in this field, it should be remembered that although geologists then were few, photographers were many.

His success came about through a robustness, a physical and mental determination to explore the significance of what he saw. And when he had done that, he wrote it down. His parents, his Granny, Auld Duncan, Susannah, Haast, Hector were major influences in his life. Together with his own experiences, they created 'The Real McKay'.

The Legend

The Real McKay became a legend in his time, and the legend expanded after he was dead. Self-taught, resourceful, tough, gruff, determined, cultured, hard-drinking, audacious, boisterous and argumentative – undoubtedly all of these descriptions were sometimes true.

Self-taught McKay surely was, but he still owed much to his early mentors, Haast and Hector. Doggedness, determination, diligence, and resourcefulness were consistent attributes, too. Audacious, irreverent, opinionated, exuberant, argumentative, and whisky-drinking – he was all of those, but not all of the time.

Legends about McKay focus on the famous 'An onion is required' report[1] and tales of his whisky consumption: whisky and porridge as sustenance in the field, the recycling of whisky containers as crates for the fossils he collected, and bottle ends ground into camera lenses. McKay certainly drank whisky but how much and how often is a matter of conjecture. One story has it that he drank half a bottle a night, mostly after he had written his report, but sometimes before. There is no evidence to support this supposition, except possibly the 'Onion' report. Similarly, the legendary image of McKay trudging off into the wilderness, leading a packhorse with a bag of oatmeal on one side and a crate of whisky on the other and returning with the crate of fossils might be overly imaginative. For example, after three months' collecting at Kaikoura, he returned to Wellington with not one, but 130 crates full of fossils. Before the mind boggles, he also noted that he used his carpentry skills to make up extra crates on wet days.

Suspicions about his whisky consumption are further fuelled by the report that J.A. Thomson began his career at the Geological Survey by organising the 700 whisky crates that then housed the collections. Kerosene crates replaced whisky crates about 1900, so the whisky crate collections must have been largely the work of Alexander McKay. He spent about 3500 days in the field. Even at half a bottle per day, his total consumption over thirty years would have produced only about 146 crates, well short of the 700 acquired by the Survey.

Further information derives from the visit of the Swiss geologist, Professor A. Heim, to New Zealand in 1901. In addition to making some superlative sketches of the scenery, Heim noted the red whisky noses of the elderly inhabitants. In 1914 his student, C.T. Trechmann, also visited New Zealand. Trechmann had heard that McKay, when in the bush, sustained himself on porridge and whisky. Remembering his professor's dictum, he observed McKay's nose carefully when he met him. Although McKay at seventy-three was indeed elderly, Trechmann noted that he certainly did not carry the red nose banner.[2] A more prosaic explanation of the crates may be that McKay, and others, called on local publicans for a supply of sturdy crates as required.

The Real McKay

Legends are based on moments, and between the moments was a man. So – who was the real Alexander McKay?

His written output provides some clues. His bibliography (Appendix 4) lists 201 publications totalling about 3000 printed pages. His first paper appeared in 1874 and his last in 1906, giving an average of just over six reports per year. His annual output fluctuated considerably, however, from a low of nil in 1880 and 1885 to a peak of eighteen in 1892.

An assessment of this outpouring is not easy. The bibliography includes brief abstracts, letters, reports duplicated by reprinting in other journals, and second editions, particularly after the end of the *Reports of Geological Exploration* series in 1894. The subsequent combination of different journals, formats, fonts, and page sizes makes converting all the raw data to equivalent 'pages published per year' unworkable, and creates problems with reference numbers, and in physically locating some material. The differences between the date written and date published add to the difficulties. Although McKay started with NZ Geological Survey in 1873 when he was thirty-two, the resulting publications did not appear until four years later. This lag before publication subsequently shortened to one or two years, but remains a factor to consider. Nevertheless some interesting aspects emerge.

His output appears to fluctuate in a cyclic manner, with high and low productivity peaks being repeated approximately every five years. A two-year running mean has also been plotted, as this results in the abnormally high or low results being 'shared' with an adjacent year. Although the peaks and troughs are reduced, and some of the vagaries resulting from irregular publication delays and other factors are smoothed, the pattern persists, suggesting regular surges of creativity or mental energy, or mood swings. Alternatively it is conceivable that McKay periodically simply ran himself into the ground. There is no obvious correlation between quantity and quality. The quality of his reports, after his initial burst of exuberance, quickly settled to an average score of around 8/10, and by 1879 it was more common for exceptions to be above rather than below the mean. Items such as abstracts and poems have not been marked, but difficulties are created if they are omitted, so they are allocated the mean as a default value. Only a small number are involved.

Unfortunately, there is insufficient information to explore fully a possible relationship between life events and these fluctuations. McKay's election as a Fellow of the Geological Society of London in 1888, an event as significant to him as a university graduation, occurs at a productive peak, but the presentation of his telephoto research in 1890 occurs at a time of no special note. Satisfaction and achievement are often anticlimactic, however, and simple answers in the life of a complex person who remains a very private individual may be wishful thinking.

Perhaps more telling is the correspondence of the production of his three poems in 1880 with a year when he produced no technical reports. Poetry is an expression of emotion and as such requires a different mindset from technical description, and can be a more revealing record of the inner man, at least at the time it is written.

The first poem, the unpublished '[Long in the strife for worldly means]', expresses an exuberant sense that life, at last, is well. The second describes a wondrous awe of nature, and the third is a score to settle. The latter two were both written when at Lake Harris (page 137). Each in turn reflects an element of McKay's psyche. Of his natural exuberance for life, there is no doubt. Although his affinity for the natural world is shared by many geologists, it is unrecorded by most, but McKay recorded it in poetry, prose, and on film. The last poem reflects his sensitivity, his awareness of his humble background, the depth of the wounds caused by von Haast, the satisfaction of his long-delayed success, and the importance to him of his ultimate qualification, his FGS.

The first recorded comments on McKay's personal attributes of doggedness and determination were by von Haast, who in 1872 described

14. THE LEGEND AND THE REAL MCKAY 191

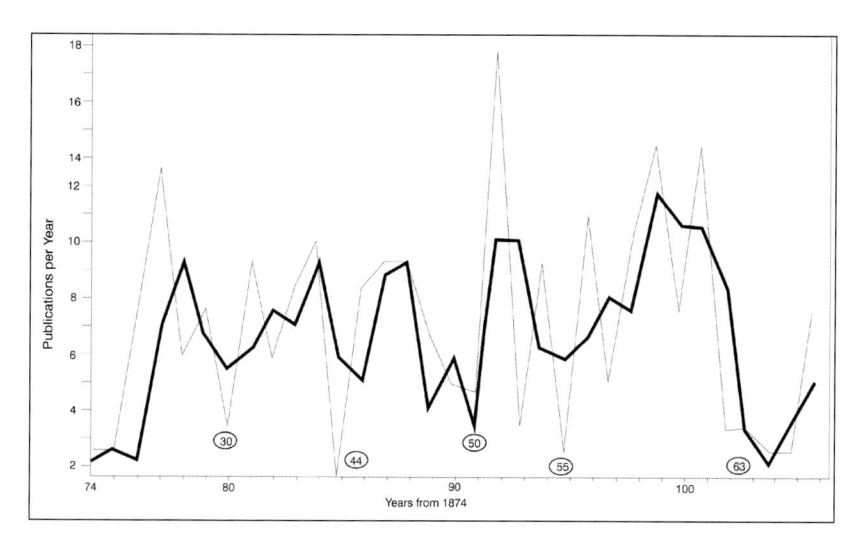

McKay's bibliography expressed in terms of publications per year. Although he began with NZ Geological Survey in 1873, when he was thirty-two, his first major reports did not appear until 1877. After that the delay between writing and publishing was normally one or two years. The running mean of every two years (heavy line) eliminates such vagaries and reduces the magnitude of isolated peaks and troughs while preserving the pattern of a productive peak every five or six years.

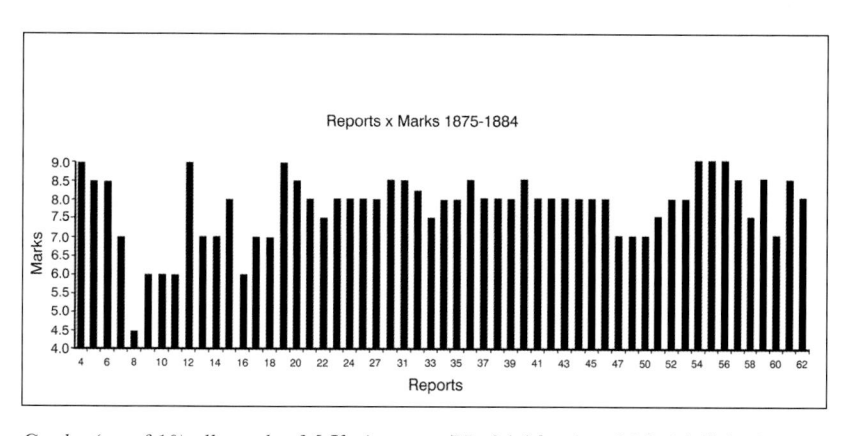

Grades (out of 10) allocated to McKay's reports 75–84 (above) and 85–94 (below).

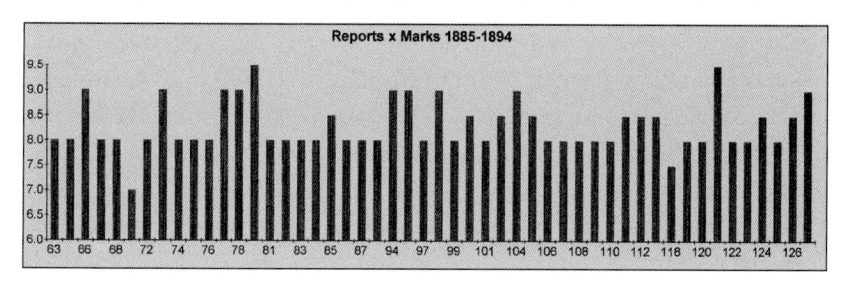

him as an 'efficient, and zealous, collector.' An early appreciation, from his colleague and friend, the Government Analyst William Skey, came in an unusual form. Skey wrote a mock elegy for him which was published in 1889, when McKay was a hale and hearty forty-eight-year-old.[3] Skey clearly knew McKay well and was familiar with much of his past, including his Scottish past. He wrote, 'Pleased with a roughness as great as his own/ How he longed to explore its recesses so lone;/ The shore barely touched, he hurries his feet/ Where the blue of the mountain with sunny skies meet.'

However, Begg and Begg[4] report McKay as 'taciturn, almost to the point of rudeness on occasions.' Unfortunately the source of this comment was not stated. A.P. Harper, a West Coaster and experienced bushman and mountaineer, provides an illustration in his Foreword to John Pascoe's book, *Mr Explorer Douglas*.[5] Harper had been holed up in the hotel on the east bank of the Otira River by bad weather and a flooded river. When the rain slackened off, he announced he was going to try to find a ford. An oldish man[6] reading a book said, 'Cheap bar-room talk.' On being told it was Mr Alexander McKay, the geologist, Harper went over and asked McKay if he was referring to him. McKay answered, 'Yes, cheap bar-room talk, find a ford!' Harper responded by informing McKay that he had been Charlie Douglas's mate (on Douglas's exploring trips in the mountains) for two years.[7] McKay stood and held out his hand: 'Sir, I apologize.'

McKay's colleagues later provided more enlightenment. James Park,

*This echinoderm (sea-urchin) lived between 27 and 25 million years ago. It was collected by McKay in the Waimate district in 1880 and later described formally by H. Barraclough Fell in 1954 (*NZ Geological Survey Palaeontological Bulletin 23, *p. 30) and named after McKay.*

Alexander McKay Falls. McKay's name is perpetuated by a waterfall, 115 metres high, in Sixteen Mile Creek, a tributary of the Shotover River. It was named by R.W. (Dick) Willett in 1938, who later became a Director of NZ Geological Survey. Photo: R.F. Entwistle

who was twenty years younger than McKay, and worked with him in Nelson and northwest Otago, regarded him very highly indeed:

> Next to Hector, McKay stands by himself as the greatest exponent of New Zealand geology. Contrary to the belief held by many of the younger generation, he was a man of high culture and wide reading ... His mind moved in two compartments – one devoted to the cold facts of science, the other crowded with images of the past and tales of adventure. Scott and Burns he could recite with effortless fluency and dramatic effect. For the rest, Ossian appealed to his Celtic strain, and he often turned to Southey's version of Amadis of Gaul,[8] a hero whose adventures and impossible triumphs gave him an unholy delight.[9]

Park also recalled McKay often carried a copy of Lyell's *Principles of Geology* in his pack and would read from it 'to his companions at night ...: "the drone of his soft monotonous voice soon lulled me to sleep ... often he chided me with sleeping instead of listening to the words of the great master."'[10]

J.A. Thomson, who joined Geological Survey two years after McKay's retirement, rated him even more highly in a glowing 'appreciation' published in the *Evening Post* two days after McKay's death:

> Hochstetter, Haast, Hector, and Hutton – the four H's have long been names to conjure with in New Zealand geology, but in the last few years the mana of Alexander McKay has increased that he is now regarded as the greatest of them all. His death removes from our midst one of the greatest original thinkers that New Zealand in her brief career has ever seen. [H]e was surrounded by a

small band of appreciative friends, and lived to see at least a partial recognition of his services to New Zealand geology. He had just enough vanity to make it a delight to yield him appreciation.[11]

McKay's professional personality was summarised by Peggy Burton: 'Perhaps the key to the extraordinary achievements of this self-educated explorer, made beyond his exceptional field surveys and into the academic theorising of the day, lay in his zest for the curious. Enthusiasm, a prodigious physical and mental health, acute observation … [an] almost naive joy in field experience …'[12]

McKay had no illusions about the validity of his conclusions about mountain-building processes, but he seems to be admitting disappointment when he wrote in his last major report: 'Although these facts were stated by me in 1885 and again in 1889, the theories which they supported … have found but little favour … the facts themselves, if they be accepted, are so with something like distrust … This is a matter of little consequence to me; the loss is not mine, and the triumph of truth is certain.'[13]

There are, however, other notable characteristics of McKay. First was the accuracy of his recording. In areas where controversy later developed, generally because attempts to relocate his fossil localities were unsuccessful, it usually transpired that McKay had been right.[14]

Second was his uncompromising integrity, a major factor in the row with Haast. And finally it seems he was a sensitive man. His interest in poetry is an indication of his delicate awareness of the beauties and ironies of life around him, and his gruffness may have been a cover for shyness. He became a respected figure, but he remembered well his humble origins.

Appendix 1
In Memoriam

McKay's name is perpetuated by a waterfall, 115 m high in Sixteen Mile Creek (page 193), a tributary of the Shotover River. It was named the Alexander McKay Falls by R.W. (Dick) Willett in 1938, who was later a director of NZ Geological Survey.

And by

the Alexander McKay Cliffs – a feature about 30 km long forming the north wall of the Geologists Range in Antarctica. It was named by the 1961–62 New Zealand Northern Antarctic field party.

And less durably by

the McKay Building of the Institute of Geological and Nuclear Science complex at Gracefield, Lower Hutt, and the McKay Geology Museum at Victoria University, Wellington, and the McKay Hammer Award of the Geological Society of New Zealand (Appendix 3).

And finally by

the McKay Club, a social group formed in 1965 to promote closer contact between the geological fraternity, and their spouses and associates. The patron, elected unanimously, was Alexander McKay, and many toasts were drunk in his name.

Unfortunately the club, like its parent body, the New Zealand Geological Survey, did not survive the frenetic restructuring of New Zealand science that marked the end of the last millennium. The name of Alexander McKay, however, will not be forgotten.

I give you a toast: *'To the memory of A Remarkable Man'.*

Appendix 2
McKay Hammer Award
Geological Society of New Zealand (Inc.)

1. To commemorate the outstanding ability and contributions to New Zealand geology of Alexander McKay, and to recognise meritorious contemporary work, the Society shall make an annual award to be known as the McKay Hammer Award.

2. A geological hammer formerly owned by Alexander McKay, and from which the award is named, shall be deposited by the Society with the New Zealand Geological Survey for safe keeping and display.

3. The award shall be made to the author or authors of the most meritorious New Zealand contribution to geology published in the previous 3 calender years. For the purposes of the award, 'a New Zealand contribution' is any contribution by a New Zealand-based author. The award shall be for one or more publications that have not already formed the basis for the award.

4. Each award shall consist of a certificate and a good quality geological hammer suitably inscribed, which shall remain the property of the winner.

5. No award shall be made if in the Committee's opinion no suitable contribution has been published.

6. The award shall if possible be presented or announced at the Annual General Meeting of the Society.

Recipients of the McKay Hammer Award

1956	G.R. Stevens
1957	C.A. Fleming
1958	M. Gage
1959	H.W. Wellman
1960	D.S. Coombs
1961	N.De B. Hornibrook
1962	B.M. Gunn & G. Warren
1963	B.L. Wood
1964	J.B. Waterhouse
1965	A. Ewart
1966	No award
1967	J.P. Kennett
1968	R. Stoneley
1969	G.H. Scott
1970	T. Hatherton

1971	D.G. Jenkins
1972	D.G. Bishop
1973–74	No award
1975	P.B. Andrews
1976	G.J. Williams
1977	I.G. Speden
1978	B.W. Hayward
1979	S. Nathan
1980	R.A. Cooper
1981	V.E. Neall
1982	G.P.L. Walker
1983	M.R. Johnston
1984	J.R. Pettinga
1985	M. McGlone
1986	C. Wilson
1987	No award
1988	I.M. Turnbull
1989	C.A. Landis & M.C. Blake
1990	C. Nelson
1991	J. Bradshaw & W. Giggenbach
1992	P.A. Maxwell
1993	B. Pillans
1994	N. Mortimer
1995	I. Wright
1996	P. Koons
1997	J.S. Crampton
1998	L. Carter
1999	P. Barnes
2000	C. Adams
2001	R.P. Suggate
2002	P. Kamp
2003	T. Little

Appendix 3
Epic Poems by Alexander McKay

My Lassie and I

I gaed at night to see a lass,
    I'll no say where nor when,
Ance by itsel haith this time was
    An' werdy o' a song.

I gaed for to fulfil a tryst,
    And kiss my lassie dear,
I was resolved and had devised
    That night of her to speir.

If e'er the thought did cross her heart
    That yet the time wad come
When we would wed and never part
    But ever be as one.

To tell her that of a' on earth
    I nothing prised mair dear
And that I deem'd her doubly worth
    A world of goud or gear.

And that while I could think a thought
    That thought wad be on her,
That love for her wad if for ought
    My heart for ever stir.

All this I had resolved to say,
    And might say muckle mair.
For wha kens what a man will da'
    When love has got him sair.

And thus inspired I took the gaet,
    A road I ken'd fu' weil
And there was nought wad turn'd me back
    E'en had I met the deil.

High with anticipation
    My heart within me throbb'd
I hugged my expectation
    Nor dream'd of being robb'd.

Tho' Januar's beat i' my face
    A trow I never felt it,
Tho' driven snaw wreath'd mony a place
    Like madness on I skelp it.

At length I reached my journeys end,
    An' Oh, how I was dumpit,
She wasna there, the clock struck ten,
    I maist deleerit jumpit.

Cauld wae the night but roun my heart
    Baith fire an' ice was heapit,
How happened it that in that hour
    I still my reason keepit?

Yet knowing I had kept my troth,
    Where was with me the blame,
"Ah," said I "this is one of them
    And they are all the same."

And sulkily my shepherd's plaid,
    I closer roun' me drew,
I gazed upon the heavens wide
    And back a glance I threw.

On the cauld grun' I thought to look
    And w' a heart grown cauld,
What reek'd I what was in the book
    Or what might Fate unfauld.

But raptures to behold I saw
    What more than worlds I prise
And smiling with a faint "ha ha"
    Straight to mine arms she flies.

I clasped her with a fond embrace,
    Each rankling thought was gane,
I gazed upon her peerless face,
    And said I'd be her ain.

But ay she said some ither ain
    For her must bar the gate.
Since I was ready off to rin,
    And her no, hardly late.

I vowed and swore by a'bove,
    I her alone did love
With that supreme affection
    Whose source is from above.

(And tho' I never do despise,
    Ae Mortal by anither,
In me for her love stronger lies
    Than d'ist for any ither.)

And sae I took her in my arms
    And was ye like to ken
How fond we were. Away alarms
    I'm the most bless't of men.

And she was fond and unco fond
    And desperate fond o' me
But she was shivering wi' the cauld
    A waefu' sight to see.

She brought me to a bonny bield,
    Beside the kitchen fire,
And this she beets wi' fourth of peats
    Until the flame grew higher.

Stript o' my boots my chilly feet
    Were at the fire warming,
I thought of nought or she of aught
    Save it might be of wiving.

In an exuberance of bliss
    All prudence disregarding,
I sought and struggled for a kiss
    Nor heeded I the warning,

That from the ben part of the house,
    We might expect invasion,
And now, for to indulge our fears
    There plainly was occasion.

What should we do? What could I do?
    Auld John, and we two thus!
The meal ark lid it open flew,
    And I, Oh, Mercy on us!

This all too soon and all alone
    She faced what was to be,
And satisfied auld limpin' John
    That there were none but she.

Nor found he aught in plain disproof,
    Of what he had been told,
Then he suggested she might be
    A-bed and from the cauld.

He went: It pleased me well, for I
    Breathed a thick atmosphere,
Of suffocating ait-meal dust,
    And death seemed very near.

I was got out and dusted well
    So soundly that Sir John
Was rousted out to come and see
    What might be going on.

Post haste I got me to the door
    Minus my boots tis true,
Which in a very searching search
    Were found, and then John knew!

Alas for me I reached my hame
    And was all day in bed
Of some disorder; but it was
    A-want of boots instead.

GLOSSARY ain=own, baith=both, beets w'forth=repaired with plenty, biggin=house, bield=place of shelter, deleerit jumpit=madly jumped, dumpit=disappointed, gairie=crag, goud=gold, gaet=road or way, rankling=painful, reek'd=smoked, rin=run, ben=inner or through, ark=storage chest, ait-meal=oatmeal, sair=sore, skelpt=move quickly, speir= speak or ask, trow=belief, werdy=worthy.

LINES WRITTEN ON A SCENE FROM LAKE HARRIS SADDLE
WEST COAST, MIDDLE ISLAND
BY
ALEX.MCKAY,
WELLINGTON:
PRINTED BY JAMES HUGHES, LAMBTON QUAY

1880

No composition of whatever kind should of itself require to be helped by an explanation. I am, however, just a little anxious about my first-born in Poesy, and fearing that it may not be quite clear to one who is not acquainted with the district to which it refers, I may be excused for giving the following explanation:

The Lake Harris Saddle, situate on the main water-shed between the Lake Wakatipu district and the Hollyford Valley, leading to Martin's Bay, is supposed to be the stand-point of the observer. We are here in the midst of one of the wildest and yet most beautiful districts in New Zealand, and moreover, the traveller cannot be here without some personal risk to himself. This is, however, forgotten in the sublime grandeur of the scenery which lies before him to the westward. From the top of the range he can hear the roar of the Hollyford (3500ft. below the level at which he stands), yet the Valley is so narrow that one might imagine a good rifle would send a bullet across it to the opposite mountains. These are the great features of the picture before us.

The Darren Mountains rise to an elevation little short, in some cases of 9000ft. above the sea. They are so thickly laden with perpetual snow and ice that they fairly the merit the name given them – *Darren* signifying white. Their slopes are so precipitous that glaciers of the first order cannot be formed, and the excess of snow is precipitated as avalanches from cliffy heights, which in many cases, are not short of 2000ft.; yet little of this ever reaches the lower slopes of the range, which are clothed with a luxuriant forest vegetation. To give an idea of the great disturbances which often take place among these mountains, I may say without any danger of being guilty of exaggeration, that while camped at Lake Harris, no fewer than 200 avalanches fell, there being during two particular days nothing but one continued roar, with the ground even at our distant stand-point, shaking as during the occurrence of a violent earthquake. Then with reference to the storm scene, I only wish it were a fable, or that I had not been there. The poem is feeble compared with the reality; but to have done this part justice, had defied a far abler pen than mine.

I may also say, that although complete in itself, the Poem has a sequel[*] which describes the personal adventures and trials of the two occupants of the "tent" mentioned in the second line of the first verse.

Alex. McKay

[*] Although McKay had undoubtedly hired a field assistant, probably a local man, it is likely that his reference to the second occupant of the tent refers to the 'spiritual' presence of von Haast, whose adventures with his recalcitrant steed are described in *The Canterbury Gilpin*.

Lines on the scene from Lake Harris Saddle
West Coast, Middle Island

Far in yon western wilderness
    A tent's white canvas shows,
Where, dungeon-like, Lake Harris lies
    Fed by exhaustless snows.

Whence, westward by a mighty plunge,
    We down and down descend
A trackless wild, all densely bushed,
    Till in the vale we stand.

Here the broad river rolls along
    Till lost in yonder lake
Whose fair expenses an honoured name
    Does from McKerrow take.

While source-ward, see, it foaming comes,
    From gloomy depths profound;
Leaping in white from yon cascade,
    Or 'twixt high walls confined.

Here, tribute-streams on either hand,
    Come rushing down the steep;
Now seen, now lost, but ever on
    Their headlong course they keep.

The Darren Mountains back the view;
    And to the left and right,
No hoary heads are there, but all
    Are clothed in dazzling white.

Christina here, a matron stands,
    And by acclaim is queen,
While yonder peak, with less expanse,
    For beauty is supreme.

There, robed in green, her skirts display
    A wealth of Nature's store;
Here, the strong birch and graceful pine
    Her lower slopes embower.

At greater height, with richer hue,
    All wild and tangled there;
Magnificence enwraps her slopes
    With many a shrub that's rare.

While, higher, flowers her mantle fringe,
    In rich profusion gay;
Till, losing these, her bust is seen
    Where streams of water play.

From ledge, or rock, in crystal sheets,
    Rolled back in clouds of spray,
These ever come, and still return,
    Throughout the longest day.

Yet higher; fields of dazzling white,
    In sculptured masses grand,
Still give, yet never waste away,
    But through long ages stand.

A lofty brow of purest white
    Yet more than these excels,
And over all a gorgeous crown
    Of icy pinnacles.

Fair over all, when shines the sun,
    Just parting with the day,
Spreads rosy hues of loveliest tint,
    That melt to softest grey.

Placid they smile when round them are
    The elements suppressed,
Here seems to be a paradise
    When Nature is at rest.

But, ah! when nursed on those fair breasts
    The wrathful storm comes down;
Woe to the traveller if his face
    Is clouded by its frown.

When mindful of the general good
    Of every form she wears,
Nature assumes her sterner mood,
    'Tis death to some she bears.

Now thick, a fog is spreading 'oer
    The lower regions fast,
While billowy clouds are onward rolled
    From yonder rugged crest.

Instinctive living Nature's mute,
    Whil'st on the loaded air
Anticipation hurries on
    The rupture to declare

At last, nursed in some mountain gorge,
    Sweeps past the whistling blast,
And now in all their fury come
    The elements at last.

The raging storm its fury wrecks
    Around those clouds clad hills,
Or worketh havoc in the bush,
    Or through the valley swells.

High overhead the waters leap
    In turbid torrents strong,
Where late a puny silver thread
    Wound gently along.

The river surges far beneath,
    And on its swollen tide
Is borne the wreck which many a creek
    Hath gathered far and wide.

Nor yet the tumult is complete,
    For, hark! yon crash and roar
Hath told us whence an avalanche
    Right to the valley bore.

Hark! yet another, and again
    The parent snowfield shakes,
And far and wide a stony wreck
    A desolation makes.

The flowers that on the mountain's side
    Sat smiling in the sun,
Bend to the blast with drooping head,
    Or quite are beaten down.

The winged life that 'oer yon heights
    So joyously careered
Have, some for ever, but all have
    At present, disappeared.

The Kea's on the mountain top,
    The Kaka's in the wood,
The Kakapo's discordant note,
    Not one of them are heard.

The Weka only, still at times,
    Maintains her evening call;
The Robin's silent, ah! his was
    The sweetest note of all.

The lesser life, beneath a leaf
　　Or stone, hath stowed away,
And still the storm but fiercer grows
　　As fades declining day.

Selected verses from *The Canterbury Gilpin* are quoted below, with apologies to McKay, who would have been furious at the excision of 309 stanzas from his epic! It was written by Alexander McKay at a camp near Lake Harris, 1879. John Gilpin was a real-life character whose exploits became legendary and featured in a well-known ballad (1872) by William Cowper, entitled *The Diverting History of John Gilpin*. The poem tells how Gilpin and his wife and children became separated during a journey to the Bell Inn, after Gilpin loses control of his horse.

　　COME, I have matter for your ear,
　　　　I have a tale to tell,
　　A song to sing, a race to ride,
　　　　And would acquit me well.

Speak of my effort what you may,
　　But read it all the same, –
Read it, 'tis written to be read,
　　Laughed at, and read again.

So much for my intent.
　　I know that I shall not escape
The charge of being personal,
　　And writing this in hate.

Yet there may be who do insist
　　They see their portrait drawn;
And, in reply, I'm bound to say,
　　"Thou art the very man."

This race began in Christchurch town,
　　The reader will not doubt;
Though where it ended has not been
　　So easy to make out.

Where Browning's Pass 'mid snow divides
　　An Alp on either hand,
The royal brood from which he sprang
　　Roamed free o'er all the land.

From hence, the wonder of the age
　　Was straight conveyed to town,
A princely Moa in the flesh,
　　A bird of great renown.

Proudly, not sixteen hands but feet,
    His head rose in the air;
His limbs were lithe, yet wondrous strength
    Was plainly seated there.

His levelled back and arching neck
    Shewed grace in every line;
His head was beauty in itself,
    His eye a diamond mine.

No gaudy plumage needed he
    To drape his majesty;
So nature, ever true to taste,
    Clothed him in sober gray.

Delighted since, at last, he had,
    A living moa found;
Sudden a thought possessed the Sage,
    That he would ride it round,

And Christchurch had a holiday
    To witness the event;
From all the bells, o'er all the town,
    Sonorous joy was sent.

The heroes of the Sumner Cave
    Were foremost in the throng;
They bore the brunt of all the strife,
    And set right what was wrong.

And now the living Moa stood
    Amid his kindred's bones,
While his huge frame was close compared,
    Adding insult to wrongs.

(Man arrogantly doth conclude,
    That he alone respects
The relics of his kind when dead;
    But mercy this suspects.)

Of Didiformis, first a leg,
    Was 'gainst his own compared;
And the due ratio of its size
    Was by the Sage declared.

See how, he cried, the South hath erred,
    And how withouten fail
My theory holds, long since I saw
    What now these facts entail.

The multiple, diameter,
    And length are not the same;
And, by this rule, 'tis needful that
    This gets another name.

Then they in triumph led him forth
    For wonder and display;
And loud and long the people cheered
    The bird in trappings gay.

A feathered biped for a steed
    The Savant had bestrode,
And sixteen stone of flesh and blood
    Were sure sufficient load.

Up Cashel street, Colombo street,
    With slow and stately pace,
A royal ride; the rider smiled
    With condescending grace.

Pealed yet again the bells, and throats
    Ten thousand rent the air,
And proudly thus our hero rode
    To halt in Market square.

O happy, honoured, much loved man,
    Enjoy while yet you may.
Thy cup of nectar's full! enjoy
    The honours of the day.

Heed not yon lowering thundercloud,
    It cannot fall on thee,
But drain thy cup, it hath no dregs,
    It holds no misery.

Freed from his fetters stood the bird,
    And in that moment free
His frame was nerved, and his bright eye
    Glowed with intensity.

He saw again his mountain home
    Rise up before his sight;
And, stirred by hope of freedom won,
    He gathered all his might

But we return. The Moa fled,
    Disdained to cross the bridge,
But sprang across the Avon's tide,
    As 'twere a two foot hedge.

Dwellers on Papanui Road
    Had never seen the like;
The women screamed, the men did stare,
    The boys yelled with delight.

Fate seemed averse. The rider's head
    Sank drooping to his breast;
But, suddenly, he seized a straw
    A feeble hope at best.

He seized the Moa by the neck,
    And sought its course to turn;
But here he found his strength was matched;
    As well had he foreborne.

But what avail to tell you more,
    Since none but one can tell
The horrors of his further ride,
    Or on his fears to dwell.

                      Dinornis Sumnerensis

SUMNER CAVE

A second unpublished, handwritten poem on the 'Body in the Cave Affair' was found by Diane Bright, a former librarian with NZ Geological Survey, in the Mantell family papers in the Alexander Turnbull Library (MS paper 83: folder 214). The handwriting and subject matter indicate it was undoubtedly written by McKay. It was labelled in a different hand 'McKay – Sumner Cave.' It was subsequently published in the *Newsletter of the Geological Society of New Zealand*, 66: 47–49.

Was it a paleolithic man
    Or was it but a maori
Or was it some unfortunate
    Not long since gone to glory

The body found in Sumner Cave
    And now in the Museum
It had broken arm: and teeth
    That much did want renewing

The world of Science does not seem
    To be agreed about it
One says 'twas there before the Flood
    Another says I doubt it

Now this looks grave and throws a doubt
    On some ones observation
Which being so it is I confess
    A serious accusation

I've read the subject carefully
    And think I understand
The true position of the case
    And what it does demand

The matter I might not decide
    But if my vote were taken
I'de give it on the winning side
    If I were not mistaken

To arbitrate so great a case
    And settle it for ever
I am ambitious I confess
    My judgement to deliver

On one great point all are agreed
    The same admits of proving
It had a broken arm: and teeth
    That much did want renewing

Tis also clear 'twas found inside
    The famous Sumner Cave
On the sou- west side close to the wall
    May yet be seen the Grave

But whether it Six or Sixty inch
    Beneath the Surface lay
Is not so clear you are asked to believe
    It might be either way

Did the ancient Neolithic man
    Disturb the Sleepers rest
Or Shoot his kitchen rubbish there
    In piles upon his breast

Could this be: and, the wakeful ghost
    The act leave unavenged
I trow not else the Spirits leave
    Their tactics lately changed

Meanwhile it seems to be quite clear
    The Body might have been
No longer in its restingplace
    And from that State 'twould seem

When Logic shows that Sixty inch
    May just as well means Six
I'll then consider I've found my way
    Out of an awkward fix

> While fifty or five hundred years
>   Would suit the case as well
> But frankly where the proofs are scant
>   How long no one can tell

Bibliography

Works by Alexander McKay

AJHR = Appendices to the Journal of the House of Representatives New Zealand

NZGSRGE = New Zealand Geological Survey Reports of Geological Exploration

TNZI = Transactions of the New Zealand Institute

Geographic keys for these publications appear on pages 144 (those to 1885), 153 (to 1895) and 162 (to 1905).

M001 McKay, Alexander, On the Hot Winds of Canterbury in *TNZI vol. 7*, 1874, pp. 105–07.

M002 McKay, Alexander, On the Identity of the Moa-hunters with the Present Maori Race in *TNZI vol. 7*, 1875, pp. 98–105.

M003 McKay, Alexander, On the Reptilian Beds of New Zealand in *TNZI vol. 9*, 1877, pp. 581–90.

M004 McKay, Alexander, Reports Relative to Collections of Fossils in S.E. District of the Province of Otago in *NZGSRGE 1873–4 vol. 8b*, 1877, pp. 59–73, 1 pl. (sects).

M005 McKay, Alexander, Reports Relative to Collections of Fossils Made on the West Coast District, South Island in *NZGSRGE 1873–4 vol. 8b*, 1877, pp. 74–115.

M006 McKay, Alexander, Reports Relative to Collections of Fossils Made in the East Cape District, North Island in *NZGSRGE 1873–4 vol. 8b*, 1877, pp. 116–64.

M007 McKay, Alexander, Report on Coal at Shakespeare Bay, Picton in *NZGSRGE 1874–6 vol. 9,*1877, pp. 32–35.

M008 McKay, Alexander, Report on Weka Pass and Buller Districts in *NZGSRGE 1874–6 vol. 9,* 1877, pp. 36–42.

M009 McKay, Alexander, Report on Country between Cape Kidnappers and Cape Turnagain in *NZGSRGE 1874–6 vol. 9,* 1877, pp. 43–53 1 pl. (sects).

M010 McKay, Alexander, Report on Tertiary Rocks at Makara in *NZGSRGE 1874–6 vol. 9,* 1877, p. 54.

M011 McKay, Alexander, Report on Wangaroa North in *New Zealand Geological Survey Reports of Geological Exploration 1874–6 vol. 9,* 1877, pp. 55–58, 1 pl.

M012 McKay, Alexander, Report on Kaikoura Peninsula and Amuri Bluff in *NZGSRGE 1874–6 vol. 9,* 1877, pp. 172–84, 3 pl. (2 geol. maps, 7 sect.).

M013 McKay, Alexander, Report on Cape Campbell District in *NZGSRGE 1874–6 vol. 9,* 1877, pp. 185–91, 2 pl. (geol. map, 6 sect.).

M014 McKay, Alexander, Oamaru and Waitaki Districts in *NZGSRGE 1876–7 vol. 10*, 1877, pp. 41–66, 2 pl.

M015 McKay, Alexander, Report on the Country between Masterton and Napier in *NZGSRGE 1876–7 vol. 10*, 1877, pp. 67–94, 2 pl. (geol. map, 4 sect.).

M016 McKay, Alexander, On the Occurrence of Gold in the Mackenzie Country, Canterbury in *TNZI vol. 10*, 1878, pp. 481–84.

M017 McKay, Alexander, Report on East Wairarapa District in *NZGSRGE 1877–8 vol. 11*, 1878, pp. 14–24, 1 pl. (map, sects.).

M018 McKay, Alexander, Notes on the Sections and Collections of Fossils Obtained in the Hokanui District in *NZGSRGE 1877–8 vol. 11*, 1878, pp. 49–90.

M019 McKay, Alexander, Report Relative to the Collection of Fossils from the Mount Potts *Spirifer* Beds in *NZGSRGE 1877–8 vol. 11*, 1878, pp. 91–109, 1 pl. (geol. map, sects).

M020 McKay, Alexander, Report on the Wairoa and Dun Mountain Districts in *NZGSRGE 1877–8 vol. 11*, 1878, pp. 119–59, geol. map, sects.

M021 McKay, Alexander, Occurrence of Moa Bones at Taradale, near Napier in *NZGSRGE 1878–79 vol. 12*, 1879, pp. 64–69, 1 pl.

M022 McKay, Alexander, The Geology of the District between Waipukurau and Napier in *NZGSRGE 1878–79 vol. 12*, 1879, pp. 69–75, 1 pl. (2 sect.).

M023 McKay, Alexander, The Southern Part of the East Wairarapa District in *NZGSRGE 1878–79 vol. 12*, 1879, pp. 75–86, 1 pl. (2 sect.).

M024 McKay, Alexander, The District between the Kaituna Valley and Queen Charlotte Sound in *NZGSRGE 1878–79 vol. 12*, 1879, pp. 86–97, 1 fig.

M025 McKay, Alexander, The District between the Wairau and Motueka Valleys in *NZGSRGE 1878–79 vol. 12*, 1879, pp. 97–121, geol. map, 2 sect.

M026 McKay, Alexander, The Baton River and Wangapeka Districts, and Mount Arthur Range in *NZGSRGE 1878–79 vol. 12*, 1879, pp. 121–31, geol. map, 7 sect.

M027 McKay, Alexander, The Geology of the Neighbourhood of Wellington in *NZGSRGE 1878–79 vol. 12*, 1879, pp. 131–35.

M028 McKay, Alexander, *Lines Written on a Scene from Lake Harris Saddle, West Coast, Middle Island*, Hughes, Wellington, 1880, pp. 1–4.

M029 [McKay, Alexander], *The Canterbury Gilpin; or, The Capture and Flight of the Moa. A Poem by Dinornis Sumnerensis. Parts I and II*, Hughes, Wellington, 1880, pp. 1–43.

M030 McKay, Alexander, Mataura Plant-beds, Southland County in *NZGSRGE 1879–80 vol. 13*, 1881, pp. 39–48, 1 fig.

M031 McKay, Alexander, Discovery of Chalk near Oxford, Ashley County in *NZGSRGE 1879–80 vol. 13*, 1881, pp. 49–53.

M032 McKay, Alexander, Of [On] the Trelissic Basin, Selwyn County in *NZGSRGE 1879–80 vol. 13*, 1881, pp. 53–74, geol. map, 4 sect.

M033 McKay, Alexander, Curiosity Shop, Rakaia River, Canterbury (Notes to Accompany a Collection of Fossils from that Locality in *NZGSRGE 1879–80 vol. 13*, 1881, pp. 75–82, 1 sect.

M034 McKay, Alexander, On the Older Sedimentary Rocks of Ashley and Amuri Counties in *NZGSRGE 1879–80 vol. 13*, 1881, pp. 83–107, 4 sect.

M035 McKay, Alexander, On the Motunau District, Ashley County in *NZGSRGE 1879–80 vol. 13*, 1881, pp. 108–18, 4 sect.

M036 McKay, Alexander, District West and North of Lake Wakatipu in *NZGSRGE 1879–80 vol. 13*, 1881, pp. 118–47, 1 map.

M037 McKay, Alexander, Coal Discoveries at Shakespeare Bay, near Picton in *NZGSRGE 1879–80 vol. 13*, 1881, pp. 147–49.

M038 McKay, Alexander, On the Genus *Rhynchonella* in *TNZI vol. 13*, 1881, pp. 396–98.

M039 McKay, Alexander, On the Younger Deposits of the Wharekauri Basin and the Lower Waitaki Valley in *NZGSRGE 1881 vol. 14*, 1882, pp. 98–106, 4 sect.

M040 McKay, Alexander, Geology of the Waitaki Valley and Parts of Vincent and Lake Counties in *NZGSRGE 1881 vol. 14*, 1882, pp. 56–92, geol. map (at end vol.), 7 sect.

M041 McKay, Alexander, The Coal-bearing Deposits, near Shakespeare Bay, Picton in *NZGSRGE 1881 vol. 14*, 1882, pp. 106–15.

M042 McKay, Alexander, On the Caswell Sound Marble in *NZGSRGE 1881 vol. 14*, 1882, pp. 115–18.

M043 McKay, Alexander, On a Deposit of Moa Bones near Motanau, North Canterbury in *TNZI vol. 14*, 1882, pp. 410–14.

M044 McKay, Alexander, On a Deposit of Moa Bones near Motunau, North Canterbury in *NZGSRGE 1882 vol. 15*, 1883, pp. 74–79 (1883).

M045 McKay, Alexander, On the Antimony Lodes of the Carrick Ranges, Vincent County, Otago in *NZGSRGE 1882 vol. 15*, 1883, pp. 80–83, 1 pl.

M046 McKay, Alexander, On Antimony Lode and Quartz Reefs at Langdon's Hill, Grey County in *NZGSRGE 1882 vol. 15*, 1883, pp. 83–85, 1 pl.

M047 McKay, Alexander, On the Albion Gold-mining Company, Hutt County in *NZGSRGE 1882 vol. 15*, 1883, pp. 85–88, 2 pl.

M048 McKay, Alexander, On an Antimony Lode at Reefton, Inangahua County in *NZGSRGE 1882 vol. 15*, 1883, pp. 89–90, 1 map.

M049 McKay, Alexander, On the Geology of the Reefton District, Inangahua County in *NZGSRGE 1882 vol. 15*, 1883, pp. 91–153, 2 maps, 14 fig.

M050 McKay, [Alexander], [Volcanic Rocks near Masterton] (Abstract) in *New Zealand Journal of Science vol. 1*, 1883, p. 521

M051 McKay, Alexander, Exploration of the Hollyford Valley, West Coast of Otago (Letter to Editor) in *New Zealand Journal of Science vol. 1*, 1883, pp. 536–38.

M052 McKay, Alexander, On the North-eastern District of Otago in *NZGSRGE 1883–84 vol. 16*, 1884, pp. 45–66, 1 map, 2 sect.

M053 McKay, Alexander, On the Igneous Rocks of the East Coast of Wellington in *NZGSRGE 1883–84 vol. 16*, 1884, pp. 71–75; *TNZI vol. 16*, 1884, pp. 547–48 (abstract); *New Zealand Journal of Science vol. 1*, 1883, p. 521 (abstract).

M054 McKay, Alexander, On the Origin of the Old Lake-basins of Central Otago in *NZGSRGE 1883–84 vol. 16*, 1884, pp. 76–81; *TNZI vol. 16*, 1884, pp. 550–51 (abstract).

M055 McKay, Alexander, On the Auriferous Quartz Drifts at Clark's Diggings, Maniototo County in *NZGSRGE 1883–84 vol. 16*, 1884, pp. 91–95.

M056 McKay, Alexander, On the Kawakawa Coal Field in *NZGSRGE 1883–84 vol. 16*, 1884, pp. 95–99, map.

M057 McKay, Alexander, On the Occurrence of Serpentinous Rocks as Dykes in Cretaceo-Tertiary Strata near the Wade, Auckland in *NZGSRGE 1883–84 vol. 16*, 1884, pp. 99–101, geol. map.

M058 McKay, Alexander, On the Relations of the Tertiary and Cretaceo-Tertiary Strata on the Coast-line between Auckland and Mahurangi in *NZGSRGE 1883–84 vol. 16*, 1884, pp. 101–06, 4 sect.

M059 McKay, Alexander, On the Geology of the Coal-bearing Area between Whangarei and Hokianga in *NZGSRGE 1883–84 vol. 16*, 1884, pp. 110–34, geol. map, 6 fig.

M060 McKay, Alexander, On the Gold Mines at Terawhiti in *NZGSRGE 1883–84 vol. 16*, 1884, pp. 135–40.

M061 McKay, Alexander, On the Geology of the Kawhia District: Preliminary Report in *NZGSRGE 1883–84 vol. 16*, 1884, pp. 140–48, geol. map.

M062 McKay, Alexander, On the Coal Outcrops on Mr Fraser's Property East of Kaitangata Lake, Otago in *NZGSRGE 1885 vol. 17*, 1886, pp. 1–5, sect.

M063 McKay, Alexander, On the Cupriferous Diabasic Rocks of the Malvern Hills, Selwyn County in *NZGSRGE 1885 vol. 17*, 1886, pp. 6–8.

M064 McKay, Alexander, On Deposits of Iron Ore near Kawakawa, Bay of Islands in *NZGSRGE 1885 vol. 17*, 1886, pp. 9–10.

M065 McKay, Alexander, On the Antimony Lodes of Endeavour Inlet in *NZGSRGE 1885 vol. 17*, 1886, pp. 10–13.

M066 McKay, Alexander, On the Geology of the Eastern Part of Marlborough Provincial District in *NZGSRGE 1885 vol. 17*, 1886, pp. 27–136, geol. map, 26 fig.

M067 McKay, Alexander, Notes on the Geology of Scinde Island and Some Parts of the Northern District of Hawke's Bay in *NZGSRGE 1885 vol. 17*, 1886, pp. 185–92.

M068 McKay, Alexander, On the Geology of Cabbage Bay District, Cape Colville Peninsula in *NZGSRGE 1885 vol. 17*, 1886, pp. 192–202, geol. map, 2 sect.

M069 McKay, Alexander, On the Age of the Napier Limestone in *TNZI vol. 18*, 1886, pp. 367–74.

M070 McKay, Alexander, The Waihao Greensands and their Relation to the Ototara Limestone in *TNZI vol. 19*, 1887, pp. 434–40.

M071 McKay, Alexander, On the Young Secondary and Tertiary Formations of Eastern Otago – Moeraki to Waikouaiti in *NZGSRGE 1886–87 vol. 18*, 1887, pp. 1–23, map, 4 fig.

M072 McKay, Alexander, On the Grey-Marls and Weka Pass Stone in Kaikoura Peninsula and at Amuri Bluff in *NZGSRGE 1886–87 vol. 18*, 1887, pp. 74–78, 5 fig.

M073 McKay, Alexander, On the Junction of the Amuri Limestone and Weka Pass

Stone, Weka Pass, North Canterbury in *NZGSRGE 1886–87 vol. 18,* 1887, pp. 78–91, 6 fig.

M074 McKay, Alexander, On the Identity and Geological Position of the Greensands of the Waihao Forks, Waihao Valley, South Canterbury in *NZGSRGE 1886–87 vol. 18,* 1887, pp. 91–119, 7 fig.

M075 McKay, Alexander, On the Mokihinui Coalfield in *NZGSRGE 1886–87 vol. 18,* 1887, pp. 161–67.

M076 McKay, Alexander, On the Geology of East Auckland and the Northern District of Hawke's Bay in *NZGSRGE 1886–87 vol. 18,* 1887, pp. 182–219, map, 6 fig.

M077 McKay, Alexander, On the Geology of the Malvern Hills, Canterbury in *NZGSRGE 1886–87 vol. 18,* 1887, pp. 230–33.

M078 McKay, Alexander, On the Geology of the Coast-line, Moeraki Peninsula to Kakanui; and Further Notes on the Geology of North-east Otago in *NZGSRGE 1886–87 vol. 18,* 1887, pp. 233–40.

M079 McKay, Alexander, [Fossil Shell from East Cape District] (Abstract) in *TNZI vol. 20,* 1888, p. 440.

M080 McKay, Alexander, Preliminary Report on the Earthquakes of September, 1888, in the Amuri and Marlborough Districts of the South Island in *New Zealand Geological Survey Bulletin 1 [1st series] vol. 16,* pp. (See also *NZGSRGE 1888–89 vol. 20,* 1890, pp. 1–16).

M081 McKay, Alexander, On Mineral Deposits in the Tararua and Ruahine Mountains in *NZGSRGE 1887–88 vol. 19,* 1888, pp. 1–6, geol. map.

M082 McKay, Alexander, On the Copper Ore at Maharahara near Woodville in *NZGSRGE 1887–88 vol. 19,* 1888, pp. 6–9.

M083 McKay, Alexander, On the Coal Outcrops in the Wairoa Valley and Hunua Range, near Drury, Auckland in *NZGSRGE 1887–88 vol. 19,* 1888, pp. 16–18.

M084 McKay, Alexander, On Certain Calcareous Rocks Occurring near Eketahuna, County of Wairarapa North in *NZGSRGE 1887–88 vol. 19,* 1888, pp. 18–20.

M085 McKay, Alexander, On the Discovery of Metaliferous Rocks in the Patua Range, Taranaki in *NZGSRGE 1887–88 vol. 19,* 1888, pp. 35–37.

M086 McKay, Alexander, On the Geology of the Northern District of Auckland in *NZGSRGE 1887–88 vol. 19,* 1888, pp. 37–57. Map, 3 sect.

M087 McKay, Alexander, On the Tauherenikau and Waiohine Valleys, Tararua Range in *NZGSRGE 1887–88 vol. 19,* 1888, pp. 58–67.

M088 McKay, Alexander, On the Limestones and Other Rocks of the Rimutaka and Tararua Mountains (Abstract) in *TNZI vol. 21,* 1889, pp. 486–87.

M089 McKay, Alexander, On the Supposed Occurrence of Two Sets of Greensand-beds at Waihao Forks, South Canterbury (Abstract) in *TNZI vol. 21,* 1889, pp. 488-89.

M090 McKay, Alexander, Remarks on Earthquakes in the Amuri District, South Island (Abstract) in *TNZI vol. 21,* 1889, pp. 508–09.

M091 McKay, Alexander, Notes on the Minerals from Stewart Island Described by Mr Skey in *TNZI vol. 22,* 1890, pp. 418–21. (Abstract, pp. 520–521.)

M092 McKay, Alexander, On the Earthquakes of September, 1888, in the Amuri and Marlborough Districts of the South Island in *NZGSRGE 1888–89 vol. 20,* 1890, pp. 1–16. (Also, *New Zealand Geological Survey Bulletin 1* [1st series], 1888).

M093 McKay, Alexander, On the Mahakipawa Goldfield in *NZGSRGE 1888–89 vol. 20,* 1890, pp. 36–44, 5 sect. (Also, *New Zealand Geological Survey Bulletin 2* [1st series], 1888, pp. 20–28, 5 sect).

M094 McKay, Alexander, On the Geology of Stewart Island and the Tin-deposits of Port Pegasus District in *NZGSRGE 1888–89 vol. 20,* 1890, pp. 74–85, map, sect.

M095 McKay, Alexander, On the Geology of Marlborough and the Amuri District of Nelson in *NZGSRGE 1888–89 vol. 20,* 1890, pp. 85–185, geol. map, 20 fig.

M096 McKay, Alexander, On a deposit of Diatomaceous Earth at Pakaraka, Bay of Islands, Auckland in *TNZI vol. 23,* 1891, pp. 375–379 (Abstract, pp. 612–13).

M097 McKay, Alexander, On a deposit of Diatomaceous Earth at the Bay of Islands (Abstract) in *New Zealand Journal of Science (new issue) vol 1(3),* 1891 pp.140–42.

M098 McKay, Alexander, On Some Means for increasing the Scale of Photographic Lenses, and the Use of Telescopic Powers in connection with an Ordinary Camera in *TNZI vol. XIII,* 1891, pp. 461–65.

M099 McKay, Alexander, On the Geology of Marlborough and South-East Nelson Part II in *NZGSRGE 1890–91 vol. 21,* 1892, pp. 1–28, 1 fig., 2 maps.

M100 McKay, Alexander, On the Prospects of Coal within the Mangahao Block, Pahiatua County in *NZGSRGE 1890–91 vol. 21,* 1892, pp. 28–30, sect.

M101 McKay, Alexander, On the Prospects of Finding Coal on the New Zealand Agricultural Company's Estate, Waimea Plains, Southland in *NZGSRGE 1890–91 vol. 21,* 1892, pp. 31–35, map, bore sects. 2 geol. sect.

M102 McKay, Alexander, On the Old Phoenix Mine, Terawhiti, Wellington in *NZGSRGE 1890–91 vol. 21,* 1892, pp. 35–38.

M103 McKay, Alexander, On the Crystalline Limestones and So-called Marble Deposits of the Pikikiruna Mountains, Nelson in *NZGSRGE 1890–91 vol. 21,* 1892, pp. 38–43, geol. map, sect.

M104 McKay, Alexander, On the Prospects of Coal near Otakaia, Otago in *NZGSRGE 1890–91 vol. 21,* 1892, pp. 43–45.

M105 McKay, Alexander, On the Prospects of Finding Coal on Rowley's Farm, near Shag Point Railway-Station in *NZGSRGE 1890–91 vol. 21,* 1892, pp. 45–50.

M106 McKay, Alexander, On the Quartz Reefs of the Nenthorn District, Otago in *NZGSRGE 1890–91 vol. 21,* 1892, pp. 50–54.

M107 McKay, Alexander, On an Outcrop of Antimony Ore on Barewood Run, Taieri River, Otago in *NZGSRGE 1890–91 vol. 21,* 1892, pp. 54–55.

M108 McKay, Alexander, On the Puhupuhu Silverfield, Auckland in *NZGSRGE 1890–91 vol. 21,* 1892, pp. 55–59.

M109 McKay, Alexander, On the Prospects of Coal at Pakaraka, Bay of Islands, Auckland in *NZGSRGE 1890–91 vol. 21,* 1892, pp. 59–63, 2 sect.

M110 McKay, Alexander, On the Geology of the Lower Waikaka Valley and the Auriferous Drifts at Switzers Diggings in *NZGSRGE 1890–91 vol. 21,* 1892, pp. 63–64.

M111 McKay, Alexander, On the Geology of the District Surrounding Whangaroa Harbour, Mongonui County, Auckland in *NZGSRGE 1890–91 vol. 21*, 1892, pp. 65–72, sect.

M112 McKay, Alexander, On the Lignites of Cooper's Beach, Mongonui, Auckland in *NZGSRGE 1890–91 vol. 21*, 1892, pp. 72–76, geol. map.

M113 McKay, Alexander, On the New Cardiff Coal Property, Mokihinui Coalfield in *NZGSRGE 1890–91 vol. 21*, 1892, pp. 76–85, map, sects.

M114 McKay, Alexander, On the Mokihinui Coal Company's Property, Coal Creek, Mokihinui in *NZGSRGE 1890–91 vol. 21*, 1892, pp. 86–97, sect.

M115 McKay, Alexander, On the Geology of the Middle Waipara and Weka Pass Districts, North Canterbury in *NZGSRGE 1890–91 vol. 21*, 1892, pp. 97–103.

M116 McKay, Alexander, On that Part of the West Coast Goldfields Lying between the Teremakau and Mikonui Rivers, Westland in *New Zealand Geological Survey Bulletin n.s. 1* [2nd series], 1892, 7 pp., 2 sect.

M117 McKay, Alexander, On the Diatom Deposit near Pakaraka Bay of Islands, Auckland in *TNZI vol. 25*, 1893, pp. 375–77 (Abstract, pp. 528–529).

M118 McKay, Alexander, Geological Explorations of the Northern Part of Westland in *AJHR C. – 3*, 1893, pp. 132–86, pls., geol. map, 4 sect.

M119 McKay, Alexander, On the Prospects of Finding Coal near Shannon, on the Wellington and Manawatu Railway-line in *NZGSRGE 1892–3 vol. 22*, 1894, pp. 1–2.

M120 McKay, Alexander, On the Maharahara Copper-Mine, Woodville, Hawke's Bay in *NZGSRGE 1892–3 vol. 22*, 1894, pp. 2–6.

M121 McKay, Alexander, On the Kumara Gold-drifts, Westland in *NZGSRGE 1892–3 vol. 22*, 1894, pp. 6–11.

M122 McKay, Alexander, On the Geology of the Northern Part of Westland and the Gold-bearing Drifts between the Teremakau and Mikonoui Rivers in *NZGSRGE 1892–3 vol. 22*, 1894, pp. 11–50, geol. map, sects. (after p. 54).

M123 McKay, Alexander, On the Puhipuhi Silverfield in *NZGSRGE 1892–3 vol. 22*, 1894, pp. 50–55, 2 sects.

M124 McKay, Alexander, On the Hikurangi Coalfield in *NZGSRGE 1892–3 vol. 22*, 1894, pp. 55–69, geol. map, sect.

M125 McKay, Alexander, On the Geology of Hokianga and Mongonui Counties, Northern Auckland in *NZGSRGE 1892–3 vol. 22*, 1894, pp. 70–90, 2 geol. maps, 11 sect.

M126 McKay, Alexander, On a Reported Discovery of Copper-ore at Karori, near Wellington in *NZGSRGE 1892–3 vol. 22*, 1894, pp. 91–92.

M127 McKay, Alexander, Geological Reports on the Older Auriferous Drifts of Central Otago in *AJHR C. – 4*, 1894, 48 pp., geol. map, 28 sect. (2nd ed. published separately 119 pp., geol map, 28 sect., 1897).

M128 McKay, Alexander, Report on the Geology of the South-west Part of Nelson and the Northern Part of the Westland District in *AJHR New Zealand C. – 13*, 1895, 28 pp., geol. map, 28 sect. (2nd ed. published separately 108 pp., geol. map, 1897).

M129 McKay, Alexander, Geology: General Report and Reports of the Special

Examinations Made During the Year 1895–96 in *AJHR C. – 11*, 1896, 51 pp.

M130 McKay, Alexander, The Geology of the Aorere Valley, Collingwood County, Nelson in *AJHR C. – 11*, 1896, pp. 4–27, geol. map.

M131 McKay, Alexander, The Prospects of Finding Workable Coal-seams at Gordon Downs, Nelson in *AJHR C. – 11*, 1896; p. 27.

M132 McKay, Alexander, The Probability of Finding Coal in the Wairoa Gorge, Waimea County, Nelson in *AJHR C. – 11*, 1896, p. 28.

M133 McKay, Alexander, The Enner Glynn Coal-mine, and the Coal-bearing Area within Brook Street Valley, near the Town of Nelson in *AJHR C. – 11*, 1896, pp. 28–30.

M134 McKay, Alexander, A Deposit of Chromate of Iron on the North-western Slopes of Mount Starveall, Waimea County, Nelson in *AJHR C. – 11*, 1896, pp. 30–31.

M135 McKay, Alexander, Wilson River and Preservation Inlet Goldfields, Fiord County, Otago in *AJHR C. – 11*, 1896, pp. 31–45, geol. map, sects.

M136 McKay, Alexander, McKenna Brothers Claim, Gulches Head, Preservation Inlet in *AJHR C. – 11*, 1896, pp. 45–47.

M137 McKay, Alexander, Deposit of Jet Coal at Maharahara, near Woodville in *AJHR C. – 11*, 1896, pp. 47–49.

M138 McKay, Alexander, Prospect of Finding Coal on the Tiraumea Estate, Upper Tiraumea Valley in *AJHR C. – 11*, 1896, pp. 49–51, geol. map.

M139 McKay, Alexander, Deposit of Lignite at Mauriceville, Wairarapa North in *AJHR C. – 11*, 1896, p. 51.

M140 McKay, Alexander, Report on the Geology of the Cape Colville Peninsula, Auckland in *AJHR C. – 9*, 1897, pp. 1–75, 2 maps.

M141 McKay, Alexander, Report on the Silver-bearing Lodes of the Neighbourhood of Blind Bay, Great Barrier Island, Auckland in *AJHR C. – 9*, 1897, pp. 75–80, plan.

M142 McKay, Alexander, *Report on the Older Auriferous Drifts of Central Otago* 2nd ed., Government Printer, Wellington. VI, 1897, 119 pp, geol. map, 28 sect.

M143 McKay, Alexander, *Report on the Geology of the South-west Part of Nelson and Northern Part of Westland* 2nd ed., Government Printer, Wellington. VII, 1897, 108 pp., geol. map.

M144 McKay, Alexander, Report on the Auriferous Rocks of the Western Slopes of the Victoria Mountains, Nelson in *AJHR C. – 9*, 1898, pp. 1–3. (Also, *New Zealand Mines Record vol. 1*, pp. 303–04).

M145 McKay, Alexander, Report on the Auriferous Character of Boatman's Creek, Inangahua Valley in *AJHR C. – 9*, 1898, pp. 3–4 (Also, *New Zealand Mines Record vol. 1*, pp. 304–05).

M146 McKay, Alexander, Report on the Copper Deposits of Omaunu No. 2, Whangaroa County in *AJHR C. – 9*, 1898, pp. 4–5 (Also, abstract in *New Zealand Mines Record vol. 1*, pp. 355–56).

M147 McKay, Alexander, Report on Further Prospecting for Coal at Kawakawa, Bay of Islands County in *AJHR C. – 9*, 1898, pp. 5–6.

M148 McKay, Alexander, Report on the Te Puke Goldfield, Tauranga County in

AJHR C. – 9, 1898, pp. 6–8 (Also, *New Zealand Mines Record vol. 1*, pp. 394–95).

M149 McKay, Alexander, Report on the Occurrence of Cinnabar in the Kauaeranga Valley, Thames County in *AJHR* C. – 9, 1898, p. 8 (Abstract in *New Zealand Mines Record vol. 1*, pp. 445–46).

M150 McKay, Alexander, Geological Survey of the Cape Colville Peninsula: Progress Report for the Year 1897–98 in *AJHR* C. – 9, 1898, pp. 8–12 (Abstract in *New Zealand Mines Record vol. 1*, pp. 43–44).

M151 McKay, Alexander, Report of Government Geologist on the Present Condition and Future Prospects of Boring for Petroleum at New Plymouth in *AJHR* C. – 9A, 1898, 2 pp.

M152 McKay, Alexander, Notes on the Auriferous Iron-sands of New Zealand in *New Zealand Mines Record vol. 1*, pp. 395–396; 446–450 (Also *Colliery Guard vol. 75*, 1898, p. 1041).

M153 McKay, Alexander, The Patua Ranges, Taranaki in *New Zealand Mines Record vol. 2*, 1898, pp. 104–05.

M154 McKay, Alexander, Petroleum in *AJHR* C. – 3, 1899, pp. 158–59.

M155 McKay, Alexander, Geological Explorations Made during 1898–99 in *AJHR* C. – 9, 1899, pp. 1–2.

M156 McKay, Alexander, Report on a Deposit of Rhodochrosite at Paraparaumu, Wellington in *AJHR* C. – 9, 1899, pp. 2–3. (*Also New Zealand Mines Record vol. 2*, pp. 217–18).

M157 McKay, Alexander, Report on Petroleum at New Plymouth, Taranaki in *AJHR* C. – 9, 1899, pp. 3–10, plan, sect.

M158 McKay, Alexander, Report on the Auriferous Deposits of the Hinemaia[i] Valley, Taupo District, Auckland in *AJHR* C. – 9, 1899, pp. 11–13. (Also *New Zealand Mines Record vol. 2*, pp. 341–42].

M159 McKay, Alexander, Report on the Supposed Gem-bearing Formation near Riverhead, Auckland in *AJHR* C. – 9, 1899, pp. 13–14, geol. sect. (facing. p. 12).

M160 McKay, Alexander, Report on Lithographic Limestone, Mangonui County, Auckland in *AJHR* C. – 9, 1899, pp. 14–15. (Also *New Zealand Mines Record vol. 2*, p. 343).

M161 McKay, Alexander, Notes on the Auriferous Iron-sands of New Zealand in 1899, pp. 15–16.

M162 McKay, Alexander, Report on the Pumice-stone Deposits of the Middle Part of the North Island in *AJHR* C. – 9, 1899, pp. 16–25, 4 geol. sect. (Also *New Zealand Official Yearbook 1900*, pp. 486–89).

M163 McKay, Alexander, Report on the Occurrence of Coal near Waihi, Auckland in *AJHR* C. – 9, 1899, pp. 25–26.

M164 McKay, Alexander, Report of Auriferous Cements at Te Puke, Tauranga County, Auckland in *AJHR* C. – 9, 1899, pp. 26–28.

M165 McKay, Alexander, Report on the District between Stratford and the Tangarakau River in AJHR C. – 9, 1899, pp. 28–30, geol. sect. (Also *New Zealand Mines Record vol. 2*, pp. 390–91).

M166 McKay, Alexander, Report on the Supposed Occurrence of Auriferous Rocks at Horseshoe Bush, near Wade, Auckland in *AJHR C. – 9*, 1899, pp. 30–31.

M167 McKay, Alexander, [Collection of Rocks and Minerals from Cape Colville Peninsula] (Abstract) in *TNZI vol. 31*, 1899, pp. 714–15.

M168 McKay, Alexander, Report on the Puponga and Pakawau Coalfields, Collingwood County in *AJHR C. – 6*, 1900, 5 pp., map, geol. sect.

M169 McKay, Alexander, Reported Discovery of Coal and Petroleum at Cheviot in *New Zealand Mines Record vol. 3*, 1900, pp. 80–82.

M170 McKay, Alexander, The Igneous Rocks of New Zealand in *New Zealand Mines Record vol. 3*, 1900, pp. 177–81.

M171 McKay, Alexander, Coal on Cape Colville Peninsula in *New Zealand Mines Record vol. 3*, 1900, pp. 217–19.

M172 McKay, Alexander, Geology of Nelson and Westland in *New Zealand Mines Record vol. 3*, 1900, pp. 220–22.

M173 McKay, Alexander, Further Notes on the Iron-ores of New Zealand in *New Zealand Mines Record vol. 3*, 1900, pp. 472–74.

M174 McKay, Alexander, Pumice-stone Deposits of the Middle Part of the North Island in *New Zealand Official Yearbook. 1900*, pp. 486–89.

M175 McKay, Alexander, Geological Explorations: General Report for the year 1900–1 in *AJHR C. – 10*, 1901, pp. 1–4.

M176 McKay, Alexander, Notes on the Glass-making Sands of New Zealand in *AJHR C. – 10*, 1901, pp. 4–5.

M177 McKay, Alexander, Report on Chrome-deposits at the Croixelles, Nelson in *AJHR C. – 10*, 1901, pp. 5–6.

M178 McKay, Alexander, Report on the Prospect of Coal at Waimangaroa Railway-station, Westport in *AJHR C. – 10*, 1901, pp. 6–7.

M179 McKay, Alexander, Report on the Supposed Coal-seams in Kaiata Range, Greymouth in *AJHR C. – 10*, 1901, pp. 7–8.

M180 McKay, Alexander, Report on Coal in Koiterangi (Camel-back hill), Kokatahi Plain, Westland in *AJHR C. – 10*, 1901, pp. 8–9. (Also *New Zealand Mines Record vol. 4*, pp. 205–206).

M181 McKay, Alexander, Report on Indications of Coal in Coal Creek, Ross, Westland in *AJHR C. – 10*, 1901, pp. 9–10. (Also *New Zealand Mines Record vol. 4*, p. 206).

M182 McKay, Alexander, Report on Indications of Petroleum at Deep Creek, Lake Brunner, Nelson in *AJHR C. – 10*, 1901, pp. 10–12.

M183 McKay, Alexander, Report on the Kaimanawa Ranges, Hawke's Bay in *AJHR C. – 10, 1901*, pp. 12–21, geol. map (at end). (Also *New Zealand Mines Record vol. 5*, 1902, pp. 367–70).

M184 McKay, Alexander, Report on the Petroleum-bearing Rocks of Poverty Bay and East Cape Districts, Auckland, New Zealand in *AJHR C. – 10*, 1901, pp. 21–25, geol. map, sects (at end). (See also *New Zealand Mines Record vol. 4*, pp. 409–13).

M185 McKay, Alexander, Report on the Correspondence of the Shoots of Gold East and West of the Moanataiari Slide, Thames Goldfield in *AJHR C. – 10, 1901,* pp. 34–36, sects. (Also *New Zealand Mines Record vol. 4,* pp. 413–15).

M186 McKay, Alexander, Notes on the Auriferous Iron-sands of New Zealand in *New Zealand Mines Record vol. 4,* pp. 321–26. (Also issued as pamphlet, Government Printer, Wellington, 18 pp.; 1901).

M187 McKay, Alexander, The Correspondence of the Reefs on the East and West Sides of the Moanataiari Slide in *New Zealand Mines Record vol. 4,* 1901, pp. 413–15, 2 fig.

M188 McKay, Alexander, The Petroleum-bearing Rocks of Poverty Bay and East Cape Districts in *New Zealand Mines Record vol. 4,* 1901, pp. 409–13). (Geol. map, *ibid. 5,* fac. p. 168 1902.)

M189 McKay, Alexander, The Older Auriferous Drifts of Central Otago in *New Zealand Mines Record vol. 4,* 1901–2 [1902], pp. 326–30, 361–65, 418–22, 457–66, 506–12 and ibid vol. 5, 1902 pp. 1–7, 49–54, 97–102, 145–49, 189–96. (from McKay, *Report on the Older Auriferous Drifts of Central Otago,* 1897).

M190 McKay, Alexander, *Report on the Recent Seismic Disturbances within Cheviot County in Northern Canterbury and in the Amuri District of Nelson, New Zealand (November and December, 1901).* Government Printer, Wellington, 1902, 80 pp., 18 pl., map.

M191 McKay, Alexander, The Gold Deposits of New Zealand: Considered in Relation to the Comparative Quantities of Reef and Alluvial Gold on the Various Goldfields of the Colony in *New Zealand Mines Record vol. 5,* 1903, pp. 357–61, 401–04, 449–52, 497–500 and *ibid. vol. 6,* 1902, pp. 1–3, 49–53, 97–100. (Also as pamphlet, Government Printer, Wellington, 75 pp. 1903).

M192 McKay, Alexander, The Igneous Character of the Carboniferous Rocks of the Tokatea Goldfield, Cape Colville Peninsula in *Transactions of the Australasian Institute of Miners and Engineers vol. 9, Pt I,* 1903, pp. 195–205.

M193 McKay, Alexander, The Igneous Character of the Carboniferous Rocks of the Tokatea Goldfield, Cape Colville Peninsula in *AJHR C. – 3,* 1904, pp. 6–9; *New Zealand Mines Record vol. 7,* pp. 268–72; *Transactions of the Australasian Institute of Miners and Engineers vol. 9,* Pt II.

M194 McKay, Alexander, Introduction [Geology of Cape Colville Peninsula] in *Rocks of Cape Colville Peninsula,* by W.J. Sollas and A. McKay, Vol. 1, 1905, pp. 1–115.

M195 McKay, Alexander, The Auriferous Ironsands of New Zealand in *New Zealand Mining Handbook,* Galvin (ed.), pp. 332–35, 1906.

M196 McKay, Alexander, Auriferous Ironsands of the West Coast in *New Zealand Mining Handbook,* Galvin (ed.), pp. 335–44, 1906.

M197 McKay, Alexander, Further Notes on the Iron-ores of New Zealand in *New Zealand Mining Handbook,* Galvin (ed.), pp. 471–72, 1906.

M198 McKay, Alexander, Parapara Haematite in *New Zealand Mining Handbook,* Galvin (ed.), pp. 483–85, 1906.

M199 McKay, Alexander, The Copper Deposits of New Zealand in *New Zealand Mining Handbook,* Galvin (ed.), pp. 497–99, 1906.

M200 McKay, Alexander, Limestones in New Zealand in *New Zealand Mining Handbook,* Galvin (ed.), pp. 547–49, 1906.

M201 McKay, Alexander, Lithographic Limestones. Notes as to their Occurrence North of Hokianga and the Bay of Islands in *New Zealand Mining Handbook*, Galvin (ed.), pp. 549–51, 1906.

M202 McKay, Alexander, 'Fragments in the Life History of Alexander McKay', MS 1177, 291p. Turnbull Library, Wellington, c. 1912 (unpublished).

Select Works Cited

Aspinall, Jerry, *Farming Under Aspiring*, Alexandra: Macpherson Publishing, 1993.

Begg, A.C. and N.C., *Port Preservation*, Whitcombe and Tombs, 1973.

Bonthron, Mrs D., *Incidents in the course of a voyage to New Zealand made in ship "Helenslee" from Glasgow in the summer of 1863*. MS C011, 30 p. Otago Settlers Museum, Dunedin.

Burton, Peggy, *The New Zealand Geological Survey 1865–1965*. New Zealand Department of Scientific and Industrial Research, 1965.

Campbell, Anna, *The Woodhead Lead Mine, Carsphairn, Castle Douglas*, Galloway: Carsphairn Heritage Group, 1997.

Cyclopedia of New Zealand, Vol. 1, Wellington Provincial District, Wellington: The Cyclopedia Company, 1897.

Dictionary of New Zealand Biography Vol. 2, 1870–1900 (1993). Department of Internal Affairs, Wellington.

Haast, H.F. von, *The Life and Times of Sir Julius von Haast, Explorer, Geologist, Museum Builder*, Wellington: The Author, 1948.

Hocken, T.M., *A Bibliography of the Literature Relating to New Zealand*, Wellington: John Mackay, Government Printer, 1909.

Hunter, Jack, *The Upper Glenkens*, Catrine, Ayrshire: Stenlake Publishing, 2001.

Lyell, Sir Charles, *Principles of Geology*, 12th edition, John Murray, London, 1875.

McClintock, A.H. *The History of Otago*, Otago Centennial Historical publications, 1949.

Main, William, *Wellington Through a Victorian Lens*, Millwood Press, Wellington, 1972.

Miller, Hugh, *The Testimony of the Rocks*. Edinburgh: William P. Nimmo, 1857.

Murray, T. 'Frae the Broomielaw to the Waitemata: diary of the voyage of the "Helenslee"'. MS 92/51, 38p. Auckland War Memorial Museum, Auckland.

Nathan, Simon, *Harold Wellman: A Man Who Moved New Zealand*. Wellington: Victoria University Press, 2005

Olssen, Erik, *A History of Otago*, Dunedin: John McIndoe, 1984.

Park, James, *Maori and Early European Explorations in Western Otago*. Dunedin: Otago Daily Times and Witness, 1922.

Pascoe, John (ed.), *Mr Explorer Douglas*, A.H. & A.W. Reed, Wellington, 1957.

Pinney, Robert, *Early North Otago Runs*, Auckland: Collins, 1981.

Pinney, Robert, *Early South Canterbury Runs*, Wellington: A.H. and A.W. Reed, 1971.

Savill, David. *Sail to New Zealand: The Story of Shaw Savill and Co., 1598–1882*. London: Hale, 1986.

Wood, June, *Gold Trails of Otago*, A.H. & A.W. Reed Ltd, Wellington, 1970.

Notes

Numerical references preceded by the letter M (e.g. M002) are to McKay's publications, listed in Appendix 4.

Chapter 1

[1] Jack Hunter, *The Upper Glenkens*, Catrine, Ayrshire: Stenlake Publishing, 2001, p. 7.
[2] Anna Campbell, *The Woodhead Lead Mine, Carsphairn, Castle Douglas*, Galloway: Carsphairn Heritage Group, 1997, p. 2.
[3] *Ibid.*
[4] *Ibid.*, p. 7.
[5] *Ibid.*, p. 3.
[6] *Ibid.*, pp. 3–4.
[7] *Ibid.*, p. 9.
[8] Alexander McKay, 'Fragments in the Life History of Alexander McKay', MS 1177, 291p (typed transcript, including 31 pp. described here as Bowker TS which fall between pp. 192 and 230 of original), Wellington: Alexander Turnbull Library, p. 4.
[9] *Ibid.*
[10] *Ibid.*, p. 3.
[11] *Ibid.*, p. 4.
[12] *Ibid.*, p. 2.
[13] *Ibid.*, p. 2.
[14] *Ibid.*, pp. 6–7.
[15] Anna Campbell, pers. comm.
[16] McKay, 'Fragments', p. 7.
[17] *Ibid.*
[18] *Ibid.*, pp. 8–9. McKay commented that this story was entirely from hearsay and that he remembered nothing of it.
[19] *Ibid.*, p. 12.
[20] *Ibid.*, p. 15.
[21] *Ibid.*, p. 9.
[22] *Ibid.*, p. 18.
[23] *Ibid.*, p. 19.
[24] *Ibid.*, p. 19.
[25] *Ibid.*, p. 34.
[26] *Ibid.*, p. 35.
[27] *Ibid.*, p. 36.
[28] *Ibid.*, p. 39.

Chapter 2

[1] McKay, 'Fragments', p. 40.
[2] *Ibid.*, p. 42.
[3] *Ibid.*, p. 41.
[4] *Ibid.*, p. 41. James Sloan was schoolmaster from 1810–53.
[5] *Ibid.*, p. 58.
[6] *Ibid.*, p. 42.
[7] *Ibid.*, p. 43.
[8] *Ibid.*, p. 44.
[9] *Ibid.*, p. 31.
[10] *Ibid.*, p. 40.
[11] *Ibid.*, p. 40.
[12] *Ibid.*, pp. 48–9.
[13] *Ibid.*, p. 51.
[14] Hunter, *The Upper Glenkens*, p. 3.
[15] McKay, 'Fragments', p. 52.
[16] *Ibid.*, p. 54.
[17] *Ibid.*, p. 55.
[18] *Ibid.*, p. 56.
[19] *Ibid.*, p. 56.
[20] The catalogue now in the Carsphairn Heritage Centre lists 421 titles, including *Geology for Beginners* by G.F. Richardson (and *Geology and Mineralogy* by William Buckland), Sir Walter Scott's Waverley novels, *Nicholas Nickleby* by Charles Dickens,

the works of Robert Burns, the works of Shakespeare in fourteen volumes, Archibald Alison's *History of Europe*, Dr Livingstone's *Missionary Travels*, John Brown's *Dictionary of Bible Characters*, Bunyan's *Pilgrim's Progress*, Cook's voyages, *The Power of Prayer*, John Williams's *The Natural History of the Mineral Kingdom*, *Philosophy of Religion*, and an atlas.

[21] McKay, 'Fragments', p. 121.
[22] *Ibid.*, p. 57.
[23] *Ibid.*, p. 59.
[24] *Ibid.*, p. 60.
[25] *Ibid.*, p. 60.
[26] *Ibid.*, p. 61.
[27] *Ibid.*, p. 62.
[28] *Ibid.*, p. 63.
[29] *Ibid.*, p. 67.
[30] *Ibid.*, p. 67.
[31] *Ibid.*, p. 69.
[32] *Ibid.*, p. 72.
[33] *Ibid.*, p. 77.
[34] *Ibid.*, p. 77.
[35] *Ibid.*, p. 79.
[36] *Ibid.*, p. 81.
[37] *Ibid.*, p. 88.
[38] *Ibid.*, p. 82.
[39] *Ibid.*, p. 89.
[40] *Ibid.*, p. 90.
[41] *Ibid.*, p. 92.
[42] *Ibid.*, p. 93.
[43] *Ibid.*, p. 94.
[44] *Ibid.*, p. 94.
[45] *Ibid.*, p. 99.

Chapter 3

[1] Burns died in the nearby town of Dumfries in 1796, some sixty years before.
[2] McKay, 'Fragments' p. 101.
[3] *Ibid.*, p. 101.
[4] *Ibid.*, p. 102.
[5] *Ibid.*, p. 102.
[6] *Ibid.*, p. 103.
[7] *Ibid.*, p. 104.
[8] *Ibid.*, pp. 104–5.
[9] *Ibid.*, p. 106.
[10] *Ibid.*, p. 105.
[11] *Ibid.*, p. 107.
[12] *Ibid.*, pp. 131–32.
[13] *Ibid.*, p. 114.
[14] Alex was apparently in ignorance of the whole affair and "like a good bridegroom stayed away from Church on that day." *Ibid.*, p. 115.
[15] *Ibid.*, p. 115.
[16] *Ibid.*, pp. 115–16.
[17] *Ibid.*, p. 117.
[18] *Ibid.*, p. 121.
[19] *Ibid.*, p. 121.
[20] *Ibid.*, pp. 133–34.
[21] *Ibid.*, p. 135.
[22] *Ibid.*, p. 136.
[23] *Ibid.*, p. 136.
[24] *Ibid.*, p. 144.
[25] Deil's Well, pp. 149–50.
[26] *Ibid.*, p. 151.
[27] *Ibid.*, p. 155.
[28] *Ibid.*, pp. 156–157.
[29] *Ibid.*, p. 158.
[30] *Ibid.*, p. 158.
[31] *Ibid.*, p. 159.
[32] *Ibid.*, p. 159.
[33] *Ibid.*, p. 159.
[34] *Ibid.*, p. 160.
[35] *Ibid.*, p. 160.
[36] *Ibid.*, p. 160. There were 315 passengers (Mrs D. Bonthron, *Incidents in the course of a voyage to New Zealand made in ship "Helenslee" from Glasgow in the summer of 1863*. MS C011, 30 p. Otago Settlers Museum, Dunedin, p. 2).

Chapter 4

[1] McKay, 'Fragments', pp. 159–62.
[2] Bonthron, *Incidents in the course of a voyage*.
[3] T. Murray, 'Frae the Broomielaw to

the Waitemata: diary of the voyage of the "Helenslee"'. MS 92/51, 38p. Auckland War Memorial Museum, Auckland.
4. McKay, 'Fragments', p. 160.
5. Bonthron, p. 16.
6. Bonthron, p. 16.
7. Bonthron, p. 23.
8. McKay, 'Fragments', p. 161.
9. David Savill, *Sail to New Zealand: The Story of Shaw Savill and Co., 1598–1882*. London: Hale, 1986, p. 80.
10. Murray, p. 7.
11. Bonthron, p. 8.
12. Murray, p. 4.
13. *Ibid.*, p. 13.
14. *Ibid.*, p. 9.
15. Bonthron, p. 26.
16. Murray, p. 15.
17. *Ibid.*, p. 25.
18. *Ibid.*, p. 8.
19. *Ibid.*, p. 2.
20. McKay, 'Fragments', p. 161.
21. *Ibid.*, p. 161.
22. Bonthron, p. 22.
23. *Ibid.*, p. 27.
24. *Ibid.*, p. 11.
25. McKay, 'Fragments', p. 161.
26. 192 nautical miles = 221 miles or 355 kilometres. Bonthron, p. 25.
27. McKay, 'Fragments', p. 162
28. Bonthron, p. 27.
29. *Ibid.*
30. The voyage out to Campbelltown in seventy-nine days was to be one of the fastest and more comfortable trips, land to land, made by the *Helenslee*, but it was another month before the fickle winds of the lee side of the South Island allowed her to reach Dunedin, after a total elapsed time of 113 days from Glasgow. On some of her later trips the *Helenslee* experienced torrid weather: in 1872 she arrived in Auckland with her cargo in a bad condition after a voyage of 142 days. In that year another ship, the *Bulwark*, took 215 days to complete the same voyage; her cargo was so damaged by breakage and saltwater that it had to be dug out of the holds. Savill, p. 94.
31. Nine passengers, including Mrs Bonthron, disembarked at Bluff. The names of eight have been recorded, but Alexander McKay is not amongst them. www.geocities.com/nzyester/shipping/passlists/helenslee.txt
32. www.angelfire.com/okz/cbluff/helenslee1863.html
33. McKay, 'Fragments', p. 162.

Chapter 5
1. McKay, 'Fragments', p. 162. Corduroy paving was made by laying branches, frequently punga (tree fern) stems, crosswise along the path.
2. *Ibid.*, p. 163.
3. *Ibid.*, p. 163.
4. *Ibid.*, p. 164.
5. *Ibid.*, p. 165.
6. *Ibid.*, p. 166.
7. *Ibid.*, p. 167.
8. McKay, Alexander, Letter from Hamiltons, 1864, in MS Papers 4409-02, Alexander Turnbull Library, Wellington.
9. McKay, 'Fragments', p. 168
10. *Ibid.*, p. 168
11. *Ibid.*, p. 170.
12. *Ibid.*, p. 170.
13. *Ibid.*, p. 170.
14. *Ibid.*, p. 171.
15. McKay, Alexander, Letter from Hamiltons.
16. Feasible if he walked at a brisk pace for twelve hours or more.
17. McKay, 'Fragments', p. 172.
18. *Ibid.*, p. 173. The Barewood Plateau is a well-preserved part of the Otago peneplain, a surface of low relief

formed when the land had been eroded almost to sea level about 130 million years ago. Earth movements commenced 5–10 million years ago, and the surface was broken by faults, uplifted, and tilted. The distinctive character of the Central Otago landscape derives from the treeless remnants of this surface.

19. McKay, 'Fragments', p. 174.
20. June Wood, *Gold Trails of Otago*, A.H. & A.W. Reed Ltd, Wellington, 1970, p. 23.
21. McKay, 'Fragments', p. 176. Twelve years after McKay was swept off his feet a fine suspension bridge was built across the Taieri River at this spot. It features beautifully crafted pillars built of hand-knapped blocks of local stone.
22. *Ibid.*, p. 177
23. *Ibid.*, p. 177.
24. Peat consists of accumulated, partly decomposed swamp vegetation. As it contains 90–95 per cent water in its natural state, it has to be cut into blocks with a spade, then stacked and dried over the summer months. Once dry, it burns well with a smoky flame and a distinctive smell.
25. McKay, 'Fragments', p. 178
26. *Ibid.*, p. 179.
27. Erik Olssen, *A History of Otago*, Dunedin: John McIndoe, 1984, p. 59.
28. *Ibid.*, p. 180.
29. A.H. McClintock, *The History of Otago*, Otago Centennial Historical publications, 1949, p. 455.
30. Olssen, p. 58
31. McKay, 'Fragments', p. 181.
32. A 'lead' is a ribbon of gold-bearing ground, usually representing a former river course or beach.
33. McKay, 'Fragments', p. 181.
34. *Ibid.*, pp. 181–82.
35. *Ibid.*, p. 182.
36. Ryan was deeply unpopular, perhaps partly on account of an incident a few months before, when Ryan's colleague, Sergeant Garvey, had perished in a snowstorm on the Hawkdun Plateau, near Clarks (the Burster or Buster) Diggings. Ryan was sharply criticised for not mounting a search more promptly. The gold-prospectors hated him for his ostentatious arrogance. Sullivan, Jim. 'Garvey legend looms large in Otago history', *Otago Daily Times*, Saturday, 25 March 2000, H27. A lonely cairn above the junction of Hut and Fraters Creek now marks the spot where Garvey succumbed.
37. McKay, 'Fragments', pp. 182–83
38. McKay, 'Fragments', Bowker TS, p. 2.
39. McKay, 'Fragments', p. 192.
40. McKay, 'Fragments', Bowker TS, p. 4.
41. *Ibid.*, p. 4.
42. *Ibid.*, p. 4.
43. Hugh Miller, *The Testimony of the Rocks*. Edinburgh: William P. Nimmo, 1857; McKay, 'Fragments', Bowker TS, p. 5. Miller (1802–56) was a self-taught geologist who started life as a stonemason. He became interested in the fossil fish he encountered in his work and developed an international reputation for his discoveries and their classification. He lived in the little town of Cromarty on the Black Isle near Inverness, where the National Trust today preserves his thatched cottage. Thirty-two years later McKay, who by then had also attained a similar measure of respectability, was to visit the short-lived New Zealand 'sister' settlement of Cromarty in Preservation Inlet.
44. McKay, 'Fragments', Bowker TS, p. 12.
45. *Ibid.*, p. 12.
46. *Ibid.*, p. 14.

Chapter 6

1. Mateship was a verbal agreement on the strength of a handshake to pool their resources until the arrangement was equally formally terminated.
2. McKay, 'Fragments', Bowker TS, p. 15.
3. Ibid., p. 15.
4. A deck (possibly temporary) running through part of the hold.
5. Ibid., p. 16.
6. Ibid., pp. 17–18.
7. Ibid., p. 18.
8. Ibid., pp. 18–19.
9. Ibid., p. 22.
10. Squatter: a runholder who had initially taken residence on unoccupied land, usually on very easy terms.
11. Ibid., p. 24.
12. Ibid., p. 25.
13. Ibid., p. 26.
14. Ibid., p. 26. Clermont was established following a significant find of gold in 1875 and is now the centre of a rich agricultural and pastoral area, with forestry and coal mining also important industries.
15. Ironically, the area eventually became an important copper-mining centre.
16. McKay, 'Fragments', Bowker TS, p. 27. The salts washed from the soils had been concentrated through time by persistent evaporation.
17. McKay, 'Fragments', p. 230.
18. Ibid., p. 230. The potentially gold bearing 'wash' is disintegrated under water in a gold pan, allowing any gold to settle out.
19. Ibid., p. 230.
20. It was during one of these near-delirious periods that his mind recalled the time when his Granny had given him a thumb-spread bannock, instead of the walloping he had expected, and he realised its significance. Ibid., p. 39.
21. Ibid., pp. 232–33.
22. Pers. comm. Dr Peter Strang to G. Bishop, 13 June 2003.
23. McKay, 'Fragments', pp. 233–34.
24. Ibid., p. 240. His illness persisted for several more weeks.
25. Ibid., p. 251.
26. Ibid., pp. 255–56
27. Ibid., p. 257.
28. Probably Wolfang Peak (see picture, p. 85), an isolated spine of volcanic rock in the undulating country of Peak Downs, about forty-five kilometres northeast of Clermont.
29. McKay, 'Fragments', p. 258.
30. Ibid., p. 259
31. Ibid., p. 260.
32. From Clermont to Rockhampton is about 400 km.
33. McKay, 'Fragments', p. 262.
34. Ibid., p. 263.

Chapter 7

1. McKay, 'Fragments', p. 264
2. Ibid., p. 265.
3. Ibid., p. 268.
4. Ibid., p. 269. When McKay wrote this account he had been absent from Scotland for fifty years and was unlikely ever to return, but he still referred to it as 'home'. My Scottish grandparents did the same, much to my childhood puzzlement.
5. Ibid., p. 272
6. Ibid., p. 273. The house was probably near Dog Kennel corner, about three kilometres on the Mackenzie side of the pass.
7. Ibid., p. 273.
8. Ibid., p. 274.
9. Ibid., p. 274.
10. Ibid., pp. 276–77.
11. Ibid., p. 279.
12. Ibid., p. 280. McKay's route

over Burkes Pass and across the Mackenzie Country is now State Highway 8, but is still known as the Bullock Wagon Trail.
13 *Ibid.*, p. 283.
14 *Ibid.*, p. 285.
15 *Ibid.*, p. 286.
16 *Ibid.*, p. 289.
17 *Ibid.*, p. 287.
18 *Ibid.*, p. 288. The Benmore Station diaries record a barrel of whisky being sent on to Lake Ohau Station on one occasion. Robert Pinney, *Early North Otago Runs*, Auckland: Collins, 1981, p. 97.
19 Removal of tails and testicles.
20 McKay later noted he spent four years exploring the Mackenzie, much of which must have been done in combination with working on the station. 'Mr. Alexander McKay.' *The Cyclopedia of New Zealand, Vol. 1, Wellington Provincial District*, Wellington: The Cyclopedia Company, 1897, p. 174.
21 William Alexander McKay, handwritten notes in the back of McKay, 'Fragments', date unknown.
22 Mary Barnes was present at the marriage of Alexander and Susannah the following year.
23 Although Susannah's *Intention to Marry* declaration indicates she arrived about this date, it has not been possible to confirm that she was on the *Countess Russell*.
24 It is possible that Susannah may have had to complete her trip on horseback, or even by boat. As Pinney notes, citing an obituary of Edmund Hodgkinson (1867), Lake Ohau was 'a very rough place with no access by road, everything having to be transported across the lake.' McKay's 'Fragments' makes it clear (pp. 283–85) that travel beside the lake was certainly possible on foot, and probably by horse in 1866. Robert Pinney, *Early South Canterbury Runs*, Wellington: A.H. and A.W. Reed, 1971, p. 152.
25 *Ibid.*, p. 152.
26 McKay, 'Fragments', p. 125.
27 Wheeler and his family had arrived in New Zealand on the ship *Zambezi* on 20 September 1863, only five days earlier than McKay. He became established rather more quickly than did McKay.
28 St Andrews Presbyterian Church, Wellew Street, Dunedin, New Zealand, *An Illustrated Sketch of the Origin and History of the Church (1861–1913)*, Dunedin: Coulls Culling, 1914, p. 16. (The photo on page 95 of the 'The Old Manse, Hillside' is from p. 19).
29 Pinney, *Early North Otago Runs*, pp. 97–98
30 John eventually settled in the North Island, and died in 1917 at the age of eighty, at Wanganui.
31 Julius Haast acquired the right to use the appellation 'von' (=Sir) when he received a hereditary knighthood from the Emperor of Austria in 1875. It was also used by his frequently quoted son and biographer, H.F. (Heinrich) von Haast.

Chapter 8

1 G.J. Williams, *Economic Geology of New Zealand: the T.J. McKee memorial volume*. Parkville, Australia: Australasian Institute of Mining and Metallurgy, 1974. 2nd ed., p. 5.
2 Cited in Wood, *Gold Trails of Otago*, p. 4.
3 Peggy Burton, *The New Zealand Geological Survey 1865–1965*. New Zealand Department of Scientific and Industrial Research, 1965, p. 14.
4 Fossils tell much more, in fact, as they record the evolution of life,

the environmental successes and disasters. The understanding of the history of our intricate world cannot be divorced from the record of the fossils.

[5] H.F. von Haast, *The Life and Times of Sir Julius von Haast, Explorer, Geologist, Museum Builder*, Wellington: The Author, 1948, p. 651.

[6] Alexander McKay, 'Dr. Haast and Mr. McKay', Letter to the Editor, *New Zealand Mail*, 3 October, 1874.

[7] Haast actively traded or exchanged New Zealand material for exhibits from overseas. Moa bones were particularly useful in this respect.

[8] Alexander McKay, Letter of 4 June 1872 to Haast, cited in Haast, H.F. von, p. 651.

[9] Sumner Cave, at Moa-bone Point, is now more closely allied with the newer suburb of Redcliffs, a community non-existent at the time of this drama.

[10] H.F. von Haast reports McKay was paid £2 and Lowman £2/2/- per week for the seven weeks. It seems unlikely that McKay would hire an assistant at a rate higher than that at which he himself was being paid: one can only wonder if the implication from Haast's report that McKay was the junior partner in the excavation was accidental or deliberate. This is one of several instances quoted here where H.F. von Haast appears to construct an image which does not gel. Haast, H.F. von, p. 722.

[11] J. Haast, Postscript in *New Zealand Mail*, 3 October 1874.

[12] Alexander McKay, Letter in *Transactions of the New Zealand Institute*, vol. 7, 1874, p. 70.

[13] In addition, von Haast may have decided the museum extensions were more important. The results of the Sumner Cave investigation and revelation of the body would have to wait until there was no risk of any scandal upsetting the delicate stages of the museum development. McKay would have had little if any conception of such politicking.

[14] James Park, 'The Canterbury Gilpin: A Notable New Zealand Epic', Letter to the Editor, *Otago Daily Times*, 16 May 1936.

[15] M002, pp. 98–105.

[16] Hector's motives in presenting McKay's paper may have been complex. McKay himself wrote later that 'Dr Hector's connection was a personal favour' (possibly to spare the inexperienced and unqualified McKay the ordeal of a public address before such an august body). Hector would have been fully aware of the quality of McKay's work since the cave excavation but, because this work was at the time unpublished, neither Haast nor anyone else would have been aware of McKay's development and potential. Professional rivalry, allied with a little mischief-making, may also have been involved, given it was an opportunity to torpedo his pet theory. Whatever the reason, Hector can hardly have been unaware of Haast's likely displeasure at the presentation of McKay's paper, although he was probably taken aback by the vindictiveness of Haast's response.

[17] J. Haast, Telegram of 14 December 1874, *Transactions of the New Zealand Institute*, vol. 7, 1874, p. 69.

[18] J. Haast, 'Researches and Excavations Carried on in and near the Moa-bone Point Cave, Sumner Road, in the year 1872', *Transactions of the New Zealand Institute*, vol. 7, 1874, pp. 54–85, 2 pl. Postscript, pp. 528–30. (Also published separately by the Times Office, Christchurch, 22 p., 1874.)

[19] The postscript is quite long. It was

[20] J. Haast, Postscript, *New Zealand Mail*, 3 October 1874.

[21] Alexander McKay, 'Dr. Haast and Mr. MacKay', Letter to the Editor, *New Zealand Mail*, 3 October 1874, plate II, p. 67.

[22] By this stage (September 1874), McKay had completed three major geological surveys and reported on all – a total of 103 printed pages, although these were not printed until 1877. In addition, he had had two papers read before the Philosophical Institute. He had come a long way in the two years since the cave excavation, making Haast's comments even more inappropriate.

[23] Alexander McKay, 'Dr. Haast and Mr. MacKay'.

[24] The shells were the accumulated debris of shellfish eaters and implied a substantial period of (intermittent) occupation subsequent to the burial.

[25] Alexander McKay, Draft Letter to R. Lowman, 4 October 1875, in MS Papers 443-3-15/12, Hocken Library, Dunedin.

[26] H.F. von Haast, p. 744.

[27] W. Mantell, motion tabled in Parliament, 19 October 1873. Cited in Haast, H.F. von, p. 740.

[28] *Nature*, vol. XIII, 6 January 1876, p. 196. Cited in Haast, H.F. von, pp. 742–43.

[29] Atholl Anderson, *Prodigious Birds: Moas and moa-hunting in prehistoric New Zealand*, Cambridge University Press, 1989, p. 103.

[30] In 1876 Hutton mentioned in a letter to Mantell that von Haast himself had been ill, and was going 'to the hot lakes'. John Yaldwyn, *GSNZ Newsletter* 117, 1998, p. 33.

[31] H.F. von Haast, p. 738.

[32] *Ibid.*, p. 748.

[33] A. McKay, Introduction. *Lines Written on a Scene from Lake Harris Saddle, West Coast, Middle Island*. Wellington: James Hughes, 1880. Reproduced in *GSNZ Historical Studies Group Newsletter* 2, March 1991, pp. 15–19. See Appendix 2.

[34] [A. McKay], *The Canterbury Gilpin; or, The Capture and Flight of the Moa. A Poem by Dinornis Sumnerensis. Parts I & II*, Wellington: James Hughes, 1880. See Appendix 2.

[35] T.M. Hocken, *A Bibliography of the Literature Relating to New Zealand*, Wellington: John Mackay, Government Printer, 1909, p. 329.

[36] James Park, 'The Canterbury Gilpin: A Notable New Zealand Epic'.

[37] MS Papers 83: folder 214; subsequently published in the *Newsletter of the Geological Society of New Zealand*, 66: 47–49.

[38] H.F. von Haast, p. 746.

[39] *Ibid.*, p. 745.

[40] *Ibid.*, p. 746.

[41] *Ibid.*, p. 747.

[42] Noel O'Hare, 'Words Heal: Literature has the power to ease our dis-ease', *The New Zealand Listener*, 10 October 1998, p. 49.

[43] McKay would have been furious at this excision of 336 stanzas from his epic! John Gilpin was a real-life character whose exploits became legendary and featured in a well-known ballad by William Cowper entitled *The Diverting History of John Gilpin* (1872). The poem tells how Gilpin and his wife and children became separated during a journey to the Bell Inn, after Gilpin loses control of his horse. See Appendix 2.

[44] [A. McKay], *The Canterbury Gilpin*, pp.

5, 7, 11.

Chapter 9

1. Alexander McKay, Letter to Haast, c. 10 March 1873, MS Papers 0242-02, Alexander Turnbull Library, Wellington.
2. *Ibid.*
3. Alexander McKay, Letter to Hector, 7 April 1873, MS Papers 0242-02, Alexander Turnbull Library, Wellington.
4. Alexander McKay, Letter to John Ingram, 25 April 1873, MS Papers 0242-02, Alexander Turnbull Library, Wellington.
5. H.F. von Haast, p. 652.
6. Duncan McKay was actually born on Sunday, 18 May. This postscript is cited in Burton, *The New Zealand Geological Survey 1865–1965*, p. 22.
7. Not only are the above sentences out of character, but the scenario of von Haast lending money to McKay for his and Susannah's fares also seems unreal, as McKay had received £15 ($2250) from Hector only three or four days before he sailed. I have been unable to find the letter quoted by H.F. von Haast, although other letters of this vintage from McKay to Haast are present in the Alexander Turnbull Library collection of Haast's correspondence. The image of the benevolent and gracious von Haast implied by H.F. von Haast appears to be without foundation.
8. McKay, Letter to Haast, 10 March 1873.
9. McKay, Letter to John Ingram, 25 April 1873.
10. William Skey, 'Elegy (On the late Alexander McKay)' in *The Pirate Chief and the Mummy's Complaint with Various Zealandian Poems*, Haggett & Percy, Wellington. 1889, p. 60.
11. M004.
12. *Ibid.*, p. 60.
13. *Ibid.*, p. 61.
14. *Ibid.*, **p. 62.**
15. A sequence of sedimentary rocks has the oldest at the bottom, with progressively younger strata superimposed on top. Uplift and folding during the process of becoming land may result in rock sequences being tilted, and sometimes stood on end (e.g. Nugget Point), or in extreme cases even being completely overturned.
16. *Ibid.*, p. 66.
17. *Ibid.*, p. 67.
18. *Ibid.*, p. 69.
19. M005, p. 74.
20. M005, p. 92.
21. *Ibid.*, pp. 86–87.
22. *Ibid.*, p. 100.
23. *Ibid.*, p. 98.
24. Sir Charles Lyell, *Principles of Geology*, 12th edition, John Murray, London, 1875.
25. Hugh Miller, *The Testimony of the Rocks*.
26. S.H. Cox, 'Report on Westland District', *New Zealand Geological Survey Reports of Geological Exploration 1874–1876*, vol. 9, 1877, pp. 63–93, geol. map, sects; 'Report on Coal Measures at Jackson's Bay', *New Zealand Geological Survey Reports of Geological Exploration 1874–1876*, vol. 9, 1877, p. 119.
27. S.H. Cox, 'Report on Westland District', p. 65.
28. M006, pp. 116–64.
29. *Ibid.*, p. 145.
30. *Ibid.*, p. 132.
31. *Ibid.*
32. M008, pp. 36–42.
33. *Ibid.*, p. 36.
34. M006, p. 132.
35. M012.
36. A telegraph cable linking the North

and South Islands was laid in 1866.
[37] M012, p. 172.

Chapter 10

[1] A detail, probably related to his developing confidence, is that on two successive reports (M021, M022) he shortened his name to Alex. He did the same again later on M026, although he then reverted to Alexander and retained it for all subsequent technical work. He used the short form when signing letters, etc., and it seems likely that he was regularly called Alex.
[2] Roger Cooper in *The Dictionary of New Zealand Biography Vol. 2, 1870–1900* (1993). Department of Internal Affairs, Wellington.
[3] M040, p. 56.
[4] M040.
[5] M017.
[6] *Ibid.*, p. 15.
[7] M019.
[8] M049.
[9] M026.
[10] M040, pp. 56–92.
[11] M033. This survey resulted in another 2700 fossils being added to the national collection.
[12] M012.
[13] M019.
[14] An attractive brachiopod fossil, sometimes present in large numbers.
[15] It had taken him a week to reach the locality; today it would take only a matter of hours.
[16] M019.
[17] This poem was found interleaved with a draft report from May 1879 by McKay on earthquakes in North Canterbury (MU 000 135110 Box 3, 20 pp. Te Papa); forwarded to the author by Rodney Grapes.
[18] He travelled by either the *Antrim* or *Mountaineer*, both paddle steamers operating on Lake Wakitipu at this time. M036.
[19] Forerunners of the back-country boom of a century later. Now more than 10,000 people per year walk the track. The river and side streams are all bridged, huts have coal for heating and gas for cooking, and there is an emergency shelter at Lake Harris.
[20] Distances in the mountains are measured in time taken, not mileage covered.
[21] This hut was demolished in 1976 to make way for one of the new breed of Department of Conservation huts. The hand-adzed heart rimu doorframe, still sound as a bell, and the heavily initialled door are now in the Arrowtown Museum. The tabletop, too, carried many names and initials, including those of some well-known geologists, but I do not remember reading A. McKay anywhere.
[22] M036, p. 119.
[23] In 1978 an able geologist and mountaineer, Ken Hyslop, elected to map the Serpentine Saddle area for his MSc thesis. He found the route north from Harris Saddle so demanding that he soon abandoned it.
[24] M036, p. 119.
[25] James Park, *Maori and Early European Explorations in Western Otago*. Dunedin: Otago Daily Times and Witness, 1922, p. 11.
[26] M036, p. 119.
[27] McKay was quite specific that their camp was at the edge of the bush on the west (Hollyford) face of the range. A. McKay, 1880. *Lines Written on a Scene from Lake Harris Saddle*, in *GSHZ Historical Studies Group Newsletter* No. 2 (March 1991), p. 17.
[28] *Ibid.*, p. 16.
[29] The lack of food, fire for warmth and cooking, and dry clothing, in wet

NOTES

30. A. McKay, 1880. *Lines Written on a Scene from Lake Harris Saddle.*
31. [A. McKay], *The Canterbury Gilpin.*
32. M036, p. 119.
33. A waterfall 115 metres high in Sixteen Mile Creek, on the eastern (Shotover) side of the Richardson Range was named the Alexander McKay Falls in 1938 (see Appendix 1 and p. 193).
34. M036, p. 131.
35. M040, p. 56–92.
36. Park, pp. 1–15. Nancy M. Adams, 'John Buchanan F.L.S (1819–1898) Botanist and Artist', unpublished manuscript. Adams's manuscript includes excerpts from John Buchanan's drafts and letters.
37. Buchanan (1819–98) was a botanist and landscape artist. He also served as a draftsman for NZ Geological Survey. He accompanied Hector on his early explorations of western Otago, and also accompanied McKay on a number of field trips.
38. Park, p. 9.
39. Park, p. 10.
40. McKay's account is written as usual in the first person and Park is not mentioned until the tenth page of the report. Park, however, makes it quite clear he was accompanying McKay at least from Waimate in November. M040, p. 56.
41. Buchanan had left Wellington on 17 December for Christchurch, on the steamer *Wanaka*, then by train to Oamaru and finally coach to Omarama. M040, p. 66.
42. M040, p. 56.
43. Neither McKay's report nor Buchanan's diary support these claims. Buchanan's diary indicates they camped at Station Creek (Maitland Stream) near the north end of Lake Ohau for only five days before returning to Benmore Station and then Omarama. See Adams, pp. 70–71.
44. Park, pp. 9–10.
45. Adams, p. 71.
46. *Ibid.*, p. 71. *Poa exigua* is a native grass only 3–4 cm high which had been discovered in the same area by Buchanan and Hector on their visit to the Matukituki in 1863. The significance of Buchanan's note on this occasion is its confirmation that McKay's interests now extended beyond rocks, but it also indicates a general spirit of cooperation, which is not apparent from McKay's accounts.
47. Poor Park seemed destined to be omitted from the accounts of both men.
48. At this stage there was no track up the East Branch and the bush had not yet experienced the depredations of introduced animals, although rabbits were beginning to make an impact on grassed areas. Jerry Aspinall, *Farming Under Aspiring*, Alexandra: Macpherson Publishing, 1993, p. 224. Park and McKay probably recrossed the river beyond Snowy Creek (Glacier Burn) and forced their way through the bush on the east side of the river until they reached Junction Flat at the confluence of the Kitchener and Matukituki. Lack of accessible rock outcrops would have required McKay to deduce what he could from the composition of the river gravels.
49. The pink piedmontite schist is prominent in the gravel of Snowy Creek (Glacier Burn), the first tributary of the East Matukituki which drains the eastern slopes of Mt Avalanche, but is less so in the second, Kitchener Stream, which drains the faces of Mt Aspiring.

M040, p. 82.
50. Hugh Macpherson and his brothers Allan and Duncan had arrived from Scotland in 1864, a year after McKay.
51. Aspinall, p. 33.
52. Adams, p. 71. Probably Scott's Bivvy, an overhanging but not entirely weatherproof rock which would have provided a cramped and slightly damp bed for three. Graham Bishop, *The Aspiring Region*. New Zealand Alpine Club (Inc.) with Moir. Rev. ed. 1989, pp. 17–18.
53. Adams, p. 71.
54. M040, pp. 82–83.
55. Adams, p. 72.
56. Park, p. 10.
57. M039, p. 91.
58. This would be quite feasible without mountaineering equipment and would have given him the view of Mt Earnslaw he mentions.
59. Park, p. 10.
60. M040, pp. 90–91.
61. Park, p. 10.

Chapter 11
1. Also called the Buster (or Burster Diggings).
2. M055.
3. *Ibid.*, p. 94.
4. *Ibid.*, p. 95. This period is now known to have affected the whole country and is known as the Kaikoura Orogeny.
5. M066, p. 27.
6. *Ibid.*, pp. 30-31.
7. *Ibid.*, p. 129.
8. *Ibid.*, p. 130. Ironically he lived for twenty years at 6 Lewisville Terrace, Thorndon, within fifty metres of the active Wellington Fault.
9. *Ibid.*, p. 132.
10. This concept, of a topography which wasn't always there, put him on a collision course with Hector, who believed the 'cover' beds had accumulated in shallow lakes and seas bordered by the present mountain ranges. Fortunately, Hector, unlike Haast, was not so blinkered that he could not see the persuasiveness of McKay's arguments and, after a cautious inspection of the evidence, he agreed, at least in principle. Isolated remnants of the cover strata occurring on top of mountain ranges – for instance in Otago and the Ruahine range of the North Island – showed that, once again, McKay was right.
11. J. Hector, Introduction, *New Zealand Geological Survey Reports of Geological Exploration 1885*, vol. 17, 1886, pp. ix–xl, pp. xii–xiii.
12. Equivalent to about $42,000 today.
13. Alexander McKay, Letter to James Hector, 21 September 1885. MS Papers 0242–02, Alexander Turnbull Library, Wellington.
14. Burton, *The New Zealand Geological Survey 1865–1965*, p. 23.
15. M077.
16. M078.
17. For McKay to go into the field without such vital equipment is like the Governor of the Reserve Bank turning up to work barefoot and without a tie.
18. Presumably the general help.
19. Legend has it that McKay used to return his fossils to the office in empty whisky cases. I suspect this story came about early in his career and the brandy case remark is an oblique reference to it. It is not known if brandy was Sir James Hector's preferred tipple. For Hector's expedition along the coast of Fiordland on board the *Matilda Hayes*, the vessel was provisioned with ten gallons of rum. Again the comment has a manic flavour, as does the remainder of the letter.

20. Alexander Mckay, Letter to James Hector, Blackley's Empire Hotel, Palmerston, 26 January 1886. MS Papers 0242–02, Alexander Turnbull Library, Wellington.
21. M074.
22. *Transactions and Proceedings of the New Zealand Institute*, 25 July 1888, vol. XXI (1889), p. 489.
23. M092.
24. *Ibid.*, p. 5.
25. *Ibid.*, pp. 9–10.
26. Personally, I gave the 'Glynn Wye' report a mark of 9.5, the highest I awarded his papers.
27. Sir James Hector, *Transactions and Proceedings of the New Zealand Institute*, 14 November 1888, vol. XXI, 1889, p. 509.
28. James Hector, Introduction, *New Zealand Geological Survey Reports of Geological Exploration, 1888–1889*, vol. 20, 1890, pp. ix–lviii, 2 pl., 6 fig, p. xl.
29. M190. The freshness of details in the photo of the fault trace (with the reclining figure) is consistent with its being taken in 1888, soon after the earthquake. The figure in the photograph appears to be McKay himself or possibly Mr Rutherford or Mr Thompson.
30. M092, p. 12.
31. M094.
32. M095.
33. M099. The Alpine Fault is one of the dramatic features of the Earth's crust. It forms the front of the Southern Alps, which seem to leap skyward behind it, from the low-lying coastal plain. Less obvious is the way the older rocks of Fiordland have been sliced through, so that one half has been shifted almost 500 kilometres north to Nelson. Like many large-scale features, the fault becomes more difficult to see, the closer one gets to it!
34. *Ibid.*, p. 27.
35. *Ibid.*, pp. 26–27. Edward Dobson was the Canterbury provincial engineer, and father of Haast's wife. J. von Haast, *Geology of the Provinces of Canterbury and Westland, New Zealand. A Report Comprising the Results of Official Explorations.* Christchurch: Times Office, 486 p., 19 pl., 4 maps, 62 sect.
36. M099, p. 27.
37. M105.
38. It is interesting that Hector accepted this report for publication, and tempting to speculate that the request for simple English came from the 'grocer from Kumara', R.J. Seddon, and was directed at Hector as much as McKay.
39. M105, p. 45.
40. *Ibid.*, p. 46.
41. *Ibid.*, p. 46.
42. *Ibid.*, pp. 46–47.
43. M115.
44. *New Zealand Gazette*, Thursday, 21 May 1891, p. 576. At the time JPs were selected on the recommendation of the local policeman.
45. M190.
46. J. Hector, 'Progress Report, 1888–1889'. *New Zealand Geological Survey Reports of Geological Exploration 1888–1889*, vol. 20, ix–lviii, 2 pl., 6 fig., p. lii.
47. M098.
48. *Ibid.*, p. 462.
49. Presumably he had been taking photographs with a standard lens before this date.
50. William Main, *Wellington Through a Victorian Lens*, Millwood Press, Wellington, 1972, p. 101.
51. The presence of the *Vjestnik* in Wellington (Lambton) Harbour is a fascinating episode in itself. In 1885–86 there were widespread fears of a Russian invasion, and when the *Vjestnik* appeared off Wellington

Heads and requested permission to enter to effect repairs, rumour was rife. Permission was granted, however, and the ship anchored offshore for nine days. Eight days after it sailed north, the eruption of Mt Tarawera occurred. The explosion was felt as far south as Christchurch, and in the Wellington area was likened to thunder out at sea. The *New Zealand Herald* reported 'From the continuousness of the firing, the loudness of reports, and the fact that there were occasional salvoes of guns, it is the impression that they must have proceeded from a man-of-war, and the supposition is that it might be the Russian cruiser *Vestnik* [sic], which was believed to be coming up the West Coast.' R.F. Keam, *Tarawera Eruption: The Volcano Outburst of June 10, 1886*. Auckland: R.F. Keam, 1985, p. 16.

[52] W.T.L. Travers, *Transactions and Proceedings of the New Zealand Institute*, 13 August 1890, vol. XXIII (1891), p. 605.

[53] Cited in Main, *Wellington Through a Victorian Lens*, p. 101.

[54] J. Hector, *Transactions and Proceedings of the New Zealand Institute*, 13 August 1890, vol. XXIII (1891), p. 605.

[55] M098.

[56] John Patterson, 'Telephoto lens. Alexander McKay and the development of the Telephoto Lens'. Unpublished MS, Geology Department, Victoria University of Wellington. Undated, p. 3.

[57] The acrimony appears to have been fuelled by third-party correspondents, one of whom (Mr A. Martin of Wanganui) made a 'scandalous accusation against me (Dallmeyer) and my firm.' Thomas R. Dallmeyer, 'The Telephoto lens', Letter to the Editor, *The Photographic News*, 16 November 1894.

[58] A meeting of the two was prevented by a quirk of fate. Dallmeyer undertook a trip to New Zealand for the benefit of his health, but unfortunately his health was not up to it and he died 'in New Zealand waters' before his ship made port.

[59] 'Mr. Alexander McKay', *The Cyclopedia of New Zealand*, pp. 174–75.

[60] He also claimed, lightheartedly, to have invented the frozen meat industry. *The Cyclopedia of New Zealand*, pp. 174–75.

[61] The legendary claim that he ground lenses from the base of circular bottles may well have been rooted in the frustration caused by the six-month delay between ordering and delivery of the necessary materials.

[62] *Transactions and Proceedings of the New Zealand Institute*, 25 July 1888, vol. XXI (1889), p. 489.

[63] I have been unable to confirm this report (Burton 1965) or determine when it occurred. Burton, *The New Zealand Geological Survey 1895–1965*, p. 22.

[64] Hector continued as Director of the Colonial Museum, and Manager of the New Zealand Institute. In 1903 he travelled to Canada for official recognition of his work with the Palliser expedition, but the occasion was marred by the sudden death of his son who had accompanied him. Hector himself died in 1907. His life and achievements were honoured by the establishment, by the New Zealand Institute (now the Royal Society of New Zealand), of the Hector medal as their major award for excellence in scientific research.

Chapter 12

[1] M121.
[2] M122.
[3] M128.

4   M099.
5   See Simon Nathan, *Harold Wellman: A Man Who Moved New Zealand*. Wellington: Victoria University Press, 2005, pp. 116–17.
6   Alexander McKay, *Report on the Older Auriferous Drifts of Central Otago*, 2nd ed. Wellington: Government Printer, vi + 119 pp., geol. map, 28 sect.
7   M135.
8   Appendix from Biggar, G.V., 'Diary of George Biggar of Croydon' [1896]. Manuscript held in the Otago Early Settlers Museum, Dunedin. Published as Appendix D in A.C. and N.C. Begg, *Port Preservation*, Whitcombe and Tombs, 1973, pp. 343–60.
9   At the time, Cromarty consisted of a hotel, two boarding houses, a sawmill, and about a dozen huts. There were no roads or pavements and going anywhere involved wading through peat bog. George Biggar saw it as appearing 'to be anything but a thriving diggings township.' Today nothing is left. For a description of Cromarty in its heyday, and a comprehensive account of the whole region, see A.C. and N.C. Begg, *Port Preservation*.
10 He noted that Preservation Inlet, being a port of call for the Union Steam Shipping Company's steamers making the yearly excursion trips to the sounds of the West Coast, 'is thus fairly well known to the pleasure-seeking or health-conserving portion of the travelling public'. M135, p. 32.
11 *Ibid.*, p. 31.
12 *Ibid.*, p. 31. The nature of these special provisions is unknown, but given that McKay was planning on periods above the bush line where there is little if any fuel, it is likely he was carrying some dried supplies which could be eaten raw or reconstituted in cold water.
13 Biggar, in Begg, *Port Preservation*, p. 346.
14 *Ibid.*, pp. 348–49.
15 *Ibid.*, p. 349.
16 *Ibid.*, p. 349.
17 Linck appears to have been a scientific assistant to McKay with some botanical and geological abilities. Biggar, in Begg, *Port Preservation*, p. 349.
18 Biggar, in Begg, *Port Preservation*, p. 350.
19 Biggar was clearly a tower of strength in such situations. As a young child, he emigrated from Scotland with his family. At the time of this incident he was forty-one, fourteen years younger than McKay.
20 Biggar, in Begg, *Port Preservation*, p. 352.
21 *Ibid.*, p. 353. In fact, McKay correctly noted that the granite extended to Prices Harbour, a further five kilometres east of Big River, but at the mouth of Big River itself there is an infaulted strip of younger (Tertiary) rocks almost two kilometres wide. This may not have been visible from their vantage point.
22 Many explorers had dogs specifically to catch ground birds. However, in 1847 Brunner's party ended up eating the dog. (See Philip Temple, *New Zealand Explorers: Great Journeys of Discovery*, Christchurch: Whitcoulls, 1985, p. 73.)
23 Biggar, in Begg, *Port Preservation*, pp. 353–54. Kiwi, kakapo, even weka, have been comprehensively eliminated from this area.
24 *Ibid.*, p. 356. A recent attempt to repeat this feat failed to get a single bite. Not only have the ground birds been eliminated, less obvious changes have occurred underwater too.
25 J. Hilton, Letter to A. McKay, August 1896. Cited in full in A. C. and N. C.

Begg, *Port Preservation*, pp. 263–64.
[26] Biggar, in Begg, *Port Preservation*, p. 360.
[27] William and May Matilda were married in Kaikoura on 7 December 1897.
[28] Duncan and Henrietta were married at the Registrar's Office, Palmerston North, on 7 September 1897.
[29] Rosa was born to Duncan and Henrietta, and William Reay was born to William and May Matilda.
[30] M194.
[31] W.J. Sollas, *Rocks of Cape Colville Peninsula, with an Introduction and Descriptive Notes by Alexander McKay.* 2 vols. Wellington: Government Printer. Vol. 1. viii + 289 pp., 104 pl. (1905); Vol. 2. vi + 215 pp., geol. map, 133 pl. (1906).
[32] When the news of the Tarawera eruption reached the Geological Survey, Park and Hector were aboard the Government Steamer *Hinemoa* within the hour, which then sailed at full speed to Tauranga. Unfortunately McKay missed the boat, probably because he could not be contacted quickly. His omission from the group was unfortunate, particularly given the photographic skills he had perfected at the time.
[33] One of three times the spire has suffered earthquake damage. M190, p. 41.
[34] *Ibid.*, p. 44.
[35] *Ibid.*, p. 57.
[36] *Ibid.*, p. 78.
[37] *Ibid.*, pp. 79–80.
[38] He may have rented an outbuilding.
[39] The original Glynn Wye report was printed in 1888 and did not contain photographs.
[40] Presumably the wife of the Glenkens runholder. Mary may have been their daughter.
[41] The gentleman in this photograph (Mr Rutherford? and his dogs?) looks to be the same as the one in the fence and trench photographs and may also be the one mentioned in his report.
[42] This is the only written indication in either this letter or his report that he was accompanied by his son William.
[43] Alexander McKay, Letter of 15 February 1902, in MS Papers 0242-02, Alexander Turnbull Library, Wellington.
[44] Dr C.D. Henry, M.B., BC, Mines document 1902/982 National Archives, p. 1.
[45] A.M. Short, Memo 15/3/1902, Mines Document 1902/982 National Archives, p. 1.
[46] Mines document 1902/982 National Archives, p. 2.
[47] A. Mason, 'The Geology of New Zealand' by Alexander McKay, *GSNZ Historical Studies Group Newsletter* No. 14, pp. 37–39, March 1997, p. 37.

Chapter 13

[1] Most of the details on her death certificate are inconsistent with her date of birth in 1835, and her presumed arrival in New Zealand in February 1867 (see Chapter 7).
[2] William was 37, and Duncan 32, when she died. Both were married and in good careers. William was briefly a geologist, and Duncan became a prominent Wellington accountant.
[3] The birth of Duncan on 18 May 1873 was registered by McKay.
[4] The report by Alan Mason in *GSNZ Historical Studies Group Newsletter* No. 10 (March 1995, pp. 5–13), p. 8, that only Skeats and Bell were short-listed, appears to be in error.
[5] The original wording was 'palaeontology', which was struck out and replaced by 'structural'. Mines

Department letter, 22 November 1904, National Archives.
6. Bell was the nephew of Alexander Graham Bell, inventor of the telephone. He married the sister of Katherine Mansfield.
7. Circular letter of the New Zealand Geological Survey, 1 September 1906. Cited in 'Alexander McKay and The New Zealand Geological Survey' by Alan Mason, *Geological Society of New Zealand Newsletter*, August 1987, p. 14.
8. J.M. Bell, Mines Department Letter, 15 May 1907, National Archives 10311.
9. *The New Zealand Mines Record*, Vol. X, No. 2, 1906, p. 67.
10. 'The Mines Department's Exhibits at the New Zealand International Exhibition, Christchurch.' *The New Zealand Mines Record*, Vol. X, no. 4, pp. 125–7; p. 127.
11. Cf Hon. James McGowan, Preface to *New Zealand International Exhibition, 1906–1907. Three Prize Essays on the Present Condition and Future Prospects of the Mineral Resources of New Zealand, and the Best Means of Fostering Their Development.* Wellington: John Mackay, Government Printer, 1907.
12. *The New Zealand Mines Record*, Vol. IX(a), No. 8, 16 March 1906, p. 360.
13. This was equivalent to about $15,000, no mean consideration. Mines Department letter, 13 January 1909, National Archives.
14. Mines Department letter, 18 October 1909, National Archives 1908/183.
15. Her death certificate states she was fifty-one at marriage, but her age at death (sixty-six), twenty years after marriage, indicates forty-five was correct.
16. 155A was presumably a semi-detached extension to 155, but the two addresses were not always differentiated.
17. Another twist is added by the fact that Alex and Adelaide were recorded there together in the Stones directory of 1908, but by 1912, after Alex and Adelaide had moved on to Kelburn, Duncan and Henrietta were ensconced in 273A, the house next door!
18. A. McKay, Letter to Peter Shankland, 30 October 1915, MS Papers 0242-02. Alexander Turnbull Library, Wellington.
19. M190.
20. Recollections of Larry Harrington. Cited in Alan Mason 'Alexander McKay, Governement Geologist', *GSNZ Historical Studies Group Newsletter* No. 10 (March 1995), pp. 5–13; p. 10.
21. A significant break in the regular succession of rock strata. *Ibid.*
22. A. McKay, 'The Jolly Beggars: A Cantata', Notes in MS Papers 0242-02. Wellington: Turnbull Library.
23. A. McKay, Letter to Peter Shankland, 30 October 1915, MS Papers 0242-02. Wellington: Alexander Turnbull Library.
24. *Ibid.*
25. *Ibid.*
26. In MS Papers 0242-02. Wellington: Turnbull Library.
27. Obituary for Alexander M'Kay. *Evening Post*, 9 July 1917.
28. *Ibid.*
29. Adelaide McKay in fact probably stayed on at Upland Road for three years. In 1920, she bought a small cottage at 24 Luxton Street, Newtown, where she saw out her days.

Chapter 14

1. M105.
2. Alan Mason, 'Albert Heim in New Zealand', *Geological Society of New Zealand Newsletter*, No. 113, 1977.
3. William Skey, 'Elegy (On the late

Alexander McKay)' in *The Pirate Chief and the Mummy's Complaint with Various Zealandian Poems*, Haggett & Percy, Wellington, 1889, p. 59–61.

4   A.C. Begg and N.C. Begg, *Port Preservation*, p. 256.

5   Arthur P. Harper, Foreword to John Pascoe (ed.), *Mr Explorer Douglas*, A.H. & A.W. Reed, Wellington, 1957, pp. ix–xiv.

6   The year was probably 1894, when McKay would have been fifty-three.

7   Charles (Mr Explorer) Douglas was a reclusive wanderer, prospector, and, philosopher, who explored much of South Westland on a semi-formal basis for the Department of Lands and Survey. There is no record of a meeting with McKay but they would have been well known to each other. Harper, Foreword to Pascoe, p. x.

8   The valiant Amadis, unbeaten by the sword, succumbed to the pen when parodied by Cervantes in his famous novel *Don Quixote*.

9   J.C. Park, 'The life and times of James Park, Geologist, Explorer, University Dean', 1934, MS 233, Hocken Library, Dunedin, p. 9.

10 Roger Cooper, 'Alexander McKay'. *The Dictionary of NZ Biography, Vol. 2, 1870–1900*. Department of Internal Affairs (ed. Claudia Orange). Wellington: Bridget Williams Books; Dept of Internal Affairs, 1993, pp. 290–91.

11 Dr J. Alan Thomson, Obituary for Alexander M'Kay, Evening Post, 10 July 1917. Thomson later (1918) wrote a rather stilted, formal obituary, which was published in *Transactions of the New Zealand Institute*, vol. 50 (1918), vii–viii.

12 Burton, *The New Zealand Geological Survey 1865–1965*, p.22.

13 M190, p. 11.

14 One of the most satisfying instances for McKay must have been when Trechmann relocated the all-important fossil in the Permian rocks of Nelson: rocks which Bell had called Jurassic and considered were upside-down! McKay's reported reaction when told of his vindication was, 'Well what did you expect?' Account of Harold Wellman published in *GSNZ Historical Studies Group Newsletter*, (1992), pp. 3–4; p. 4.

INDEX

References to illustrations are in **bold**.

Abbey Rocks 123–24
Acheron, HMS **58**
Acheron River 150
Alexander McKay Falls **193**
Alma Heights 42–43
Alpine Fault 154, 161, 163
Alpine Rock Studies Expedition (1974) 135
'Amalgamated beef' 62
Amberley 171, 173
Amuri 74; district 154, 172; limestone 147
Amuri Bluff 115–16, 184
aneroid 149, 166
Aorangi Mine 163, 168
Aorere Valley 100
Ashburton 74, 87, 102, 130
Ashley 127
Ashley Gorge 96, 184
Aspiring Hut 140
Atlantic Ocean 52
Auld Guffie 44, 48
Australia 9, 10, 34, 37, 45, **52**, 75, 77–85, 184
autobiography *see* 'Fragments'
avalanches 88, 136
Awatere Fault 147; Valley 150
Ayr **14**
Ayr Advertiser 32, 37

Balclutha 64–65, 117
Bald Peaks 164
Ballantine, Mary 43
Balyando 79, 82
Bank Burn 42; *see also* Benloch Burn
Banks Peninsula 105
Bardennoch Hill **14**, 23
Barefell Pass 150
Barewood Plateau 68

Barker, Dr A.C. 107–08
Barnes, Mary 93, 95, 173
Barnes, Susannah 10, **93**, 94–96, 116, 169, 177, 180–81, 185, 188; *see also* McKay, Susannah
Barraclough-Fell, H. 192
Bass Rock 57
Bay of Islands 154, 157, 180–81
Beechey, R.B. **58**
Bell, James Macintosh 178, 179
Ben Ohau Range 89, 96, 139
Benloch Burn 42
Benmore Station 90
Big River *see* Lake Hakapoua
Biggar, George 163–65, 167–68
Black Peak 141
Blackley's Hotel 160
blankets 34, 63, 69, 84–85, 88, 91, 124, 165–66
Blenheim 74
blowholes 117, 166
Blue Gums Accommodation House 87
Bluff 51, 59, **60**, 136, 168, 184
Boat Landing Bay 167
Boby's [Bobby's] Creek **103, 104**
'Body in the Cave' affair 105–14, 116, 127–28
Bonthron, Mrs David 51–54, 56–58
Bowen 78
Braidenoch **14,** 15, 22, 23–26, **24, 25,** 46, 181, **182**; Hill 22
Branch River 145
Brett, Colonel De Renzie James 111
Briery, Geordie 35
Brighton 117
Brisbane 78, 81
Broken River 127
Broomielaw **50**, 180
Brown, Captain William 51, 56, 58
Bruce 87
Buchanan, John 101, **121**, 138–42, **146;**

Buchanan Collection 126, **142**, **176**
Buller 127
Burdekin River 79
Burke, Michael John 90
Burke's Pass 86, 88–90, 96
Burns, Robert (Robbie) 34, 37, 41, 43, 193
Burton, Peggy 194
bushrangers 79
byres (small paddocks) 15, 33
Byron, Lord G.G. 37, 41

Cairn Avel **14**
Cairnsmore/Cairnsmuir **14**, 31
California 33, 99
Cameron Flat 140
Campbelltown *see* Bluff
camps 82, 131, 135, 137, 139–40, 165
Canada 178
Candlemas 30
Cannibal Bay 117, **118**
Canterbury Museum **98**, 100, 102–03, 105, **107**, **156**, 184
Canterbury Plains 105
Canterbury Gilpin, The 112–14, 137, 190
Canterbury Provincial Geologist 98, 100–01
Canterbury 97–98, 100, 127, 129, 184
Cape Colville 168, 170
Cape of Good Hope **52**
Cape Palliser 129
Cape Verde Islands **52**, 55
Carlin's Cairn 46
Carminnows farm 45, 48
Carnavel farm 22
carpentry trade 41, 45, 62
Carsphairn **14**, 15–17, **17**, **18**, 19, 20–22, **24**, 26, 30–32, 34–37, 41, 44–46, 48–49; environmental issues 19; Heritage Centre 16; McKay cottage 14–16, **17**, **18**; Salutation Inn 15–16, **17**, 27; Mackenzie Country compared 19; Tinklers Loup **19**
Cascade Creek 140
Castlemaddy **14**, 46
Cathcart, Colonel McAdam 20–21
Catlins 117, **118**, 121–22
Cavendish River 167

Central Otago 70, 90, 99, 122, 143, 145, 157, 163
Chalky Inlet 167–68
Chelmsford 93, 177
Cheviot 154, 170–71, 173; earthquake 170–73
children 26, 29, 30, 36–37, 51–52, 56
Christchurch 61, 74, 94, 96–97, 100, **104**, 105–06, 115–16, 130, 139, 148, 171, 177; International Exhibition 178
Christmas celebrations 73, 87, 130
church **14**, 16, 30–31, 44, 61, 96; Auld Kirk 18, 22, 29, 30; Free Church 21
Clarence 74; Fault 147; River 150
Clarendon 65
Clark's (the Buster) Diggings 143, **145**
Claud Hamilton 87
clays 41, 79, 155; claystone 41–42
Clennoch **14**, 36
Clent Hills 102
Clermont 78–79, **80**, **81**, 83
Clinton **120**
cloth calico 68, 71, 125; plaids, shepherd's 22, 36
clothing 23, 29, 32, 54, 63, 69, 82, 88, 124; moleskins 46, 70; oilskins 124
Clutha Ferry 117; River **64**, 99, 120
Clyde River **50**
Clydesdale district 41
coal 77, 96, 97, 99–102, 124, 143, 149, 153, 155–56, 160, 170, 184; seams 96–97
Coal Burn **164**
Coal Island 165
coalfields Drury 99, 100; Puponga 161
Collingwood 99
Colonial Museum *see* Dominion Museum
Conway 74
Cook, Capt. James **57**
Coromandel 99, 100, 168–71, **171**
Cotton, Charles 187
Countess Russell 93
Cowan, John 44
Cox, Herbert 123, 125, 130–31, 133, 148
Craigengillan Estate 15
Crawford, James 149

Creek Hut 103
creeks, blackwater 124
Crimean War 42
Cromarty 163, **164**, **165**, 167–68
Cromwell 99
Croydon 168
Cunaris Sound 167
Curio Bay **118**
curling 29, 32
Curry, Leezy 43
Cuttle Cove 168

Dallmeyer, Thomas 159
Dalmellington 16, 46, 48
Dannevirke 169, 177
Darcy Stream 89
Darran Mountains 136
Dart Glacier 141; River **134**, 145
Deadmans Track 134, 136
death 16, 33, 72, 160, 183–4, 193
Deil's (The Devils) Well see Green Well of Scotland
Desolation Island **52**, 55
Deugh River see Water of Deugh
diaries 35, 37, 51, 57, 123, 163, 168
diggers 71, 74, 77, 143, 145, 166
Dinornis Sumnerensis 112
discoveries 20, 34, 57, 107, 111, 123, 158, 179; claystone 41–42; gold 34, 41, 67, 99; lead ore 20; telephoto lens 185
disease gastric disorders 22, **27**; malaria 82–83; measles 53; medicines 32, 82, 101; typhoid fever 22; whooping cough 53
Dobson, Edward 154
Dobson River **86**, 90, 139
Dominion Museum 115, 169, 184–85
Dominion 169, 184
Dootson, Adelaide 180–83, 185
Dootson, John 180
Douglas, Charlie 192
drownings 32, 122
'Drumness' 181, **182**, 185
Dumbarton 51
Dumfries **14**, 16; Dumfrieshire 48
Dunedin 8, 10, 65, **66–67**, 73–75, 94–96, 116–17
Dunn, Johnnie 79

Dunstan 72
Dunstan Road 69
Duntroon 139
Durnscaw farm 34, 44
dykes (stone walls) 15

Earle, Henrietta 169
earthquakes 147, 150–51, 153–54, 170–72; effects 157; fault lines 150–51; horizontal movement 150
East Cape 116
Edinburgh **14**
Education Act (1877) 61
education, family 21, 30, 93, 138, 168, 177
eels **124**, 125
Eglinton Valley 137
Elephant Hill 139
emigration 10, 49, 50, **50**, 177; arrives Bluff 51, 59, 60, 136, 168, 184; *Helenslee* 50–51, **52**, 53, 55, 57, 59, 164, 184; hygiene 53–54; medical inspection 60; sailing conditions 55–59; shipboard life 51–53, **53**, 54–56, 62, 94
Empire Hotel 148
employment 45, 48, 70, 84, 97
Encyclopaedia Britannica 20, 32
engravings 53, 146
Equator **52**, 55
Evening Post 184, 193
excavations 105, 108, 110; cave 105, 107, 166
explosions 13, 38, 63

families 15, 18, 33, 96, 103, 168–70, 172, 177, 181, 183
farm animals cattle 22, 90, 120; bulls 33, 35–38, 159; bullocks 23, 62, 89; cows 33, 35–38; goats 120; horses 48, 73, 79, 83, 89, 102, 131–32, 172–73, 187; lambs 45, 91; pigs 54; sheep 45, 71, 78, 83, 85, 91, 120
farms 32–34, 45, 56, 75, 87, 182; farmers 33, 45, 48, 96; farmwork 33–39, 42, 46–47, 61, 92, 117, 180; crops 37, 47, 91; haymaking 33, 36, 42, 44; shearing 78, 91

faults 68, 137, 147, 150, 151, 154, 161; faulting and folding 126, 137, 143, 147, 151
Ferguson, Jean 42
Fiordland 161, 163, **164**, 167–68, 170
fireplaces 15, **18**, 149
Firth of Clyde 50, 55
Flanagans Saddle **86**
floors 15, 26, 53, 63, 125, 141
Fog Peak 141
food 45, 53–55, 71, 89, 94, 96, 103, 105, 117, 137–38; bannock loaves 26, 28; bread 30, 54, 68, 71; butter 24, 26, 30, 54, 71, 77, 140; cheese 24, 26, 71, 138; cooking **18**, 26, 54–55, 93; flour 54, 125, 141; meat 71, 90, 141, 167, 184; oatmeal 54, 125, 141, 188; poisoning 22; porridge 26, 188–89; potatoes 21, 24, 26, 41, 46, 54–55, 73
fords 38, 124, 192
forests 50, 61–62, 68, 70, 99, 122
fossils 9, 42, 102–03, **104**, 119, 123, 130, 138, 149, 160, 163, 176, 179, 188, 194; ammonites **142**; collectors 102–05, 115, 121, 143, 187; corals 42; ferns 131; fish **126**, 127; gastroliths 103; gastropod 176; graptolites 168; *Kawhiasphinctes* **142**; marine reptile **103**; mesosaur **104**; photography **176**; saurians **156**, 184; serrate 168; skeletons **103**; wood 117
Foveaux Strait 57, 59
'Fragments in the Life History of Alexander McKay' 11, 21, 41, 45, 46, 47, 51, 53, 77, 79, 91, 181
fuels 70–71, 92, 96, 99
Fullerton 71–73
Furmiston farm 33, 44–45

Gabriel's Gully **67**
Gairy Crag 23
Galloway **14**, 15, 19, 33; hydroelectric scheme **19**
Garryhorn Farm **14**, **17**, 37–39, **38**
Geological Society of London 149, 184, 190
Geological Society of New Zealand 175
geological periods Cretaceous **142**; Devonian 123; Jurassic **142**; Pliocene 154; Silurian 42; Triassic **142**
geologists 9, 10, 42, 97, 99, 101–02, 126, 129, 151, 174, 178–79, 184, 187, 188, 189–92
geology 13, 23, 32, 41, 59, 97, 99, 101, 102, 119, 122–23, 129, 131, 140, 143, 145, 147, 149, 157, 161, 181
'Geology of New Zealand' 174–75
girls 29, 30, 35, 42–43, 45, 169
Gisborne 185
glaciers 92, 184
Glasgow **50**, 51, 56, 180
Glenkens homestead 173
Glenmuck Bridge 46
Glenomaru 117
Glynn Wye 150–51, 154, 157, 187; earthquake **150**, 151, **152**, 153–54
Glynn Wye Station **150**, **152**, 154
gold 13, 32–34, 41, 48–49, 61, **67**, 71–75, 79, 83, 99–102, 143, 153, 161, 163; prospecting 78–79, 163; rushes 61, 99
goldfields 61, 65, 73, 74
Gordon, Mary 48
gorges 19, 90, 117, 125, 132, 134, 145–46
Government Analyst 116, 178
Government Botanist 121
Government Geologist 161, 163, 165, 167–69, 171, 173, 175, 179
GPS devices 122
Grace Burn 167
Gracefield 146, 179
Gracie, Samuel 47
grandparents 16, 22–24, 26, 33, 35, 37
granite 31, 34, 101, 163, 167–68; country 46, 164
'Granny' (Jenny Welsh) 22–24, **25**, 26–28, 30–34, 37, 188
graves 110, 168, 185
Great Barrier Island 170
Green Island 75
Green Islets Peninsula **164**, 166–67
Green Well of Scotland 30–32, 47–49, **47**
Greymouth 122–23

Greystone Inn 16
Grovetown 74
Guffie, David 65
Guffie, William 72
Gulches Head 168

Haast, Heinrich F. von 110, 112, 113
Haast, Julius von 97, **98**, 99–103, 105–14, 115–16, 127, 154, 188, 190, 193–94; *see Mauisaursis haasti*
Haast Pass 138
Hakatere Station 130–31
Hales, Chas 169
Hales, Emma 169
Halfway Bush 65
Hamilton, Jock 35, 46
Hanmer region 150, 157
Harper, John 44–45, 192
Harris Saddle **134**, 137
Hastings, Rab 15–16, 31
Hastings, Robert 41
Hawkes Bay region 102
Heathcote River 105
Hectors Col 140, **141**
Hector, Sir James 99, 101–02, 112–13, 115–17, 121–23, 126–27, 129–30, 138–39, 147–49, 151, 160, 184–85, 188, 193; 'Body in the Cave' affair 105, 109, 112, 116, 127–28; earthquakes 147, 150–51, 153–54, 170–72; expresses confidence in McKay 147–48; fish fossils **126**, 127
Hedrass, J.F. 95
Heim, Professor A. 189
Helenslee 50–59, **52**, **53**, **57**, 164, 184
Henderson, Patrick 51
Henry, Dr C.D. 174
Hillside Manse **95**
Hochstetter, Ferdinand 99, 100, 193
Hocken, Dr T.M. 112
Hodgkinson, Edmund 90–91, 93–96
Hodgkinson, George 90, 92, 94
Hokitika 87, 124, 154
Hollyford Valley **134**, 136
Holm Bridge 47; Farm 46; Hill 41; House 38, 45
Hope Fault 150
Hopkins River **86**, 139

Horse Range 73
houses 15–16, 20–21, 23–24, 27, 33–34, 39, 41, 45, 48, 72, 79, 83, 88, 172; Kelburn **182**; Lewisville Terrace 157, **158**, 169; *see also* 'Drumness'
Hughes, John 112
Hunter River 78
'Hunter and the Hunted' **107**
Hutton, Prof. F.W. 149

Ida Range **145**
Imperial College 138
Invercargill 59, **60**, 61–63
Irishmans Creek **86**, 89
Isthmus Sound 167–68

Jackson Bay 124
Jane Coves 167
Janets Peak 149
'Jimmy the Needle' 73
Johnson, Peter 57
Jollies Pass 150

Kahiku Range **120**
Kaiapoi 96
Kaikoura coast 74
kakapo 167
Katikati 170
Kawhia Harbour **142**; region 100, 129
Kekerengu 74
Kerguelen Islands *see* Desolation Islands
Kinloch 134, 137
Kisbee Bay **165**
Kiwi Burn 164–66
Knockengorroch 41
Knockgray 45; Craig **14**, 42; farm 44–45
Kumara 161
Kurow 139

Lake
  Ellesmere 87
  Hakapoua (Big River) 122, **164**, 167
  Harris 112–13, 134, 135–37, **136**, 190
  Kiwi **164**
  Middleton 90
  Nerine 134–35, **134**
  Pukaki **86**

Lake, contd
  Tekapo 86
  Wakatipu 129, 134, 137
  Wanaka 139–40
Lake Ohau 86–97, **86, 93**, 139, 177; land title 91; marriage 92–95; meets Haast 97; assistant manager 94
Lake Ohau Station **86**, 91–97, **92, 93**
Lawrence 99
Leeston 87
Legislative Council 110
Leithfield 74
lenses *see* photography
Leslie Hills Station 154
Lewis Pass 138, 150
Linck, C.W. 163, 165–66, 168
Lindis Pass 139
Lines Written on a Scene from Lake Harris Saddle, West Coast, Middle Island 112, 137, 190
Livingstone Mountains 137
Loch Doon **14**, 45
Loch Ken **14**, 19
Logan's Station 64
Long Sound 167
Lookout Point 65
Lort Stokes, Captain J. **58**
Lowman, R. 105, 108, 110–11
Lyell's *Principles of Geology* 123, 193
Lyttelton 87, 116, 149

Mackenzie Basin **86**; Country 19, **86**, 88, 90, 96, 184
Maclaurin, J.S. 178
Macpherson, Hugh 140
McAdams, Robert 173
McClellan, Agnes 15
McCrae, Rab 63
McCrae, Alex 36
McCrae, Jock 36
McGowan, Hon. James 174
McKay, Adelaide (née Dootson) 181
McKay, Agnes (née Mclellan) 16, 21
McKay, Alexander achievements 13, 187–88, 190; 'Body in the Cave Affair' 105–14, 116, 127–28; brother John 63–72, 73–74, 87, 96; death 183–84, 193; emigration 51–59; family 168–70, 177–78; gold seeking 71–74, 77–82; health 82–83, 164–66, 174–75; houses 157–58, **158**, 169, **182**; legend 188–94; marriage 92–96, **95**, 178; meets Haast 97; works for Hector 115ff.; obituary 184–85; personality 149, 155, 183, 188, 190–92; poetry 112–14, 133, 137, 190, 197–210; portraits front cover, **186**; reading 193; retirement and remarriage 180–83; searches for work 62–63, 75, 88; unfinished mss 183; will 185–86; winding down 177–83; *see also* photography
McKay, Alexander adolescence emigration 49–50; farmwork 33–39, 42, 44, 45–49, 61, 92, 117, 180; literary interests 41–44; love 41, 43–44, 45; pranks 32, 37–39, 44, 47–48; reading 29, 32–33, 37, 42, 45
McKay, Alexander childhood 15–16; Candlemas 30; Granny's influence 22–23; geological interests 23, 42; health problems 22–23; learns to read and write 24; school days 29–33; Scottish heritage 27, 30, 34; siblings 15, 18, 21; thrashings 29
McKay, Alexander, employment Assistant Geologist 148–49, **153**; Field Geologist 129–41, 143–48, **144**, 161; Fossil Collector 102–14, **103, 104**, 115; Government (Mining) Geologist 161–75, **162**, 179; Lake Ohau 87–97; NZ Geological Survey 115ff.; publications **144, 153, 162**, 189–91, 213–24
McKay, Alexander, travels Australia 77–85; Catlins 117–21; Cheviot 170–73; Coromandel 170; Fiordland 163–68; Glynn Wye 150–54; Lake Ohau 87ff.; Marlborough 145–49; Poverty Bay 125–28; Routeburn and Hollyford 134–38; Rowley's Farm 155–57; Waitaki to Matukituki 138–41; West Coast 122–25
McKay, Catherine (Kate) 21
McKay, Duncan 21, 37, 116, 168–70, 177, 181

McKay, Elizabeth 34
McKay, Henrietta (née Earle) 169–70, 177, 181
McKay, James 21
McKay, Janet 16
McKay, John 16, 21, 96
McKay, Margaret 16, 21
McKay, May Matilda (née Maxton) 169
McKay, Susannah (née Barnes) 10, 92–96, **93**, 116, 169, 177, 180–81, 185, 188
McKay, William 16, 21, 170–71, 179
McKay, William Alexander 96
McKay, William Sloan 15, 29
McMurtie, Duncan 73
Maerewhenua 139
Main Divide **134**
Maitland Stream 90
Malvern Hills 139, 148
Maniototo County 143
Mantell, Hon. W.D.B. 110, 112, 127–28, 149
Maori 22, 61, 105, 106–07, 126, 137; grave **109**
maps 10, 76, 122, 125, 151, 153–54, 162
Marlborough 145–48, 154
Martin, Josiah 158
Martinmas 35, 37
Maskell, William Miles 112
Mason, Alan 175
Masterton 129
Mataura 64
Matukituki Valley 138–40, **141**
Mauisaursis haasti **103**
Maungatua 65
Maxton, May Matilda 169
Meade River 145, **146**
Melbourne 63
Middlemarch 68
Milburn 65
Mile Creek 193
Milton 65
mineral resources 70 143, 154, 156, **162**, 163, 170, **171**, 179, 181
miners 20–21, 32, 37, 41, 48, 71–73, 87, 99, 161, 163, 170, 174, 178, 180, 183
Mines Department 160–61, 178, 184; Minister 170, 174, 183

mining 20, 34, 145, 168
'Moa-bone Cave' 105–14, **106**, 184
moa hunters 106–08, 115
Moeraki–Kakanui coast 148
Molyneux Bay 117
money 26, 37, 54, 63, 70, 75, 82–83, 94, 96
Morning Star Goldmine **165**, 168
mosquitoes 62, 82, 125
Motutara Point **142**
mountain-building processes 145, 147, 187, 194
mountains 48, 59, 74, 84, 89, 91–94, 96, 122, 138–39, 145, 147, 161, 163, 192
Mowbray Street School 168
Mount
    Alta 139
    Ansted 140–41
    Aspiring 139–40
    Avalanche 140
    Cargill 74
    Cook **86**, 88
    Edward 140–41
    Hopkins 139
    Huxley 139
    Iron 139
    Maitland 139
    Potts 129–31
    Somers 87, 130–31
    Tarawera 13, 171
    Tongariro 100
    Tyndall 140
    Vesuvius 100
Mt Aspiring Station 140
Mullocky Gully 74
Murray, Thomas 51, 54–55
museums 42, 101, 105, 108–11, 160, 169, 178, 184
Muzzle River 145, 156

Narrows 167
Naseby 72–73, 75, 143
Nelson 49, 74, 99, 100, 129, 154, 163, 168, 193
Neolithic burial mounds **14**
neo-tectonics 151
Neumann Range 139
New Plymouth 157

New River 62
New South Wales 77
New Zealand 60, 87, 93, 149, 175, 179, 183–84, 187, 188; geology 100, 160, 179, 187, 193–94
New Zealand Geological Survey 10, 116, 129–30, 144, 148, 170, 178–79
New Zealand Times 184
Newcastle 77–78
newspapers 10, 37, 42, 166
Niger Peak 141
North Auckland 143
North Col **134**
North Island 13, 101, 125, 154; McKay's travels **144**, **153**
Novara 99, 100
Nugget Point 117, **118**, **119**

Oamaru 73, 102, 129
Ohau Range 89, 94; River 89
Old Man Range 69
Omarama 139; Station 96
'Onion Report' 189
onions 24, 26, 125, 155–56
O'Reilly, Mick 77, 83–84
Orepuki 166
Otago peneplain **68**
Otago region 49, 61, **68**, 74, 89, 101, 116, 122, 138, 143, 161, 184–5, 193
Otago Retreat, entrance **165**
Otago Daily Times 112
Otago goldfields 87
Otago Harbour 77
Otapiri Gorge 133
Otira River 192
Outram 65
Oxford Hills 139

'Palace Hotel' 68
Palliser's expedition 101
Palmerston 73, 148, 160
Palmerston North 149
Papanui 74
Park Pass 135
Park, Professor James 112, 123, 135, 138–41, 149, 160, 192–93
Peak Downs 84
Peak Springs 79

Pearl Flat 140
peat 18, 38, 42, 70
Pembroke (Wanaka) 139–40
penguins 105, 166
Philosophical Institute of Canterbury 100
Philosophical Society 143
photography 13, 151, 154, 157–60, 173, 179–80, 185–86, 187; telephoto 13, 157–60, **158**, **159**, 185–87
photomicrographs 170, 187
Picton 74
Pig Island 77
poa exigua 140
poetry 41, 43, 113, 190, 194
poets 9; 35, 41, 139
Polen, Dr D. 111
police 72, 110–11, 157
Polmaddy **14**, 22
poplars, McKay **92**
Popotuna (Kuriwao) Gorge 117
population 15–16, 20–21, 54, 59, 151, 163
porridge *see* food
Port Chalmers **67**, 93, 177
Port Molyneux 117
Port Pegasus 154
Potts River 131–32
Poverty Bay 125–28
powder, blasting 20, 39, 48
Preservation Inlet 163, **164**, **165**, 167–68
Prince Edward Islands **52**, 55
Princess Burn 164
Puketoi Station 71
Puti Point **142**
Puysegur Lighthouse 168; Point **164**, **165**, 166

Queensland **76**, 78, 85
Queenstown 137

railways 61, 187
Rakaia District 127, 130; River 74, 87
Rangitata River 74, 131–32; Valley 130
rats 77, 125
Read, Gabriel 99
reading 29, 32–33, 37, 42, 45, 193
Retro Creek 83–84

INDEX 251

Revolver Bay **165**; Hill **165**
Rhinn of Kells **24**, 46
Rialto 77
Richardson Mountains 137
rifles 136, 171
river beds 78, 126–27, 131, 156
Riverton 62
Roaring Bay **119**
'Roaring Forties' 55
Robertson, Captain 167
Rock and Pillar Range 73
Rockburn River **134**, 135
Rockhampton 83, 85
rocks 23–24, 57–58, 68, **68**, 70, 74, 101–03, 117–18, 120–23, 125–27, 170–71, 179; breccia-conglomerate 155; crystalline 154; gold-bearing 145, 161, 170; granite 31; green 140; greywackes 101, 130; hard siliceous 100, 123; limestone 101–02, 139, 147; low-grade metamorphic 138; pink quartzites 140; quartz 143, **145**; red 140; schists 137; *spirifer* beds 130–31; Triassic 119, 123; volcanic 57, 74
Rocky Gully 131–32
Routeburn Flats **134**, **135**, 137; hut **135**; River **134**
Routeburn Station 137
Routeburn Track 134, 136, 138
Rowley's Farm 155–57, 160
Royal Geographical Society 185
Roy's Peak 139
Ruamahunga 129
Ruapehu 180
Rutherford, D. 154

Salutation Inn 15–17, **18**, 27
'Samaritan's house' **86**
Scott's Bivvy **141**
Scotland 9, 10, 13, 15, 29, 30, 47–49, 184
Scrimgeour, Rev. Robert 95–96
Seddon, Richard (King Dick) 160
Semple, Rev John 31
Serpentine Saddle 134–35
Shag Valley 109, 149
Shag Point 102, 149, 160, 184
Shag Point Railway Station 155

Shankland, Peter 180
Shaw, Alexander 33
Shaw Savill Line 51, 54
sheep *see* farm animals
Shepherds' Arms Hotel 157, **159**, 181
shepherd's hut **86**
shipboard life 51, **53**, 54–56, 62, 94
Shotover River 137, 141, **193**
Silver Stream 65, 74
Sixteen Mile Creek **193**
Skey, William 116, 160, 192
snowstorms 45, 69, 88, 132, **136**
Solander, Daniel **57**
Solander Islands **52**, **57**, 58, 164
Sollas, Professor W.J. 170
Somerville, William 37–39
South Island 58, 99, 122, 127, 138, 154, 163; McKay's travels **144**, **153**
South Malvern 149
Southern Alps **86**, 88, 130, 154, 161, 184
Southland 56, 102, 129–32
Southland Syncline 118, **120**, **121**
spar minerals 41
St Andrews Presbyterian Church **95**, 96
St Peter's Church 180
Star Lane 45
Station Creek (Maitland Stream) 90
steamers 59, 61, 73–74, 83, 85, 115, 117, 124, 134, 137, 163, 168, 187
Stewart, Aggie 30
Stewart Island 59, 143, 154
stoats 120, 125
Stokes, Captain J. Lort 58
Strang, Dr Peter 82
stubbornness 73, 89
sugar 26, 30, 54, 119, 141, 171
Sumner Cave 105–14, **106**, 108, **109**, 184
Sutherland, Duncan 96
swags 63, 69, 79, 87, 96, 165–66
Swale River 145
Sydney 78, 83, 85, 87
synclines 121, 155–56, **155** *see also* Southland Syncline

Taieri Gorge 74; Ridge 69, **70**, 71; River **69**
Tait, Christina McDougall 181

Tank Gully 131
Tapuaenuku 147
Tautuku Bay **118**
Tautuku Beach 117
Te Aroha 170
Te Oneroa 168
Te Waewae Bay 163
Tekapo Station 88
telephoto lens *see* photography
Temuka 74
tents 62, 65, 71–73, 83, 117, 120, 125, 134, 136, 165–66
Testimony of the Rocks 74
Thomson, J.A. 189, 193
Timaru 73, 123
Tinklers Loup **19**
Townsville 78
Travers, W.T. 112, 158
Trechmann, C.T. 189
trees 14, 17, 46, 63, 89, 92–93, 167
Trotter's Gorge 73
Tuhawaiki Island 117, **118**
Tuparoa 126
tussock lands 120, 122, 141

Upper Pomahaka 64

Vancouver 151
Vjestnik 13, **158**
volcanic rocks 57, 74; eruptions 13, 171
Von River 137

wages 35, 49, 90, 92, 94, 115–16, 178
Waikato Heads 100
Waikiekie Creek 183
Waikouaiti River 74
Waimate district 108, 192
Waipao River 185
Waipara River 127, **156**
Wairarapa 129
waird (enclosures) 33, 36

Waitaki River 73, 138; Valley 129, 138
Waiwera River 119
Wakamarino 87, 184; River 73
Wallace, Jock 45
Wangapeka 129–30
Wanlockhead district 41
Ward's Brewery 96
water 20, 77–79, 91–92, 99, 124, 131, 164–66; closets **53**; holes 78–79; pumps 15–16; races 20; rationing 55; wheels 20
Water of Deugh **14**, 19, **19**, 31, 34, 41, 47
waterfalls 104–05, 193
Waterhead farm 33–36; Hill **14**
Weka Pass 127, 156
weka 125, 167
Wellington 10, 61, 102, 117, 122, 124, 127, 130, 140–41, 148, 168, 173, 180, 185; Harbour **158**
Wellington Philosophical Society 108
Wellman, Harold 161, 187
Welsh, Jenny 22
Wenlockhead 34
West Coast 102, 116, 121–22, **124**, 125, 127, 129, 137–38, 163, 185, 192
Westland 99, 161
Westport 123
Wheeler, Edmund 94
wheelwrights 20–21
whisky 9, 30, 38, 43, 188–89
Wight, James 48
Willett, R.W. (Dick) **193**
Wilson River 164
Wilson, William 34
Wilson, Bess 34–35, 43–44, 49
Wilson, Elizabeth 16, 34, 44
Wilson River **164**
witches 31–32, 48
Wolfang Peak **85**
Woodhead **14**, 20–21; lead mine **17**, 35